The Aliens Rugby Football Club

R.U.F.C

SEFTON

Alias the Aliens

Sefton

RUGBY UNION FOOTBALL CLUB

Alias

the

Aliens

Congratulations on your great Season

David Bohl.

D. P. Bohl B.Sc

SERENDIPITY

Published in 2003 by
Serendipity
Suite 530
37 Store Street
Bloomsbury
London

British Library Cataloguing-in-Publication data
A catalogue record for this book is available from the British Library

ISBN 1 84394 066 3

Printed and bound by Alden Group, Oxford

Acknowledgements

Geoff Daley for gathering and supplying most of the source material.

The Commonwealth War Graves Commission for helping to find our military casualties.

Contents

Sefton RUFC – Committee Minutes 1923–25

D. P. BOHL B. Sc

CONTENTS

SEFTON
R.U.F.C.

(ALIAS THE ALIENS)

Sefton RUFC — 1972–2002

Memories of Sefton

Team Photographs

D. P. BOHL B.Sc

CONTENTS

SEFTON
R.U.F.C.

(ALIAS THE ALIENS)

Preface

L ITTLE DID I KNOW that the purchase of a 'Black Widow' flatbed scanner for a £178 in 1990 was to become the start of a long and enjoyable project to retrace the roots of Sefton Rugby Union Club in Liverpool.

With a heavily laden shoe box full to the brim with photographs, newspaper cuttings and exercise books, the air thick with the smell of garlic, a certain Geoff Daley spoon fed me the first of the treasures – a programme of the Aliens Club Dinner from 1907. In wonderful Scouse phraseology, "Scan darrin," he barked, to which I picked myself up off the floor after a brief bout of Garlic Shock Syndrome and replied "Certainly, sir," and here we are now, twelve years on.

OUR FREDDIE

The book is dedicated to the members who scratched and scraped their way through two world wars to keep the game of rugby union alive and kicking in the heart of Merseyside. I am particularly indebted to the diligence of founder member and club secretary F.J. Applebee, without whose efforts the club's rich history would undoubtedly have been lost. Many thanks are also due to the current membership who have had to rattle and shake 'the old grey matter' for dates and names.

Liverpool 2003
D. P. Bohl

The Founder Members of
The Aliens 1907

Back Row:- R.J.ADAMS. E.E.BOND. A.L.WALKER. J.W.HETHERINGTON. D.J.SLOSS
W.A.STEWART. W.ROCHESTER. J.WOOD. F.J.HANEY. J.D.JOHNSTONE.
Sitting 2nd Row:- W.THOMAS. A.DAVISON. J.W.A.TAYLOR. R.W.JONES. R.T.ROBINSON.
Standing:- H.TOLSON. H.N.BELL. Front Row:- H.W.MITCHELL. E.P.BYWELL. F.J.APPLEBEE. J.FAIRLEY.

Team	Season	Name	Age	Row		Home	Occupation
Aliens 1907/08	1907/08	R. J. Adams	25	B/R	✓	Barnsley	Teacher
		E. E. Bond	25		✓	Lancaster	Teacher
		A. L. Walker	21		✓	Batley	
		J. W. Hetherington	28		✓	Yorkshire	Schoolmaster
		D. J. Sloss	22			Liverpool	Mech. Engineer
Colours		W. A. Stewart	21		✓	Carlisle	
Black/Emerald		W. Rochester	31		✓	Morpeth	Schoolmaster
		J. Wood	22		✓	Crewe	Teacher
		F. J. Haney	22			Widnes	Teacher
		J. D. Johnstone	22		✓	Carlisle	Teacher
		W. Thomas	23	M/R	✓	Cardiff	Teacher
		A. Davison				Nottingham	
		J. W. A. Taylor	20			Liverpool	
		R. W. Jones				Liverpool	Teacher
		R. T. Robinson			✓	Burnley	
		H. Tolson	23	Standing	✓	Holmfirth	Teacher
		H. N. Bell			✓	Dewsbury	
		H. W. Mitchell	23	F/R	✓	Bristol	Teacher
		E. P. Bywell			✓	Liverpool	
		F. J. Applebee	25		✓	Slaithwaite	Teacher
		J. Fairley	23		✓	Barnsley	Teacher

Condensed History

THE CLUB WAS FORMED IN 1907 under the name of the 'Aliens' by a number of school teachers, none of whom was a native of Liverpool, and membership was at first restricted to members of the teaching profession.

In the first season every game was played on the ground of their opponents and out of eighteen games played, seven were won, ten were lost and one was drawn. Economy was strictly observed and the total expenditure for the season amounted to three pounds, nineteen shillings and two pence halfpenny. The assets at the end of the season consisted of one ball and two jerseys.

The first ground, occupied in 1908-09, was that of the old Clubmoor Cricket Club. In the following season the restriction of membership was removed and the club moved to a larger ground in Townsend Lane where it remained until the outbreak of the 1914-18 war. During this period steady progress was made under the auspices of chairman R.L.Knipe. The 'Aliens XVs' of all the local senior clubs were played, the 1st XVs of many well known Lancashire and Cheshire Clubs, and in 1912-13 and 1913-14 Birkenhead Park granted first team fixtures. World War 1 led to the club being suspended as most of the members volunteered for active service.

In 1919 several of the old playing members decided to reform the club, and although only eight were available, fixtures were arranged for 1919-20 season. Proposals to change the club name to 'Tuebrook' and 'Mersey' were rejected and on August 31st 1920 a motion was passed to rename the club 'Sefton' after their first landlord Lord Sefton. In 1922 F.D.Outhwaite became its first Life Member. The membership grew rapidly and, after one or two moves, the club secured a ground in Meadow Lane, West Derby,

with changing facilities in the Hare and Hounds Hotel, where it remained until 1929, when it acquired its present ground. This was made possible by the enthusiasm of the numerous playing and honorary members in those years, whose activities built up a substantial ground fund. With the help of loans from the Rugby Union and the Lancashire County Rugby Union the club was able to purchase this ground.

Once again the club was progressing steadily, but the outbreak of war in 1939 again caused its suspension of activities. The ground was requisitioned as a heavy anti-aircraft gun-site and it remained requisitioned until long after the war.

After the war ended enough space was secured for one playing pitch and a number of pre-war players worked hard to make it fit for play in the 1946-47 season. Despite the handicap of a poor ground and the invasion of the pavilion by squatters, the efforts of both old and new players helped to keep the club alive.

After prolonged negotiations with the War Department work on restoring the ground and pavilion was started in September 1951, and by December 1952 the ground was reopened on the thirteenth of that month by Councillor Hedley A. Williams (deputising for the Lord Mayor of the City, Alderman A. Morrow), a game being played against Davenport R.U.F.C. (now Stockport RUFC) to mark the occasion. The club facilities in this period were possibly better than most Merseyside Rugby Football Clubs, but very modest by today's standards.

Two years later saw the building of the stand, this built to specifications drawn up by Messrs O.G.Thomas, Liverpool Architects, the building work for this project being undertaken by the club members themselves. The wooden cladding has long since gone, but still it does afford some protection on wetter days.

Throughout the fifties and sixties the club regularly fielded four sides each week, with regular fixtures against Orrell, Leigh, Widnes, Winnington Park and West Park.

(ALIAS THE ALIENS)

These clubs are now playing in leagues well above ourselves at present, however, history, they say, does repeat itself; well maybe!

1967 was well celebrated, this being the club's Diamond Jubilee, a club dinner was held at the Strand Hotel in Liverpool. The function was attended by many well known rugby personalities of the period. Throughout the sixties dinner dances were held at the Mecca Rooms, Sefton House in Liverpool, and for the less well off, Dance Hops held at the very popular NUR Club on Dean Road, Liverpool.

In the season of 1969, plans were drawn up for what is now the present changing rooms and bath area and after many deliberations the 1973 season brought the grand opening. This coincided with a new bar (not the present one) which was situated in the vicinity of the emergency exit. Our present bar, known as the Tom Donnelly Bar from which members now derive their pleasure was bought from Broadway Conservative Club in 1975. Further club improvements were made in the 1979-80 season when the front extension was built. This has greatly enhanced the aesthetic values of the club, and even more so in recent years, with the interior decorations.

In the early 1970s Sefton hosted the St Margaret's Baseball Team, the diamond being situated on the top two pitches.

In the season of 1983-84, Sefton won the Liverpool Cup in a hard fought match against Merseyside Police. The venue was the former Liverpool RUFC's ground at Aigburth. The score-line, Sefton 26 Merseyside Police 3. The competition unfortunately has gone out of existence.

Radical changes were made to most clubs' fixture lists in the 1986-87 season. This was brought about by the formation of the leagues.

In the early nineties Sefton hosted two summer seasons of Aussie Rules Football, the Liverpool Blues formed up of local antipodeans and rugby lads trying to keep fit. They played teams from as far as London, Birmingham and Bristol.

D. P. BOHL B.Sc

The season of 2002-03 sees Sefton maintaining a place in the Lancashire-Cheshire League. Over the years Sefton's Committees have been both diligent and calculating in their efforts to make the club facilities to what they are today, and they are to be commended for their accomplishments. However we now at Sefton are reaping the rewards of our forebears both on and off the pitch.

What of the future? Sefton Rugby Club has a lot to offer, we have to explore the possibilities of expanding our facilities to cater for our ancillary sporting sections, namely youth rugby, cycling and aerobics

On a final note, Sefton's management team, players and members will continue to welcome not only seasoned rugby players, but potential players to share and enjoy our facilities here at Sefton.

In 2007 the club celebrates 100 years!

(ALIAS THE ALIENS)

The Dawning of the Aliens

The Story of Sefton RUFC
by Club Historian A.G. Daley

INTRODUCTION AND BACKGROUND

IN RECORDING the following paragraphs relating to the history of Sefton, thanks is first given to David Applebee, son of the most prominent founder member, F.J. Applebee, affectionately known as 'Freddie' when referred to in the following passages. David, his only son, born in 1924, used to listen to his father's stories of the characters and events at the club and, having an excellent retentive memory, has disclosed his stories for a biographical setting for the following opening chapters.

David played for Sefton's First XV for a number of years in the fifties but, unfortunately, after some disagreements he left to play for Hightown.

Having retired as a civil servant from the Liverpool passport office in the eighties he now maintains good health, and enjoys his regular rounds of golf, playing at Huyton golf club with his old friends. The family home is still his residence in Twig Lane, Huyton.

Founder Member 'Our Freddie'

Acknowledgements are given to members who have contributed to these pages; tales that would be unheard of if they were not requested. One such senior contributor was Jack Daybell, who joined Sefton in the late forties. I can recall his telephone call to our home looking for a game, my instructions from my father being, "If anyone is looking for a game, to meet at the Rocket Hotel at 12.30 on Saturday."

Jack, a former Liverpool headmaster, served Sefton well, playing mainly at stand-off half. He played in the First XV, was captain of the Second XV for five consecutive seasons, and fulfilled his role as Fixture Secretary for a similar period in the fifties and early sixties. Eventually he was honoured with position of club president for the statutory two years from 1968-70. He is also one of four Sefton club trustees. A first-rate club man he now lives in Bolton and is still in contact with the club.

Peter Moloney and John Davies, two fine former captains, have also contributed their own recollections which I regard as 'treasured history.' Thank you!

David Bohl joined Sefton as a young man in the late seventies, always willing to lend a hand in any of the club's working parties. He has collated the club's photographs and history from 1907 to present day, this from memorabilia handed down and preserved over the years, and from minutes of meetings. With this material he has formed our Sefton website. David, locally referred to as 'Ned' (given to him for his impressions of Spike Milligan's Goon Show), has by his deliberations spurred me on to recall my memories of events, this before my memory gets too faded.

Extolling David's attributes one step further, David is not alone. Our current Chairman of Rugby, Paul Hood, is also responsible for bouncing Sefton into the twenty-first century by creating our initial website, possibly one of the best sites of a junior rugby club in the country featuring every known aspect of Sefton: photographs, events, reports, results, league records, and much more, not forgetting of course the topical newsletter 'The Seftimes'.

(ALIAS THE ALIENS)

In compiling these records one must not overlook the fact that the club over the years has had many fine representatives. Men of great character, these people, players and officials alike, are a reflection on the present day committee and players. In recording the history of our club, unfortunately not all names can be included and apologies are extended to those members to whom this applies.

Unhappily, we have recently lost a good club man with the death of our Chairman Brian Eden. Chairman for almost six years, also serving the club in other departments over many years, Brian died in hospital on the 19th November 2002. He will be sadly missed.

THE FORMATIVE YEARS

THE CLUB WAS FOUNDED in the year 1907 by a number of school teachers, none of whom was a native of Liverpool, and membership was restricted to members of the teaching profession. In 1910 the Club became open. Mr F.J Applebee was in the main the guiding light in the club's development, a man of exceptional character who lived for sport. I consider myself fortunate in having met him, although at the time he was well into retirement.

At the turn of the century London and Liverpool paid higher rates of pay for school teachers than other parts of the country. As a result many teachers came to Liverpool from other towns. One of these teachers was Mr F.J Applebee, born in 1882 at Hollins Farm, a hill farm outside the village of Slaithwaite in the West Riding of Yorkshire. His father was a church worker for the Church of England. He was a true cockney, having been born in London within in the sound of Bow Bells.

As a boy Freddie, as he was later known, took a keen interest in cricket and rugby, and was eventually awarded a place at St John's College, Battersea, London. He gained blues in both cricket and rugby, being captain of the rugby team playing at stand-off half more often than not.

When Freddie graduated in about 1905 he became a teacher and decided to come to Liverpool. He joined New

SEFTON
R.U.F.C.

Brighton RUFC and played for them for about two years. Numerous young teachers from out of town used to congregate at public houses in the city before they left to play for various clubs in the district.

It seemed that one Saturday Freddie raised the question, "Why don't we form a club of our own? " So the first steps were taken to register a club with the Rugby Football Union and organise fixtures. As the club had no formal identity and the early members came from outside Liverpool it was decided to call it the 'Aliens F.C'.

In the first season of 1907 every game was played on the grounds of their opponents, and out of eighteen games played seven were won, ten lost and one drawn. Economy was strictly observed, the total expenditure for the season amounted to three pounds nineteen shillings, and two pence half-penny and the assets at the end of the season consisted of one ball and two jerseys.

Freddie had a very close friend, namely Hector Munroe, a Liverpool Solicitor who knew Lord Sefton's agent and it was through him that they were given a field to play on subject to the payment of a small rent. This field was near the Parish Church of West Derby, the exact location not being known, and no more information can be found. It is quite probable that this field was used for a very limited time. It is rather unfortunate that records have been lost.

The first ground occupied in 1908-09 season, was that of the old Clubmoor Cricket Club. In the following season the restriction of membership was removed, and the club moved to a larger ground in Townsend Lane, where it remained until the outbreak of the 1914-18 war which led to the club's disbandment, as most members joined the forces. Steady progress was made during this period. The Aliens XVs played all the First XVs of many well known Lancashire and Cheshire clubs, and in the 1912-13 and 1913-14 seasons Birkenhead Park granted first team fixtures.

EXTRACTS FROM THE MINUTES

AT A MEETING HELD at the Clubmoor Hotel on December 19th 1912 Eccles RFC had written to decline fixtures for the season 1913-14 as they were offering fixtures to another club. A Hot Pot Supper was arranged for February 1st.

At a meeting held on 4th April 1913 the committee proposed that the annual subscriptions should be 15/- (75 pence), 12/6d if paid in full before November 1st, this for playing members, 2/6d for existing honorary members, future honorary members 5/-, ground ticket holders 2/6d. These proposals to be put forward for the next annual meeting.

Aliens final general meeting held at the Bee Hotel 31/8/1920: a leakage of gate money reported by the assistant secretary at the Preston Grasshoppers game, more efficient checks to be made in the future.

1920 - six more jerseys to be ordered, Liverpool City Council demanded four pounds ten shillings for use of the dressing rooms. It was also reported that Southport requested a weak team be fielded for their forthcoming game.

David Applebee, son of Freddie, can remember his father's conversations and recalls the following information.

Hector Munroe was appointed solicitor for the club. He was a very good friend of Lord Sefton's agent, which came in very handy as time went on.

The selection of club presidents did not commence until the season of 1912-13, the first gentleman to fill this honour was the Director of Liverpool Education Committee James. G. Legge. Little is known of this man, but it seems that in the early days persons of note were invited to fulfil this position.

Fred Outhwaite, a renowned club member, emigrated to South Africa in or around 1922.

W.B.Croxford joined Sefton from Heaton Moor RUFC. This gentleman was a well known columnist writing for the *Liverpool Daily Post* on rugby and cricket interests.

D. P. BOHL B. Sc

SEFTON
R.U.F.C.

Dr Rumjahn, was a very early member playing for the club from about 1910. When he was too old for rugby he took to playing hockey, playing in goal for West Derby Sports Club. The ground was situated behind our present stand on the other side of the brook, running parallel to and the length of our ground. It was sold in the 50s for housing, now Harbern and Winterburn Close are situated there.

We then came to the Great War of 1914–18, the club went into hibernation for that period, many members were killed in the conflict, interestingly eight of these had played at full-back.

Members Fallen in Action			Members Returning with Decoration	
Lieutenant	F. Venmore Military Cross		Captain R.W. Jones	Military Cross & bar
Lieutenant	N. Howe		Sergeant F. King	Military Medal & bar
CSM	Isaac		Sergeant S.J. Kay	D.C.M.
Lieutenant	J.G. Williams		Private R.A. Roberts	Military Medal & bar
Lieutenant	A.L. Williamson			
2nd Lieutenant	J.H. Weights			
2nd Lieutenant	H. Tolson			
Sergeant	R.G. Griffith			
Lance Corporal	A.E. Hickling			
Private	G.P.S. Brown			
Private	C.A. Beverley			
Private	J.B. Humphrey			
Private	W. Johnson			

REORGANISATION AFTER HOSTILITIES

IN 1919, several of the old playing members, including Freddie, decided to reform the club. Although only eight were available, fixtures were arranged for the 1919–20 season. The membership grew rapidly, and after one or two moves the club secured a ground in Meadow Lane, West Derby, where it remained until 1929 when it acquired its present ground. This was made possible by the enthusiasm of the numerous playing and honorary members whose activities built up a substantial ground fund and enabled the club, with the help of loans from the English Rugby Union, to purchase this present ground. It provided three good pitches and before the war five teams were run. The first district 'Sevens' were held, and the annual carnivals were more than local events.

It was around this time that the club decided to change the name of the club from The Aliens to Sefton RUFC. The

Jack Dawson

Roger O'Donnell

Walter Croxford

Jack Birchall

name 'Alien' was not popular in post-wartime Britain. Sefton was chosen as Lord Sefton had rented them their first ground.

As previously stated David was born in 1924 and resided in Inigo Road, Old Swan. One of his first recollections of his father, Freddie, was when his dad was practising his cricketing skills by throwing small potatoes at the local cats in full song on the back yard wall.

David recalls his first visit to our present ground in Thornhead Lane when he was about eight years old. In those days the embankments were created by the council. They were made from household rubbish and were eventually covered with a layer of ashes and finally landscaped. The method used to convey the material to build these two embankments was via a railtrack from the bottom of the lane at Leyfield Road. The rail trucks were loaded and manually propelled up the lane. It must have taken some time as on their completion they stood at an approximate height of eighteen feet, eventually to subside as the ground compacted over the years.

Sefton had quite a few players of outstanding quality who went on to become well known:-

Jack Dawson, a forward in 1932 for Sefton, turned to league and played for Great Britain and Hull in 1934–35, he also played against France in 1935, against the great full back Puig Aubert.

A player by the name of White went on to play in a rugby league cup final with Widnes.

D. P. BOHL B.Sc

SEFTON
R.U.F.C.

Roger O'Donnell, from Cork Constitution in Ireland, played for Lancashire, as did W.B. Croxford and S. Dumbell, with W.H. Masheter playing for Cumberland.

Arthur Stephens

Jack Birchall was apparently one of the finest wingers Sefton had seen, according to Freddie's reminiscences a bit like Billy Boston, a renowned league player. Jack was offered £100 to turn professional and play for Salford by the great Lance Todd, the Salford Manager. He, however, did not take up the offer, in his own words, "too much like hard work!"

E.P. Jones was one of the club's finest forwards prior to the Second World War.

Fred King

Herbert Balmer was also a member prior to the Second World War, he went on to become Deputy Chief Constable of Liverpool, he featured in many famous murder cases.

Arthur Stephens was considered to be one of the finest captains in the club's history, he went out to South Africa as an agricultural manager. He told Freddie that rugby saved his life. When out hunting with two native assistants, they were charged by a small herd of buffalo. The two natives made it up the nearest tree, Arthur did not make it and as a final resort hurled himself to the ground, and apart from severe bruising lived to tell the tale. "I hurled myself to the ground just like I used to when diving on the ball in a rugby match" were his words.

Bert Brownbill

Treacle Carr

Treacle Carr, at scrum half was one of the strongest players, only about five feet tall, you would see about eight forwards

Arthur Stephens
on Safari

in a maul moving towards the try line and at the bottom would be Treacle plodding along with the ball.

Another character, a colleague of Freddie's, was Fred King, a Liverpool headmaster, and a great sprinter as well as a rugby league player. He ran 100 yards in 10.3 seconds pre-war. Pupils and parents referred to him as the galloping headmaster as he never seemed to walk.

Bert Brownbill, another keen player, became a career dame in pantomime. He had a long career on the stage appearing at the Pavilion Theatre, The Empire, and the Prince of Wales Theatre in London. Bert played his part in organising Sefton's various Concert Parties, this to raise club funds in the twenties. Dave Applebee recalls that in 1936 he met Bert wearing the first pair of suede shoes he had ever seen.

Joe Fawley, a renowned imbiber, a grand chap, who had a great reputation for his drinking habits. After a Sefton versus Kersal game he was challenged by Kersal's 'best drinker' to a drinking marathon. After a while the Kersal rival fell asleep, Joe finished the evening off by eating a full bottle of mixed pickles. Later that year Joe went out to Canada, borrowing a five-pound note off Freddie who saw him off. His last remarks were, "Don't worry, you will have it back when I have made my fortune." Freddie laughed and said "Pigs might fly!" Joe was never seen again but was reported killed in action in the First World War. Freddie could still laugh as he related the story sixty years on.

Cec Adams played for Sefton in the 1920s era as a second row forward. Cec recalls the ground being acquired in that period, and it was the members who furbished the club house, his particular job in the procedure was mixing the concrete for the baths. The baths were situated in the area now forming the committee area and storeroom. Cec was born in 1907 and died in August 2000, a good age.

D. P. BOHL B.Sc

SEFTON
R.U.F.C.

Although having spoken to him quite often on the phone, it was unfortunate that the opportunity to meet him never arose. He in his own words was rather too old to be standing around watching games. His nephew, Barry Evans was chairman of Wirral RUFC in recent years and he was responsible for passing on some 1920s Sefton photographs for which I was very thankful.

In 1929–30 when Randolph Churchill was put up for election, Sefton provided 20 bouncers for his protection. Possibly a few more would be required in present days.

In 1932 the club obtained a very large dog to guard the club in mid week. It seems that it was a Great Dane. For some strange reason he was quite friendly with club members, but had a bad habit of biting visiting officials. He was last seen heading towards Lord Sefton's Estate.

As the years passed, World War Two arrived and Sefton's ground was requisitioned by the War Office, the area to be made into a heavy anti-aircraft gun site. It was a sad time for all the club members receiving call up papers, some of whom said their last farewells to family and club mates.

POST SECOND WORLD WAR

IN 1946 Freddie retired from teaching and handed the control of the club to others with Jack Moore continuing his role as club secretary. Tom Daley, formerly with Port Sunlight prior to the war, joined the committee to be accompanied by F.R. Barry, J. Birchall, E. Morrison, A. Spencer and Barney Wall; a good team!

In 1946 the clubhouse and ground were still under the control of the government and were still manned by the army. This was the first opportunity for the post-war club enthusiasts to visit Sefton. During the hostilities the Royal Artillery had two heavy anti-aircraft gun emplacements adjacent to each other in the area which is now occupied by the first team pitch. I have been led to believe that the task for this gun site was to defend the Western Approaches. During the war the Docks at Liverpool and Wirral were heavily bombed, as was our chippy!

(ALIAS THE ALIENS)

ANTI-AIRCRAFT GUN SITE

EARLY IN 1946 I was 10 years old and visiting the ground for the first time with my father, Tom Daley, who was accompanied by a few former club stalwarts. The Crown Inn was now past its 3pm closing time, this on one very wet and dull Saturday afternoon. The entourage had with prior permission come to inspect the ground with a view to forming a pitch for the following 1946-47 season. The ground at this time had not been released by the War Office, the only space available was the bottom of the ground which was covered in tank traps. 'Tank traps' – a description from the Chambers dictionary specifies to be 'an obstacle large enough to stop a military tank'.

However my father said, "Look son, we are going to the bottom of the ground to have a look around, it is too muddy for you." He then asked the duty sergeant if I could stay with him.

The Sergeant, an amiable man asked me if I would like to see the gun emplacements before they were demolished, which seemingly, was going to be the next day. He explained on the way that the anti-aircraft guns had previously been removed from their mountings and the charges for the demolition were in place.

At the first of the two very large constructions in the ground, what confronted me was a deep hole open to the elements. It is very hard to judge the size, but past members have said that the banks had to be levelled to accommodate the emplacements. The concrete steps leading down were no wider than three feet, they hugged the wall to what seemed to be an interminable depth. The worst thing was that there was no handrail for support. Down we went, the sergeant leading the way and pointing out the explosive charges emerging from drilled holes in the concrete. Going down those steps, to say the least, was very disturbing. We eventually got to the bottom where he went on to explain the gun mountings and other points of interest. The sergeant led the way on an uneventful but frightening

D. P. BOHL B.Sc

return journey, remarked to me when we reached the top, "Well son, if you ever visit this club again in future you can always say that you were last out of the ground." These words I have never forgotten, and I always feel privileged over this occurrence. An attempt has been made to give the reader an impression of what the gun-site resembled, this rough sketch minus the anti-aircraft guns is shown on page 131.

The Second World War hostilities now over, the people of Liverpool attempted to return to some sort of normality, their lives having been in turmoil since 1939. Liverpool council had the enormous task of rebuilding the city and docklands, this area having suffered some of the heaviest bombing in the country with large stretches of the town completely flattened. This caused a large number of families to become homeless, or 'bombed out' as they used to say.

THE SQUATTERS

EARLY ONE SATURDAY during the summer of 1946 those of the committee who had telephones were alerted to the fact that the club house was occupied by squatters. It turned out that no sooner had the remnants of the army personnel vacated their billets than they were replaced overnight by a contingent of Liverpool refugees. On the morning of crisis I was not allowed to accompany my father, a job for the men it seemed. A posse of players and committee assembled in the Crown Inn to discuss tactics while one or two of the fitter forwards did a reconnaissance and reported back. It was not very clear as to what went on that day, but all I was told was that everything was in order. Fortunately for the club the pavilion was the only habitable building on Sefton's property. All the army huts were sited on the land now occupied by Blackmoor Park Infant School.

In 1946 the first post war pre-season games got under way with matches against Dunlops and Preston Grasshoppers. The first post war game on home ground was a second team fixture against Rockferrians. That season started with

the club surrounded by our uninvited guests, but no trouble ever occurred. The vacated army encampment, consisted of numerous billets, occupied now by these homeless men, women and children. An access road had

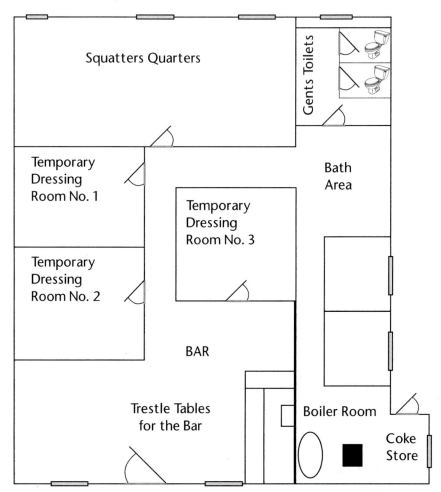

been formed by the army through this camp from Leyfield Road to Sefton's land, bridging the brook at the rear of the club. To walk down this road was an experience not to be forgotten, a typical refugee camp with washing lines, barking dogs, squawking hens, utter chaos. All the men seemed to have motorbikes which were unaffordable to most people at that period in time, and one has to make one's own mind up as to the authenticity of ownership.

At this time it was necessary to ensure the players were

D. P. BOHL B.Sc

afforded some privacy. At first removable screens were used. After a while temporary dressing rooms were erected, as shown in the diagram. At the side of the clubhouse was a large E.W.S tank (Emergency Water Supply). This provided a fine bathing facility for numerous youngsters, skinny dipping and frolicking about in the cold water, the majority as naked as the day they were born.

The club occupants consisted of a man and his family, complete with dog. They seemed to be settled in the living quarters, confined to an area approximately twenty square yards. A few house rules had to be enforced, to quote Les Wilkinson, "Do not use our coal, you have your own rations. Do not remove the wood from the walls." He kept a strict eye on this as the evidence presented itself in the weeks to come. The bottled beer crates never seemed to be touched; he was possibly tee-total.

Each Saturday morning my job was to light the fire for the bath water and get the messages from the local shops. The saddle-bag on my bike was large enough to carry the requirements of paraffin, tea, sugar, milk and thirty jam tarts. These tarts were for the players, fifteen yellow and fifteen red, some fussy players insisted on a particular colour. As there was no gas or electricity there were gas mantles for the tilly lamps. These had to be lit before the game finished, and hung up in strategic positions around the club. The last one was for the squatter, as it was he who made the tea, boiling the water on his coal fired stove, with tea, sugar and milk being provided. A reminder that in those days of austerity, food as such, was rationed.

One story recited to me by Fred Telfer, who was bar chairman in the late 40s is as follows. We were playing Warrington that day, I was refilling the lamps, as usual, when the paraffin spilt. It was cleaned up and I thought no more of it. In those days all the beer was bottled, Fred of course had to choose that particular trestle table to upturn the glasses, ready to serve. Well everything was contaminated with paraffin, I was not very a popular lad for a while after that.

The gentleman squatter suddenly disappeared, to be replaced by a woman with three or four young children. This move was conducted in a clandestine way, again overnight. One story I recall about this lady was when returning from the grocers with the tea and sugar. She said, "Put it over there on the window ledge, the tea is already made." On the ledge were mounds of used dried tea. When challenged she replied, "Yes, we have the fresh tea during the week." I was rather shocked that she had the temerity to do such a thing. I said, "I will speak to Jack Moore." Then she came out with a tirade of abuse, reminding me that she had to feed her kids on meagre rations with no one to help her. As her anger gave way to tears, I beat a hasty retreat. For years later, she was talked about in the bar as the 'Lady of the Night' as certain members were rumoured to be returning to the club when it was shut. All the squatters disappeared in the early fifties, rehoused possibly to Kirkby.

GAMES START AGAIN

THE ONLY AREA AVAILABLE for a pitch was at the bottom of the ground situated left to right. The committee and a number of former pre-war players worked hard to establish this pitch which was completed for the 1946–47 season. Even so, for many years the referee quite frequently had to stop the game to allow the players to dig out lumps of concrete and spikes which were gradually coming to the surface. It was always the normal thing for the captain to arm himself with a shovel and pick for this purpose. Bernard Houghton was one of the better diggers, his record still stands at excavating one armoured tank, two howitzers and a set of cymbals. On a more serious note, Bernard has completed twenty years as fixture secretary, this is a great achievement for a good club man!

With the government gradually releasing its forces, Sefton's numbers increased and were able to sustain two teams. The first game that season was a Second XV playing on the 13th of September, unfortunately no results for this are available. The rest of the ground was in complete dev-

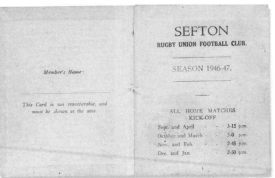

SEFTON
R.U.F.C.

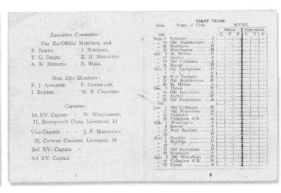

astation. Huge mounds of earth and mud, and massive slabs of concrete littered the area, barbed wire, spikes, this all part of the relics of the former gun-site. Compensation for this undertaking was funded by the government under the heading of 'war damages'. The committee used to despair of ever getting the ground back to some sort of normality. The wooden clubhouse, with windows on all sides, was in a good state of repair and was well maintained as it was used for accommodation during the war period.

RURAL AREA

THE RURAL BACKDROP to the ground consisted mainly of farmland fields and stretched as far down as Princess Drive, the following areas were now being built upon:

- § Deysbrook Barracks with houses for their married quarters.
- § Deysbrook Lane with its extensive farmland, council houses and new roads.
- § Multi-storey flats, Winterburn Heights, built overlooking

(ALIAS THE ALIENS)

Sefton's ground, a blot on the landscape for years. They were demolished in the late 90s to most people's approval. The building of these flats had brought a lot of inconvenience to the club over the years.

The bottom pitch, as it became known, was played upon until the re-opening of the ground in 1952. This was when the first team pitch and the present banking was reinstated to its pre-war situation. In 1948–49 with three teams and few reserves available, the need for a further pitch arose. It was quickly solved when a local farmer offered to rent a piece of land on the road which is now known as Bevins Lane, adjacent to 'Melwood', Liverpool Football Club's training ground. Access was made from the bottom left hand corner of our ground. Jack Moore sought me out one Saturday morning to help him mark out a pitch. In fact that day was my first introduction to the game, with him lending me his boots and jersey. The players very kindly kept me under their wing, looking after me throughout the match.

The washing facilities at the club were quite basic, two baths, the hot water was heated by a coal fired boiler, this having to be lit each Saturday morning with paper and wood brought from home. Away games were not so luxurious. Orrell for instance had a tin shack at a YMCA ground, West Park used the school cloakrooms with sinks and cold water and Ormskirk played on local council park land, the changing facilities at a local pub named the 'Eureka'. In a semi-derelict building in the yard, the washing arrangements were very primitive. They consisted of four tin baths in the open air. It must have been a pretty sight to any observer, each bath being supplied with a fresh bucket of luke warm water at irregular intervals in turn. The water carrier was probably the pub landlord. The rear of the pub was a two-storey building with all the curtains drawn. But to the observant bather the blinds would twitch occasionally. The Ormskirk lads would say, "Don't worry it is only the landlady, she will be serving you when they open at half five." Curiously we waited an hour for her to open, not really worth the wait as she was not a pretty sight!

D. P. BOHL B.Sc

SEFTON
R.U.F.C.

Most of the old boy clubs at this time were poor so it was ruled that we would not play them. Although there were one or two exceptions to the rule, works teams were also banned mainly because of a possibility of ungentlemanly conduct. There were few cars to travel to games in those days, it was either train or hired bus. Secretary Jack Moore would be at 'the meet' armed with a fistful of tickets to dole out. The meet would be Exchange Station for games against Hightown, Southport, Orrell, Shrewsbury, Rockferrians, Wirral, and Wallasey. For distant games it was a Crosville coach meeting at either the Rocket Hotel or St Johns Lane by Lime Street.

TRIBUTES TO THE CLUB'S REBUILDERS

SECRETARY JACK MOORE joined Sefton in September 1924, an accountant by profession, he was secretary to the area Meat Marketing Board and to various meat companies in the North West. He possessed the acumen of being capable of adding a column of pounds, shillings and pence in his head accurately in seconds. Over the many years as secretary it is unfortunate that minutes of meetings held were not recorded to the standard of his predecessor Freddie (he created fine hand written notes which form part of our valuable records). After the war, he had his fair share of work corresponding with government departments in getting things back to some normality. Jack, in his playing days, was a full back, usually fulfilling his role in the lower teams. His eyesight was not as good as it might have been, and his pals used to pull his leg when he caught a ball, "Jack your hearing is remarkable! " Angrily Jack would reply with a few impolite expletives, as he was not a guardian of linguistic purity.

In January 1950 Jack made an application to Liverpool Corporation for an electric supply to the club. An associate of one of the committee, an electrician, did the preliminary wiring, allowances being made for one kilowatt of lighting and nine kilowatt for water heating. An agreement was drawn up by H.J. Davis Bethren & Munroe, Sefton's

(ALIAS THE ALIENS)

solicitors and Mr George Endicott, the occupier of number 17 Lisleholme Road to install the necessary metering and cabling from his property to the clubhouse. Poles had to be erected to carry cabling across the hockey ground, permission for this was granted by the Deysbrook Club, an annual acknowledgement of three pound three shillings was agreed with the owner of the property. It seemed that George's wife was not too happy with this arrangement as she wanted something out of the deal so it was agreed that a turkey be afforded at Christmas every year. Problems arose from time to time with the limited supply as Sefton overloaded the system, the phone ringing most weeks with complaints from the Endicotts declaring that the electric meter was bouncing off the wall. Jack, usually dealing with these problems would promise Mrs Endicott another turkey to keep her quiet. It is thought Mrs Endicott finished up with enough turkeys each Christmas for all her family.

Jack left the club in 1958 after serving the club as secretary for twenty-six years. He was also credited with the honour of life membership. It was later announced, after a life as a bachelor that he married a lady golfer whose former husband was a Wirral Golf Club captain.

AS A PLAYER Barney Wall was not too particular over the condition of his kit, often neglecting to wash it. When hanging up his boots in the late forties he took on the responsibility of Club Chairman. He then adopted the habit of checking players for the state of their kit, reprimanding them if they wore white shorts or had dirty boots. He had further sporting interests, playing water polo in goal for Everton Swimming Club who were based at the former Dovecot baths on East Prescot Road. Throughout the history of the club the Chairman had always been nominated by those present at a particular meeting. At the 1948 AGM Barney was the first person to hold that position on a seasonal basis. He completed ten years at this post, and was president for two further years.

D. P. BOHL B.Sc

SEFTON
R.U.F.C.

EACH SUNDAY lunchtime the committee and their associated friends met for a drink, usually at The Rocket Hotel. Stringent times prevailed with the usual shortage of cigarettes. On one occasion Barney, when visiting the gents, was caught finishing a sly smoke. Being ignorant of the fact he had been spotted, Tom Daley sidled up to him and deftly relieved him of a prized packet of twenty from his jacket pocket. Returning to the company Tom began handing them out to the party. "Thanks!" said Barney, accepting a cigarette. "It's a pleasure", replied Tom, "You can hang on to the packet, they are yours, I've left you a couple". With that Barney didn't say a word. Unfortunately, shortly after the conclusion of his presidency, Barney died.

A MASTER BUILDER by trade Fred Barry, a quiet unassuming man, worked as an overseer for the Liverpool Warehousing Company, maintaining mainly dockyard buildings. He was a fine rugby player, a second row forward, playing in the first team for two or three years before retiring. Fred is responsible for much of the existing building work that is still evident today; brickwork to perimeter walls, removing all the windows, this literally boxing in the club to prevent vandalism, and building the much admired fire place in the early fifties. He was also responsible for organising the players in the concreting of the stand, all completed for our bi-centenary celebrations in 1957.

LES WILKINSON, as dedicated a club member as he was to his job as a Liverpool City Land Surveyor, worked hard for the club, always on the lookout for ways things could be improved. He inspected the work carried out by the contractors who were responsible for reinstating the ground, ensuring that it was up to standard. He introduced the collapsible touch-line flag to Sefton, this maybe as he was regularly running the line, realising the possible dangers of a fixed flagpole. Les, with his knowledge of city sports grounds made a comparison of Sefton's to Goodison Park and found both were of similar acreage. A confirmed bach-

elor, it seemed all his time and effort was centred on Sefton. Deservedly he was appointed as an Honorary Life Member in the fifties, and a club trustee. In 1989, at a good age, he died to be remembered as a good servant of the club.

Jack Wilson, a former Stafford club member and former county player with Staffordshire, joined Sefton in the early fifties. This upon being transferred by English Electric to work in the area. A senior engineer he was responsible for many design features for his company. On joining the club he soon found himself on the executive committee and eventually was appointed a trustee. He proved a great asset to the club over many years.

George Nelson, a former pre-war first team player of note and pre-war treasurer, held the office of County Representative for twenty-three years. A club life member, he was conferred as President on two occasions, 1950-52 and 1974-76, something unique at Sefton, as his club record reveals. He was a man with distinctive qualities, no less.

All Pals Together
Back Row: Alf Roby, Les Wilkinson, J.F.Moore, J.P.Williams (Captain),
Front Row: a guest, Tom Daley, L.McLoughlin, Barney Wall,
J.C.Parkinson, Fred Barry, Bob Alexander
(Note: Only bottled beer in those days)

D. P. BOHL B.Sc

It would not be fitting if a word or two were not mentioned of the club's former groundsman and caretaker, Alf Hughes. A man of particular note, who lived in Lisleholme Cresent, he was formally employed with the West Derby Hockey Club, our old neighbours. This gave him access to his job via his back garden gate, diligently working for the club throughout the late fifties until his retirement in 1975. He at that time presented a trophy to the club with the inscription 'Player of the Year'. A generous gift, to some people a little ornate. Alf was not a rugby player, but a fine gentleman!

JIM ALEXANDER

JIM WAS BROUGHT UP in East Yorkshire and educated at Bridlington School where his sporting activities included rugby and cricket, rugby being his first choice. After further education at Birmingham University he joined the army and went to Sandhurst and was commissioned in The Duke of Wellington's Regiment. He was later transferred to the West Yorkshire Regiment, playing rugby at every opportunity. His battalion was sent to France a few days after D-Day in 1944 where they encountered some of the fiercest fighting in the Normandy campaign. Many good men lost their lives and Jim was severely wounded. For a time it looked as though his rugby days might be over, but he recovered and was again back on the rugby field.

Upon leaving the army Jim returned to Birmingham University to complete his degree in Chemical Engineering. Finding employment in the area he joined Erdington RUFC. In 1953 he moved to Liverpool taking up a post at BICC Prescot. At the age of 31 and in the twilight of his rugby career he sought out Sefton. Jim played regularly for his new club at prop-forward for the first fifteen until he suffered a serious shoulder injury, which ended his rugby-playing career. Not deterred, he took to refereeing and whilst he became known as strict but fair, in one of his

Jim Alexander

earlier games refereeing Sefton's third team, he blew his whistle and called "*Our ball, Sefton.*"

Over the years Jim served in many offices, including the executive committee, chairman, president, treasurer and chairman of selection. He took over the role as treasurer for a second period from Doug Herd, a member of the club who was tragically killed one morning on his way to work. During Jim's husbandry as treasurer for over fourteen years the club built up a healthy bank balance.

When Jim was chairman of selection he consulted the first team captain, Bill Jones whist he was still sitting in the bath! That was typical of Jim, always willing to give help, support and encouragement to others both on and off the field.

One cold night in February 1989, Jim went to the club to discuss proposed changes to the kitchen facilities. He was about to go home when he suffered a fatal heart attack. He had always prayed that he would die quickly and God granted him his wish, at the place he dearly loved, Sefton.

D. P. BOHL B. Sc

The Aliens – Committee Minutes 1912–20

Report for Season 1912–13

Report for season 1912–13

The first team played 24 matches, 9 of which were won, 3 drawn & 12 lost. They scored 291 points against 281 by their opponents. The chief scorers were W. B. Croxford 14 tries, W. J. Trist 11 tries & R. W. Jones 7 tries.

The second team played 20 matches, won 7 drew 3 & lost 10, scoring 159 points against 234. Their chief scorer was J. King, 6 tries.

During the season the club held four social gatherings, with fair results financially. Great credit is due to the Entertainments committee for their work – work which should help to bring the men more in touch with each other, & so strengthen the "club" feeling between the members. While all have worked well to this end, I wish to draw your attention to the vast amount of hard work which has been cheerfully borne by the entertainments secretary, H. N. Ellis, & to ask you to join with me in a very hearty vote of thanks to him for the efficient way in which these socials were managed.   J. J. Appleton

Player Statistics 1912–13

AGM Cash Statement 1912–13

CASH STATEMENT.

RECEIPTS.				EXPENDITURE			
Overdue Subscriptions		£6	5	0	Balance due Hon. Treasurer 1911-12	£8	5	8½
Vice-Presidents' "		3	18	0	Washing Towels	2	10	6
Hon. Members' "		6	5	0	Wash-bowls, Lemons, &c.	1	11	5
Playing Members' "		27	0	6	Jerseys	1	13	0
Jerseys		4	12	0	Rugby, County and Referees' Unions	2	1	6
Gate Money		3	1	5	Rent for Ground	15	0	0
Members at Princes Rd.		0	10	0	Groundsman's and Gatesman's Wages			
		51	11	9	and Expenses	5	19	0
Profit on Teas		2	10	0	Printing and Stationery	5	6	9
" Entertainments		1	3	0	Football Material	1	17	0
					Dressing Rooms	3	5	0
					Sundries	0	11	2
					Postage and Correspondence	5	14	3½
						53	14	10
					Balance in Treasurer's hands	1	10	5
		£55	5	3		£55	5	3

J. J. Appleby
Hon. Treas.

Audited and found correct— F. KING,
HAROLD B. ELLIS

D. P. BOHL B. Sc

Newspaper Game Reviews 1912–13

Notes on the Barnsley Game by their Club Secretary Mick Marshall

SEFTON
R.U.F.C.

THERE ARE TWO HUGGARDS mentioned in the report. The Rev'd R Huggard (referee) was our founding president and there is a load of information about him on our website at: HTTP://WWW.BARNSLEY RUFC.CO.UK/HUGGARD. HTML.

The other one, I can only assume to be one of his sons. I did not realize he played for the club. It is a shame that his first name is not mentioned. The Reverend lost two sons in the first war, one in France and the other in Gallipoli (unusual as that battle was mainly fought by the ANZACS). There is a significant connection with our club and the two Barnsley Pals regiments of the first war. I have read extensively about the regiment and when I saw the name Kell in your match report it rang a bell.

The other names (Harris, Dickinson and Nesbitt) are probably as follows. The Harris could be either Frank or Herbert Harris and the Dickinson (first name unknown) all served with the Plymouth and Portsmouth battalions, strangely enough at Gallipoli.

The Nesbitt is a cleric, one of around four or five in the team at that time. Barnsley was formed from a couple of church sides, as was the norm in those days

ALIENS LOSE TO BARNSLEY.

The Aliens had an attractive tit-bit for their supporters at Clubmoor on Saturday, when they entertained the Yorkshire Cup semi-finalists. Unfortunately, Barnsley were minus several of their regular men, and the Aliens very sportingly lent them a couple to enable them to put a full team in the field.

In the opening half the home team had the greater portion of the attack, but failed at the critical moments, when a cool head would have been invaluable. Their forwards on many occasions made much ground, but as a rule an ill-directed pass or a knock-on brought the movements to an untimely end. Yet they did most of the attacking for their side, and it was the forwards who initiated the movements which resulted in the scoring of their two tries—Bob Jones getting one in each half. The Barnsley forwards were a lusty lot, and played the typical kick-and-rush game in menacing style, although they were not so progressive as their opponents. Kell, at full-back for the visitors, played a capital game, and his defence was always sound. Harris and Dickinson were a pair of hard-working forwards. Huggard, however, was the best man on the side, his fielding under extreme difficulties being excellent. Rumjahn was again at back for the Aliens; he fields well and kicks with judgment. Croxford was the best three-quarter on view, and Bayliss and Ellis are a serviceable pair of halves. Forward, Jones, although a little unorthodox perhaps, was easily the best of the home vanguard.

At the interval Aliens deservedly led by a try to nil, scored by Bob Jones after a prolonged spell of attacking by the home team. The second half was pretty even, and Barnsley were lucky to score from a try which to all appearances was offside. Kell scored again for the visitors and converted his own try. Jones again got through for the Aliens; and the Rev. J. Nesbitt counted for Barnsley. On the whole, however, the home team were distinctly unlucky to lose, the result being: Barnsley 11 pts. Aliens 6 pts. The Rev. Mr. Huggard, chairman of the Yorkshire Union, officiated as referee.

Daily Post, 31 March 1913

ALIENS OVERCOME LIVERPOOL A.

The Aliens were much the better side in their match with Liverpool A, at Clubmoor. Their forwards packed and scrummaged better, and their three-quarters always looked the more convincing line. Liverpool A, who were weakly represented, had the ball as often as their opponents, but they lacked the ability to press their attacks home to a successful issue. Against a less resolute defence they would probably have done better, but from start to finish the tackling of the Aliens was particularly sound.

In the first half Madoc-Jones scored, after a scrambling run by R. W. Jones, who carried the ball up to the line and parted at the right moment. Ellis converted from a difficult angle, and this proved to be the only scoring in this half. The Aliens continued to have the best of matters on the resumption, and a fine passing movement among the forwards ended in Madoc-Jones scoring again for the home team. Ellis took the kick, but failed to improve on the score. The finest effort of the match, however, came from Cocks, who, receiving in midfield, handed off man after man, and scored a splendid try. Ellis again failing. Liverpool were by this time a well-beaten team, only Thomson being able to make any impression on the home defence. Gabrielson, Grant, and Thomson were Liverpool's best men, while the Aliens were well served by Griffith, Cocks, and Armitt. The final score was: Aliens 1 goal 3 tries (11 points), Liverpool A nil.

MILT

Daily Post, 3 February 1913

The Aliens.

I am indebted to Mr. F. J. Applebee, the hon. secretary and treasurer of the Aliens, for a complete record to date of his club. The claims of the bigger games prevent my paying a visit to Townsend-lane, Clubmoor, but one of these days I hope to give the club a surprise visit. A characteristic of the present team is their enthusiasm the whole game through. Happening of this important type in Rugby football are numerous, as instanced by the fact that in late September Preston Grasshoppers led the Aliens by 17 points to nothing, and at the finish the result was a draw. On Saturday last at Furness the home team scored 5 goals, a dropped goal, and a try, and the visitors to all intents, were subdued to defeat. In the second half the Aliens played like giants and registered a goal and 3 tries.

This is the type of rugger to set the spirit of enthusiasm moving. W. B. Croxford, R. W. Jones, H. M. Ellis, and F. J. Applebee are representative of that type, and a compliment to the men generally is well deserved.

Yorkshire's Visit.

"Oval" in the *Express* 9 November 1912

ALIENS DEFEAT WATERLOO.

At Waterloo the home "A" team fell victims to the Aliens after a keen struggle, although the visitors were rather lucky to claim winning honours. Waterloo in the first half were more than a match for the Aliens, Thornton goaling from a mark and Penny a little later getting over with a capital try, which Fontannaz failed to improve on. The home side at half-time held an advantage of 6 points to nil. On turning round, however, the Aliens rather early crossed the Waterloo line twice with converted tries, and later added an unconverted try; while Waterloo, in reply, could only manage 5 points, though up to the finish it looked odds on the home lot piercing the visitors' defence again. Hearty tackling, however, by the Aliens kept their line clear, and enabled them to run out victors by 15 points to 11 points.

Courier, 18 November 1912

ALIENS OVERCOME LIVERPOOL UNIVERSITY.

The Aliens thoroughly deserved their success against the Liverpool University, although they played below their best form. The 'Varsity opened strongly, and looked like walking away with the spoils, but once they got a grip of the game the homesters were more convincing. Their forwards were smarter in their combination, and showed a better understanding. The visiting forwards were a disjointed lot, working in fits and starts, but even at their best they never compared with the Aliens for judgment and understanding. The Aliens did all the scoring in the first half, Croxford scoring the first try after a fine individual effort by Johnstone, the veteran cleverly intercepting a 'Varsity pass. Ellus failed to convert from a difficult angle. After a clever passing in the first half, Croxford securing the ball between the posts for Bishop to convert. The 'Varsity improved in the second half and scored tries through Lee and Anderson, Moore failing to improve on either kick. A feature of the game was the strong tackling and kicking of the 'Varsity back.

Daily Post, 30 January 1913

✝RUGBY UNION.

THERE WAS SOME GOOD FOOTBALL AT DALTON ON SATURDAY AND FURNESS WON.

Railway Meadow, Dalton, was the scene of a splendidly contested match on Saturday, when the Liverpool Aliens were pitted against Furness. There was a capital attendance, both on the field and on the "free" grandstand on the boundary of the railway line. Here a good crowd gathered and witnessed the match without putting their hand down for the threepenny bit. Surely the committee of the Furness Club can effectually prevent this free view of their matches by the provision of rolls of canvas or some other material stretched across the embankment wall. I commend this step to the committee. It was said (I may as well say that my friend Joe said it) that the gate in the field and out of the field in the lane) was a record. I don't dispute it Joe. To the match. Furness had a representative side out, with the exception of A N. Widdop, who was doing duty for the county. Liverpool was not fully represented, and picked up three subs in Dalton, in the persons of Molly Riley, J. Hunter, and J. Lawrence, who were in the forward rank.

DALTON AND LINDAL MEN WERE PLAYING.

I noticed two other fellows I knew, viz. Jack Helme, from Lindal, and George Corkhill, from Dalton, who live and work in the Mersey city, and are regular Alien players. Furness made a fine burst in the first half, the Aliens seeming not to have got into their stride. Perhaps they had not cast their railway legs. At any rate Furness was the better team and tries were scored by Wilf Brown, Tommy Brown, Gillott, and Harry Brown; Teasdale kicking three goals out of four attempts, Wilf Brown also dropping a goal. At the interval Furness had 22 points to nil. But what a change, a sensational change, I should say, came over the aspect of affairs in the second half. Furness had evidently shot their bolt, for they were over played in the second half, and Liverpool put up 14 points. Croxford scored three times and Helme once. Twist kicked one goal. It was a peculiar match, for in the first half there was only one team in it and that was Furness, and in the second half there was only one team and that was the Aliens.

THE GAME WAS A CAPITAL ONE.

Barrow Paper, 9 November 1912

D. P. BOHL B.Sc

Membership Handbook Season 1912–13

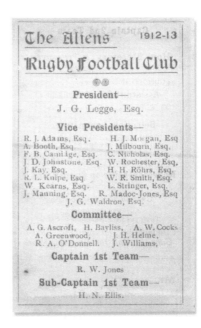

The Aliens — 1912-13

Rugby Football Club

President—

J. G. Legge, Esq.

Vice Presidents—

R. J. Adams, Esq.	H. J. Morgan, Esq
A. Booth, Esq.	J. Milbourn, Esq.
F. B. Camilège, Esq.	C. Nicholas, Esq.
J. D. Johnstone, Esq.	W. Rochester, Esq.
J. Kay, Esq.	H. H. Röhrs, Esq.
R. L. Knipe, Esq.	W. R. Smith, Esq.
W. Kearns, Esq.	L. Stringer, Esq.
J. Manning, Esq.	R. Madoc-Jones, Esq
	J. G. Waldron, Esq.

Committee—

A. G. Ascroft, H. Bayliss, A. W. Cocks
A. Greenwood, J. H. Helme,
R. A. O'Donnell. J. Williams,

Captain 1st Team—

R. W. Jones

Sub-Captain 1st Team—

H. N. Ellis.

Captain 2nd Team —

W. G. Flint

Hon. Secretary & Treasurer—

F. J. Applebee,

44 Guernsey Road, Stoneycroft, Liverpool,

Assistant Sec. & Treas.—

O. E. Bayliss, 16 Priory Rd., Anfield

Selection Committee—

R. W. Jones.	W. G. Flint
H. N. Ellis	F. J. Applebee.
W. B. Croxford,	A. G. Ascroft,
O. E. Bayliss,	J. D. Johnstone.

Representative on County Com.

W. B. Croxford,

GROUND—TOWNSEND LANE.

DRESSING ROOM—
Townsend Lane Council Schools.

*Clubmoor or Cabbage Hall Cars to
Cabbage Hall for Dressing Room*

Mr ....

....

FIRST TEAM			
DATE.	CLUB.	Ground	Result
Sept. 14	Oldham	Home	
,, 21	Birkenhead Park	Away	0 — 32
,, 28	Preston Grasshoppers	Home	14 — 17
Oct. 5	New Brighton "A"	Away	
,, 12	Liverpool University	Away	
,, 19	Chester College	Home	
,, 26	Southport Olympic	Away	
Nov. 2	Furness	Away	14 — 7
,, 9	Eccles	Home	
,, 16	Waterloo "A"	Away	
,, 23	Liverpool "A"	Away	
,, 30	Eccles	Away	
Dec. 7	Hamilton	Home	
,, 14	Birkenhead Park 2nd	Home	
,, 21	Cosmopolitan	Away	
,, 28	Waterloo "A"	Home	0 —
Jan. 4	New Brighton "A"	Home	
,, 11	Furness	Home	
,, 18	Southport Olympic	Home	
,, 25	Liverpool University	Home	8 — 6
Feb. 1	Liverpool "A"	Home	11 — 0
,, 8	Preston Grasshoppers	Away	
,, 15	Ashford House	Home	
,, 22	Cosmopolitan	Home	
Mar. 1	Hamilton	Away	
,, 8	Chester College	Away	
,, 15	Oldham	Away	
,, 22	Ashford House	Away	
,, 29	Barnsley	Home	

Report for Season 1913– 14

Season 1913-14

The past season has been a disastrous one both
as regards finance & results. We finished the season
with a deficit of £13. 1. 5, the first team won 8
matches lost 19 scoring 165 points against 395, and
the 2nd team won 5 drew 1 lost 14 scoring 145 points
against 292.

The experiment of running a 3rd team resulted in
failure.

The season however was not without its bright side.
We had in our teams many men who were new to the
game. They were not expected to win many games,
& they certainly fulfilled those expectations. Still
they have youth on their side & among the novices
are some men, who with a little luck, will go
far in the game. They will commence next September
with the advantage of a season's experience & with
the advent of several new men, coupled with the
retention of the services of most of the older hands
the future of the club looks very bright. If only
a little more keenness can be infused into the
team, the report at the end of next season will

be much pleasanter to write & to read

This year the entertainments committee has
not been supported as it might have been. Our
entertainments should be a source of considerable
revenue to the club, & they will be if the
members will give us their whole-hearted support.

In conclusion I wish to thank those officers
who have given up so much time to the well being
of the club, in particular that much maligned
body the selection committee, the entertainments
committee & its secretary, Mr Knife for turning
out so frequently in all weathers to referee the
second team games, Mr Milbourn for many actions
which have lightened my own work, & Mr H. Baylis
for taking over the duties as treasurer when his
brother had so unfortunately to give them up.

J. Appleby
Hon. Sec.

The Aliens v Birkenhead Park 20th September 1913

SEFTON
R.U.F.C.

Branscombe's Original Programme
(Established 1882. The oldest Programme in Great Britain).

GRAND FOOTBALL MATCH,
Saturday, September 20, 1913.

At Birkenhead Park.   Kick-off 3-30.

THE ALIENS. Red and White.

RIGHT WING	FULL BACK.	LEFT WING
	R G Griffiths	

THREE QUARTERS.

J Rumjahn   H von Mergershausen   R Cubbin   J H Weights

HALF BACKS.

W B Croxford (capt.)   *J Hessey Anderson*
~~H N Ellis~~

FORWARDS.

S J Bishop	F Outhwaite	A Roberts	W J Trist
R A O'Donnell	E B Ringrose	J R Williams	D Sloss

( )

L G Wall	T C Hughes	G C Burrell	C Oke'l
R C Lindsay	H D Pain	C A McHutcheon	F Wilson

Forwards.

J C Barber   J S Jowett

Half Backs.

E D L Gonner   V H Kempson   J P Pomeroy   J L Roe

Three Quarters.

F H Heyworth

LEFT WING.	Full Back.	RIGHT WING.

Birkenhead Park.

P. Branscombe, Printer, 113. Borough Road, Birkenhead.

RUGBY METHOD OF SCORING.—A try, 3 points; Goal from try, 5 points; a Dropped Goal (except from Mark or Penalty Kick), 4 points; Goal from a Mark or Penalty Kick, 3 points; In case of a goal from a try, the try is not counted.

Newspaper Game Reviews 1913–14

BIRKENHEAD PARK'S GOOD START

Birkenhead Park made an excellent start with Aliens as visitors. Of course, it was expected that they would win, and even 2 goals 8 tries to a try was not a colossal score for the occasion; but it was in the way the team shaped that satisfaction came, and for an opening game the play was quite good. Skipper Lindsay finds himself with a capital lot of fellow-forwards, among whom G. C. Burnell, H. D. Pain, L. G. Wall, and F. Wilson were, perhaps, the most prominent on Saturday, but they worked well together. The chief weakness was not keeping the eye on the ball—not an easy thing to do at all times—but in loose work they were capital. J. S Jowett, a new half from Loretto, did well in the stand-off position, with an occasional touch of nervousness almost inevitable in a first game with a new club; and J. C. Barber was good as ever in working the pack. At three-quarter H. H. Kempson's heady work was of value, and so, too, was the cleverness and dodginess of J. P. Pomeroy and his partner, J. L. Roe. E. D. Gonner, on the left wing, lost some good opportunities, but also made good openings. On the other side it was defence that was tested, and Weights, Croxford, Von Mergershausen, and R. Griffiths, the full back, did some good things, but the Park combination was too much for them. Anderson and M'Cubbin had several good dashes, and the forwards all worked hard.

In the second half Aliens had one good spell of attacking, the sole result being a well-worked try which fell to Trist; but on the whole the Park were the pressers, and put on 3 tries in the first half and 7 in the second, the scorers being J. L. Roe (3), G. C. Burnell (2), J. P. Pomeroy, E. D. Gonner, H. D. Pain, C. A. M'Hutcheon, and F. Wilson. Practically all of the tries resulted from combination among the backs or company play by the forwards, but Wilson got his through the smartness with which Lindsay snapped up the ball in touch and threw it out before a full line-up could assemble. On the whole play the Park prospects seem good, and even against the "international" team on the other side of the river they will make a good show if they can put out full strength for the occasion.

ALIENS v. NEW BRIGHTON.

New Brighton were visited by the Aliens to-day, this being the team's opening engagement. Frank Edwards was the referee, and New Brighton made the first incursions and got to close quarters, but relief came, and the Aliens approached midfield, only to be put on their defence by a spirited run on the part of Chester.

Hostilities prevailed close to Griffiths' charge, and several minor breakaways took place, but the visitors could not raise the siege, and eventually R. D. Nesbitt used his strength and rushed over, the goal kick failing. Later on Chester ran in another try, and this was followed by another from Stead, but neither were augmented. A free kick was well taken by Dwyer, who landed a goal. Stead was the next tryist, and Morgan scored full points. The score at the interval was:—New Brighton 17pts, Aliens nil.

In the second half Stead, Armstrong and Dwyer scored for New Brighton, and Williams for the Aliens. Not one of the four tries were converted.

Final.—New Brighton 26pts, Aliens 3pts.

New Brighton's Auspicious Start.

A hastily-arranged fixture between New Brighton and Aliens gave the former club an opportunity to get into harness on the closing Saturday of September, and if the Brightonians can be judged on their initial performance the club ought to have a fairly good season. Against the Aliens the forward line was not of a sensational composition, but probably the quality of the Aliens scrummagers rather upset their play. Behind the scrum, however, New Brighton were extremely fast and occasionally clever, and by gradual stages they accumulated a total of 26 points against 3 points scored by the Aliens. In the opening half R. D. Nesbitt, Chesters, and Stead (2) scored tries, two being converted by Morgan, and Dwyer kicked a penalty goal. After the interval Stead got his third try, and Dwyer forced his way over the Aliens' line. For the visitors Williams was the only player to make an impression, and his try was well deserved. Stead, Eskrigge, Chesters, and T. R. Cook were prominent in the winners' attack, and R. D. Nesbitt, the veteran forward, was the leading scrummager of the side. For the Aliens Griffiths at back played well, and Jones was the outstanding threequarter; At half-back Croxford put in a lot of good work, and the forwards held the scrum without, however, giving the rear ranks enough opportunities to turn the run of the game. Teams:—

New Brighton—Morgan, Stead, Lee, Eskrigge, Chester, T. R. Cook, G. N. Cook, R. D. Nesbitt, Dwyer, M'Cann, Simpson, Armstrong, Roberts, Westrupp, Quinsey.

Aliens—Griffiths, T. Jones, Weights, Bellamy, Ramjohn, Croxford, Ellis, Parry, Sloss, Roberts, A. Roberts, Kaye, Outhwaite, Ringrose, Williams. Referee, Mr. F. H. Edwards.

Post 29 September 1913

NEWS THROUGH THE TUNNEL.

Birkenhead Park started the season with a sort of preliminary canter, having an easy thing on with Aliens, but the latter played a capital game against heavier metal. They were tryers all the way, they lasted well, and their defence was really good; but the Park won by 2 goals 8 tries to 1 try. As a matter of fact, most of the tries were so smartly worked that almost any defence would have been hopeless. Skipper Linsay put in a notable one towards the finish by a bit of work which no defence could have countered. The Park pack as a whole was good, but it was the clever work of J. C. Barber as scrum half that did the damage. He got his men going in fine style, and Jowell, the Loretto boy, did very well at stand-off. J. P. Pomeroy was himself at three-quarter, and J. L. Roe on his wing got three tries. Kempson is a very strong point on the Park line, and is always resourceful. E. D. Gonner was unfortunate over the line, but got one try. G. C. Burnell played a fine forward game, and had a couple of tries, the other scorers being Pomeroy, Pain, M'Hutcheon, and F. Wilson.

D. P. BOHL B.Sc

SEFTON
R.U.F.C.

ALIENS' HEAVY REVERSE.

At Clubmoor, on Saturday, the Aliens met by no means a representative team in Vale of Lune, but were, nevertheless, heavily beaten. The home pack were quite as good as the visitors for three-parts of the game, and then went all to pieces, during which time the visitors ran in six tries from forward rushes, two of which were due to faulty work by the home back. In the first half, aided by a strong wind, the Aliens were constantly pressing, but the "threes" were terribly weak and threw numerous chances away through lying in a bunch and trying to walk the ball through instead of opening out and swinging the leather about. As a consequence it was close on the interval when Roberts scored their solitary try.

Afterwards, Croxford and Kay both made a mull of good openings. With the assistance of the wind the visitors dominated the play, and Bond, Wilcock, Helm, Corless, and Oglethorpe (twice) crossed the home line, Salthouse goaling from the last try, although a good kicker would have majoried at least three of the other tries. Result: Vale of Lune, 1 goal 5 tries (20 points); Aliens, 1 try (3 points).

Daily Post 23 March 1914

THE ALIENS' DEFEAT.

The Aliens visited Heaton Moor and were defeated by 3 goals 3 tries (24 points) to nil. Heaton Moor were the better-balanced team, and their combination was the main factor of the Aliens' defeat. Cameron was the first to score from a forward rush, and E. Copley scored the next two tries after some fine passes between the backs. In the second half Whitehead, Cameron, and Summersgill scored. Kelly kicked two goals and E. Copley one. The Aliens were unfortunate to be beaten by so many points, as the game was not as one-sided as the score would suggest. W. R. Croxford was many times dangerous, but was too fast for his colleagues, and the chances that he made could not be utilised. F. H. Anderson and G. Horridge played cleverly at half-back, and gave their three-quarters many openings which they failed to materialise owing to lack of combination and some fine defensive play. J. H. Weights played a fine game at full back, and on several occasions cleared his lines cleverly. W. B. Croxford was the outstanding three-quarter. He made many fine attempts to score against his old colleagues, but received little assistance. S. Sloss, E. Kendrick, and S. S. Jones were prominent in the forwards. The Heaton Moor team gave a fine all-round exhibition, and it would be hard to individualise; but Cameron in the forwards and Kelly at half were at the top of their form.

Daily Post 30 March 1914

ALIENS' WELCOME WIN.

The Aliens broke the "spell" which has remained so long on their homeland at Clubmoor by a brilliant 25 points to 3 victory. Southport were weakly represented, their team including eight reserves, Twy being absent from the pack, and Gifford much missed at half-back. Aliens opposed them with an exceptionally strong combination, which included Hessey-Anderson, the Lancashire half-back, and Von Mengershausen, Manchester University and ex-South African three-quarter. Aliens asserted themselves early, as after three minutes H. Anderson obtained from a five yards' scrum, and eluding Grimshaw, Wainwright, and Mackintosh "docked" safely. Later Anderson's astuteness enabled Ellis to slip through unmolested. After dominating the scrum the Aliens heeled out to Anderson, who artfully enabled the veteran Croston to get in near the posts, Bishop later cleverly negotiating the major points. Following a line-out, Trist also traversed the Southport lines. Von Mengershausen engineered a bright venture, and parted to Croxford, who worked the oracle once more. Aliens thus had 19 points to their credit at the interval.

Olympic resumed with the wind in their favour, and soon managed to catch their hosts napping. Following a five yards' scrummage Grimshaw got away with the oval to Baldwin, who got home smartly, and thus scored Southport's solitary try. The homesters, however, continued to dominate, and further tries came from Anderson and O'Donnell. The outstanding feature of the game was Anderson's irrepressibility.

Daily Post 15 January 1914

second half. Eskrigge, Stead, Short, and Nesbitt were the pick of the side.

ALIENS LOSE AT LANCASTER.

The visit of the Aliens to the Vale of Lune at Quay Meadow, Lancaster, provided a hard-fought game, which was in every way much closer than local supporters had anticipated. The Aliens had a good weighty pack, and though the Vale were more successful in gaining possession, the Aliens were wonderfully good in the loose, and their outsides, if not brilliant, played quite a useful game. Croschord, the ex-Lancashire three-quarter, was a tower of strength for the visitors, and with Ellis started many dangerous attacks. Mudge, at half-back, also played a skilful game for the Aliens, cutting through and giving dexterous passes. The Vale greatly missed their captain at scrum-half, M'Namara, who usually plays stand-off, making an indifferent substitute, and marring to a large extent the work of the Vale backs. The splendid work of the Vale forwards was always in evidence, and it is a curious feature that all the tries were obtained by forwards. W. Pinch scored for the Vale from a forward rush in the first three minutes, and O'Donnell, the Lancashire trial forward, equalised. Regan put the Vale ahead in the second half, the kicks all failing. The Vale backs gave a poor display, Atkinson, at full back, being quite a failure, and if his mistakes had not been well covered he would have jeopardised the Vale's unbeaten home record. The result was a win for the Vale by 2 tries to 1 try.

RIVAL 'VARSITIES AT CALDERSTONES

The meeting of the rival 'Varsities of

Daily Post 15 December 1913

The Committee Minutes 3rd September 1914 – WWI
The Club is Suspended

One Fixture: v. Germany.

The Aliens R.F.C.—As the majority of their
players are on service, have only one fixture,
viz., that v. Germany

Committee Meeting held at Clubmoor Hotel
3 . 9 . 14.
Present Messrs Knife, Applebee, Cowper,
R.N. Ellis, T. Madoc-Jones, Smith

It was decided that as so many of the playing
members had volunteered for active service, that
the club should be suspended during the
period of the war.

World War 1– Military Casualties

Pte G.P.S. Brown	Cpl C.A. Beverley	2nd Lt H. Tolson
www.cwgc.org.uk	www.cwgc.org.uk	www.cwgc.org.uk
detailed.asp?casualty	detailed.asp?casualty	detailed.asp?casualty
=843260	=340445	=1589673

D. P. BOHL B.Sc

THE LATE SECOND-LIEUTENANT
WILLIAMSON.

WOUNDED OFFICER'S ADVENTURES.

Second-Lieutenant Robson, of the Black Watch, who prior to the war was a schoolmaster in Liverpool, has been wounded, and is in the Stationary Hospital, Abbeville. His condition is reported as satisfactory.

He has served on the staff of Birchfield-road Council Schools and Emmanuel Council Schools. He was a member of the Aliens Rugby Football Club and of the Anfield Cricket Club.

The officer was in Brussels when the war broke out, and with difficulty escaped in the guise of a Belgian peasant, entering the Dutch frontier at Aloat with a number of Belgian refugees. Reaching Ostend, he was fortunately able, amid thousands clamouring to get away, to find a berth on board a vessel leaving for England. This was owing to the hospitality of a lady whom he knew, who had secured a stale cabin. After returning to England he joined the Scots Guards. He took part in many important engagements with his regiment.

DIRKDALE OFFICER

SEFTON
R.U.F.C.

2nd Lt J.H. Weights
www.cwgc.org.uk
detailed.asp?casualty
=576937

2nd Lt A. Williamson
www.cwgc.org.uk
detailed.asp?casualty
=455093

2nd Lt. J. Robson

LIVERPOOL OFFICER HONOURED.

LIEUTENANT VENMORE RECEIVES THE MILITARY CROSS.

It is officially announced that the Military Cross for conspicuous bravery has been awarded to Lieutenant J. Frederick Venmore, of the 14th Royal Welsh Fusiliers.

On the night of January 30 last Lieutenant Venmore was on duty as patrol officer in front of the British trenches in France, when a sentry in the firing trench reported that three men in an advanced listening post had been wounded. Two of these men were just able to crawl back to the British lines over the barbed wire, but the third man was too seriously wounded to follow, being shot through both legs. Lieutenant Venmore volunteered to go to his assistance, and took with him a non-commissioned officer (Corporal William Williams, a Carnarvon man), who is also awarded the Distinguished Conduct Medal.

They went out under heavy fire over the parapet, and after great difficulty successfully brought in the man over the wire and two ditches. This brave action was succeeded by a further gallant act on the following morning, when a message was received that a man had had his arm blown off at another listening post, practically unapproachable by daylight. Lieutenant Venmore again undertook to go to his aid, once more taking with him Corporal Williams. They crawled across the open ground in the face of heavy machine gun fire. The sufferer was reached, his wounds attended to, and he was subsequently brought to safety. Both the officer and his companion were most highly congratulated by the brigade and divisional officers.

Lieutenant Venmore, a son of Mr. James Venmore, a Liverpool citizen and a justice of the peace of the city. He is twenty-seven years of age, and was educated at the Liverpool College and at Hill Hall School. He subsequently studied architecture at the Liverpool University, and was engaged in that profession in Liverpool until at the outbreak of war he enlisted as a private in the 3rd Battalion of the Liverpool "Pals." He received his commission in the 14th Royal Welsh Fusiliers in December, 1914, and proved himself a most capable and popular officer.

Lieutenant Venmore's well-earned distinction will give great pleasure to his many friends in Liverpool and in North Wales.

Pte W. Johnson
www.cwgc.org.uk
detailed.asp?casualty
=796339

Lt J. F. Venmore
www.cwgc.org.uk
detailed.asp?casualty
=548492

(ALIAS THE ALIENS)

BRAVE WORDS.

Lance-corporal A. E. Hickling, of the King's Liverpool Regiment, died in France from wounds. He was first assistant-master at St. Lawrence Schools, Kirkdale, and a member of the choir of Holy Trinity Church, Walton Breck. He was educated at Deacon's School, Peterborough, and at St. John's College, Battersea, where he was popularly known as "Pete." Here he had a most successful career, gaining the Government certificate with a double first-class, and was a member of the college first teams. As "Pete" he was known to a wide circle of admirers in Liverpool, who mourn the loss of a valuable friendship which stood every test, but the

Lance.-Cp. A. E. HICKLING loss is greatest to the boys of his old school. A few days before he was wounded he wrote:—"I am afraid we are bound to have losses in the next few days, and if I am among the number I hope my friends will remember what an infinitely small thing the loss of one life is in comparison with the principle for which we are fighting; and, therefore, my wish is that you should not grieve for me, but rather that you should be proud that I have an opportunity of falling in the same cause as so many of our St. Lawrence boys have done."

L. Cpl A. E. Hickling www.cwgc.org.uk detailed.asp?casualty =21507

Lt J.G. Williams
www.cwgc.org.uk
detailed.asp?casualty
=554216

SILENCED MACHINE-GUN.

HOW LIVERPOOL SCHOOLMASTER WAS KILLED

Sergeant Griffith, who was for eight years an assistant-master at St. Anne's School, Stanley, has been killed in action. He was well known as a member of the Alloa Rugby Football Club, and had obtained much repute as an artiste; he was a pupil of the Liverpool School of Art. A comrade describes his death as follows:—Some of the platoon had been mown down by a German machine-gun, which was enfilading from the right flank. Sergeant Griffith mustered a few men, who, to his shout of "Come up, boys," dashed at the enemy and put the squad out, not without, however, the loss of the sergeant, who fell mortally wounded. He was noticed to be lying alongside a German officer. Brave little Bob Griffith! I take my cap off to his memory.

Sgt R.G. Griffiths
www.cwgc.org.uk
detailed.asp?casualty
=787685

Jack (Lt Williams) sang at The Hot Supper on Feb 1st 1913 (see below)

Bob (Sgt Griffiths) sang at The Hot Supper on Feb 1st 1913 (see below)

The Man behind . . . . R.G. Griffiths.

Thy Sentinel am I . . . . R.G. Griffiths.

I fear no foe . . . . Jack Williams.

D. P. BOHL B.Sc

World War 1 – Military Decorations

Capt. R.W. Jones
Military Cross
and Bar

Lt J.F. Venmore
Military Cross

Sgt S.J. Kay
Distinguished
Conduct Medal

Sgt F. King
Military Medal
and Bar

Pte R.A. Roberts
Military Medal
and Bar

Note: The
Distinguished
Conduct Medal was
the second highest
military award next
to the Victoria Cross

Cartoon of H.N. Ellis – 1916

(ALIAS THE ALIENS)

The lack of 'beer' & the price of the substituted beverage having shell-shocked the majority of the members present, the customary vote of thanks to Captain R. W. Jones for occupying the chair was omitted.

J. M. Hourn

List of Members Fallen in Action.

Private G. P. S. Brown full back.   L'Cpl. A. E. Rickley
         C. A. Beverley.   "   "   C. S. M. Isaac.
         J. B. Humphrey   "   "   Lieut. J. G. Williams
Lieut.   S. Venmore   "   "
         N. Howe   "   " & forward.
2nd Lieut J. H. Weighto   "   "
Sgt.   R. Griffith   "   "
Lieut.   Ax. Williamson   "   "
         It is a singular fact that every one of our
fallen playing members had occupied the full back position.

Pte W. Johnson Forward. Missing at Flers Oct. 1916.
2nd Lieut. H. Tolson Wing¾   "

D. P. BOHL B.Sc

The Committee Minutes 17th October 1919 — New Ground at Eaton Road

SEFTON R.U.F.C.

General Meeting held at Victoria Hotel
October 17th 1919

Present Messrs Sloss, Croxford, Snele, Owen,
Applebee, Bellamy, Knife, Ringrose, Jones,
Williams, Milbourn, R. T. Robinson, J. Robinson,
Bate, Hemingway, T. H. Caswell, W. Caskell,
Taylor, Helme,
Chairman Mr. R. L. Knife.

1. The Secretary Reported that the committee had an
   option on two grounds one at Ford Station, the
   other at Eaton Rd West Derby, with
   dressing accommodation at 'Oliva House'

   It was agreed to take the Eaton Rd
   Ground at a rental of £15, & to pay the
   caretaker at 'Oliva' House 5/- per match
   for all necessary arrangements. This amount
   to include washing of towels.

2. Mr D. Sloss kindly promised to see that forms
   were supplied for use in the dressing rooms.
   & was duly thanked by the meeting for doing so.

Oliva

'Oliva House' was built in 1855 by
The Consul of Wittemburg, J.A. Bencke
of Oliva. It used to occupy the area
of shops opposite Walkers Field on
Eaton Road, West Derby.

The Committee Minutes 16th April 1920 – O'Donnell plays for Lancashire

Comittee meeting held at Gainsboro' Cafe 16.4.20

Present: Messrs Knife, Milbourn, Kay, Williams, O'Donnell, Taylor, Applebee.

Minutes of previous meeting read & confirmed. The following new members were elected.

A HARD TACKLE.—O'Donnell (Possibles) tackled by Russell (Probables) in the Lancashire Rugby Union trial match at Manchester. [Daily Mail.

Daily Mail 25.10.20

Messrs J. R. Williams & R. Kaye Dixon were appointed auditors.

One of our members R. A. O'Donnell played for Lancashire v Northumberland & scored two tries. His play was highly commended in the press. S. Dunbell, an alien trained player, now with University appeared v Durham, & F. Outhwaite was first reserve v Cheshire

D. P. BOHL B.Sc

Report for Season 1919–20

SEFTON
R.U.F.C.

Season 1919-20

The past season opened under depressing circumstances. After making the necessary arrangements for the continuation of the club we were faced with unexpected difficulties. We failed to obtain a suitable ground with convenient dressing accommodation. Our playing members numbered eight but we raised the number to fifteen & commenced our matches. As there had been no preliminary practices we were heavily beaten. In the first half of the season, the first team played 8, lost all & scored 14 points against 152. In the second half season they won 4, drew 1, & lost 7 scoring 82 pts against 79. Three of the 7 losses were by the narrow margin of a goal kick.

The second team had somewhat similar results. They won 4, lost 12, & scored 108 points against 333, but as this team contains several very promising & very young players, the prospects for the team are decidedly bright. *

We were very fortunate in numbering amongst our members several players of the old Hamilton club, & it was mainly due to their accession, together with a good influx of old boys from Liverpool College, that the club was enabled to continue.

AGM 31st August 1920 –
Proposed name change to 'Sefton'

of the old name, it was agreed that from the date of the meeting the Club should be called The "Sefton" Rugby Union Football Club.

The meeting closed with a vote of thanks to the chairman for his services.

President.
J. G. LEGGE, ESQ.

Vice-Presidents.

W. B. CROXFORD, ESQ.   H. MARSHALL, ESQ.
H. PLENLEY, ESQ.   J. MILBOURN, ESQ.
J. FOX, ESQ.   H. J. MORGAN, ESQ.
R. F. HARDING, ESQ.   C. NICHOLAS, ESQ.
J. D. JOHNSTONE, ESQ.   J. H. RAWS, ESQ.
R. W. JONES, ESQ.   W. R. SMITH, ESQ.
J. KAY, ESQ.   L. STRINGER, ESQ.
W. KEARNS, ESQ.   J. W. A. TAYLOR, ESQ.
R. L. KNIPE, ESQ.   J. G. WALDRON, ESQ.
R. MADOC-JONES, ESQ.   I. R. WILLIAMS, ESQ.

Captain.
J. H. HELME.

Sub-Captain.
F. OUTHWAITE.

Hon. Team Secretary.
W. B. CROXFORD, 6 PALLADIO RD., STONEYCROFT.

Hon. Treasurer.
J. MILBOURN, 165 MOSCOW DRIVE, STONEYCROFT.

Hon. Secretary.
F. J. APPLEBEE, 40 INIGO RD., STONEYCROFT.

Committee.
J. R. WILLIAMS, D. SLOSS, S. J. KAY,
D. BELLAMY, H. N. ELLIS, R. A. O'DONNELL,
S. P. G. UPWARD, J. H. OWEN, H. E. SNAPE.

FIXTURES.

	1ST TEAM.		2ND TEAM.	
1919.				
Oct. 11.				
„ 18.	Waterloo "A"	L		A
„ 25.	L'pool Univer.	L		A
Nov. 1	St. Helens O.B.	L		A
„ 8.				
„ 15.	Southport	H	Southport	A
„ 22.	L'pool Univer.	L H	L'pool Univer.	L A
„ 29.	New Brighton	L H	New Brighton	L A
Dec. 6.	Cosmopolitan	L H	Cosmopolitan	L A
„ 13.	Rainhill	L A	Cosmopolitan	W H
„ 20.			Waterloo 3rd	L H
„ 27.				
1920.				
Jan. 3.	New Brighton	L A	New Brighton	L H
„ 10.	Southport	W A	Southport	L H A
„ 17.		A	B'head Park 3rd	L H
„ 24.	Cosmopolitan	L H	Cosmopolitan	L A
„ 31.	Bowdon Rangers	H		
Feb. 7.	St. Helens O.B.	H	St. Helens O.B.	L A
„ 14.	Heaton Moor	A	B'head Park 3rd	L H
„ 21.	Waterloo "A"	W H	Waterloo 3rd	W A
„ 28.	Bowdon Rangers	A Co		
Mar. 6.	Chester College	H	Rainhill	A
„ 13.	Heaton Moor	L A	Wis Hin's Team	W
„ 20.	B'head Park 2nd	D A	Cosmopolitan	H
„ 27.	Chester College	L A	Collegiate School	H
Apr 3.	Heaton Moor	L H		
	Rainhill	W	A	

Newspaper Cuttings 1919–20

NOTE: Heaton Moor fixture probably because W.B. Croxford originally came from there.

SEFTON
R.U.F.C.

UNIVERSITY'S WIN.

Liverpool University, who were again playing at Calderstones Park on Saturday, got the better of the Aliens by 6 points to 5. Neither side was at full strength. The 'Varsity were without Hope, Woodson, and Reid, who were selected for the county trial, and the Aliens were minus their captain, Helm, who was injured last week, and Outhwaite, who was also in the Probables v. Possibles game at Fyldesley.

The game on the whole was rather scrappy, but there was plenty of attractive incident and two casualties, one in either fifteen. Johnson, one of the 'Varsity three-quarters, was just about to cross the Aliens' line when he was brought down heavily and had his collar-bone broken in a melee. He played on for a few minutes before retiring to the pavilion. The Aliens lost Sloss, who went off with a ricked back.

The scoring opened like a bolt from the blue. The Aliens were having a desperate fight on their own line, and the 'Varsity seemed on the ace of scoring, when the ball was suddenly got away to King. The wing three-quarter, whose remarkable turn of speed was the subject of frequent comment, was unmarked, and capped a dash nearly the whole length of the field by grounding under the 'Varsity posts. M'Diarmid converted, and the Aliens' 5 points lead was not wiped out till after the interval. The second half saw the 'Varsity maintain a persistent attack which, but for an excess of individualism, would have meant at least three tries. Indeed, so far as actual points were, the home side owed their victory to Turner, who kicked two capital penalty goals and narrowly missed a third. M'Diarmid was quite the outstanding feature among the Aliens, for whom Hemmingway, King, and Corlett did well. Burton, Oldham, Flynn, and Cook were the most noticeable men in the 'Varsity colours.

Result: Liverpool University, 6 points; Aliens, 5 points. Teams:—

Liverpool University.—M. Laren; H. R. Coster, A. Wilson, J. R. Johnson, and D. J. Cook; J. P. Flynn and R. S. Turner; J. B. Oldham, S. Dumbell, L. Armour, W. Burton, D. A. Wells, A. R. Mann, J. V. Stephens, and Parry-Jones.

Aliens.—R. Hemmingway; T. King, D. Bellamy, S. J. Kay, and O. Robinson; W. J. Barber and J. M'Diarmid; D. Sloss, J. Williams, H. Daulmen, R. A. Roberts, H. E. Snape, E. B. Ringrose, R. L. Corlett, and W. H. Varley. Referee, Dr. Smith.

Liverpool Daily Post 27 October 1919

WIN FOR ST. HELENS OLD BOYS.

Aliens visited St. Helens on Saturday to play the newly-formed Old Boys' team. The journey to St. Helens was made four short of the full team. St. Helens were at full strength and keen on the game, so that the Aliens were quite overplayed. Four of the Cowley Schools team turned out to complete the Aliens' team. Old Boys played with the wind in the first half, and a grand run by E. Woods, who is proving the star three-quarter for St. Helens, put Watson over for a try. Aliens were let down at forward, and in the opening period further tries were scored by Heaton and Brown (2). Lyon kicked a penalty goal, and Perkins improved Heaton's try, so that Old Boys led at the interval by 19 points to nil. In the second half, Greenough, Watson, Heaton, and Mavity scored for St. Helens, and Davies kicked a goal.

Result: Old Boys 35 points, Aliens nil.

St. Helens have a good side, and the forwards on Saturay had an easy task, pushing the weakened Alien pack off the ball and over-running the defence. Snape, Bellamy, Barber, and Hemingway strove hard to make some impression, and Outhwaite led the forwards well, but without avail. Woods was splendid among a good lot of backs. Mavity worked hard and effectively behind the scrum. Perkins, the energetic secretary and captain, directed his team well, but passed very wildly.

Teams.—Old Boys: J. Davies; T. Lyon, W. Heaton, E. Woods, A. Greenough; H. Mavity and A. Perkins; S. Brown, W. Grime, T. Mahon, J. Foster, J. Watson, W. E. Pennington, J. Molyneux, and A. Waywell. Aliens: Snape; King, D. Bellamy, Kaye, and Robinson; Hemingway and Barber; Outhwaite, O'Donnell, F. G. Bellamy, J. Williams, Dodd, Bashill, Bickerstaff, and Tickle.

Liverpool Daily Post 3 November 1919

SEFTON v. HEATON MOOR.

The game between Sefton and Heaton Moor, at West Derby, was scrappy in more senses than one, both sides exhibiting undue heat. Play throughout was almost wholly confined to the forwards, neither line of threes showing anything like cohesion. In the first half Ellis kicked a penalty goal for Sefton, but Ramsden replied with two tries for Heaton Moor which, however, remained unconverted. Both sides were level at half-time with 6 points each. There was little between them in the second half until Hallet ran over and gave Heaton Moor victory by 9 points to 6 after a rather poor game.

1920–21

The Aliens Club Dinner 3rd April 1909

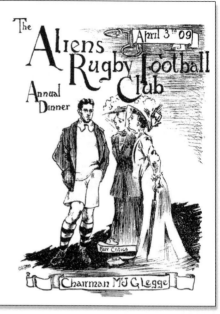

MENU

Soup
Mock Turtle

Fish
Boiled Cod, Oyster Sauce

Entree
Fricasse of Chicken
Jugged Hare, Red Currant Jelly

Joints
Roast Sirloin Beef, Yorkshire Pudding
Roast Pork, Apple Sauce,
Vegetables

Sweets
Plum Pudding
Stewed Fruit and Custard
Cheese and Biscuits

Part First	Part Second
Quartet ... ... *"The Old Brigade"* ... ... _____	Quartet ... ... *"The Goslings"* ... ... Bridge
The Athena Male Voice Quartet:	**The Athena Male Voice Quartet.**
Alto – Mr C. G. STEIN. Baritone Mr ROHAN KOLESAR.	
Tenor – Mr BICKERTON HUGHES. Bass – Mr CHARLES ARCHER.	Song ... ...*"The Romany Lass"* ... ... Stephen Adams
	Mr G. D. Kermode.
Song ... ... *"Even bravest heart may swell"* ... Gounod's *"Faust"*	
Mr S. Ralph Smith.	Song ... ... *"The Gallant Salamander"* ... D'Auvergne Barnard
	Mr Charles Archer.
Song ... ... *"O Song Divine"* ... ... Gordon Temple	
Mr Bickerton Hughes.	Violin Solo ... ... Selected ... ... _____
	Mr E. Partoon.
Violin Solo ... ... (a) *"Romance"* ... ... Svensden	
(b) *"Hungarian Idyll"* ... ... Keler Bela	Song ... ... *"Mountain Lover"* ... ... Squire
Mr E. Partoon.	**Mr Bickerton Hughes.**
Mr S. Partoon at the Piano.	
	Song ... ... (a) *"Absent"* ... ... ___ ...
Song ... ... *"Lanagan's Log"* ... ... _____	(b) *"Two Eyes of Gray"* ... ... _____
Mr Charles Archer.	**Mr Rohan Kolesar.**
Song ... ... *"I'll sing thee songs of Araby"* ... Frederick Clay	**Mr Bert Sayers** will talk to you.
Mr G. D. Kermode.	
	Song ... ... *"The Windmill"* ... ... Herbert Nelson
Mr. Bert Sayers will talk to you.	**Mr S. R. Smith.**
Song ... ... *"Yeoman's Wedding Song"* ... ... _____	Song ... ... *"Three for Jack"* ... ... _____
Mr Rohan Kolesar.	**Mr Tom L. Jones.**
Song ... ... Selected ... ... _____	Quartet ... ... (a) *"Absence"* ... ... Hatton
Mr W. Scott	(b) *"Evenings Twilight"* ... ...
	The Athena Male Voice Quartet.
At the Piano – - - Mr J. S. Gough	

D. P. BOHL B.Sc

Aliens Smoker 5th December 1909

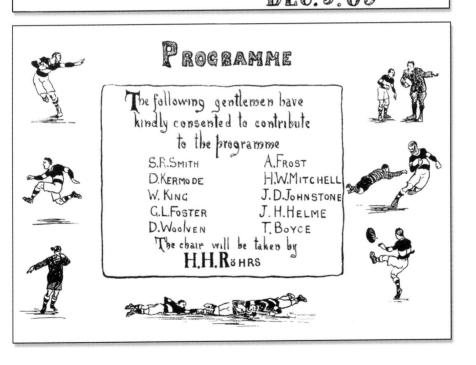

Bohemian Concert 14th December 1912

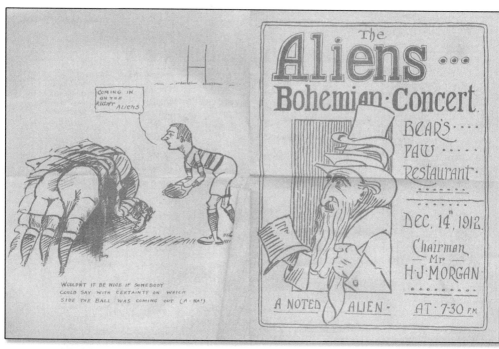

Aliens Hotte Potte 1st February 1913

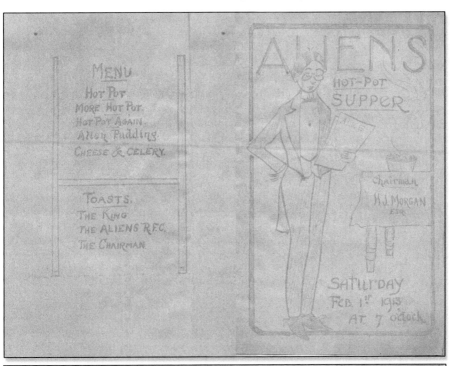

MENU
Hot Pot
More Hot Pot.
Hot Pot Again.
Alien Pudding.
Cheese & Celery.

TOASTS.
The King
The Aliens R.F.C.
The Chairman

ALIENS
HOT-POT
SUPPER

Chairman
H.J. MORGAN
ESR

SATURDAY
Feb 1st 1913
At 7 o'clock

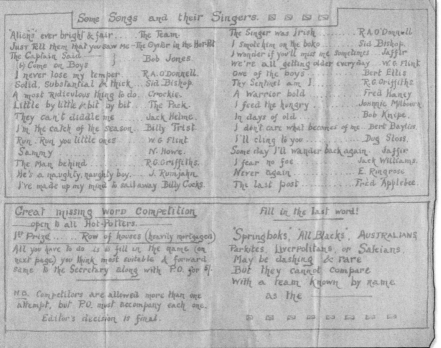

Some Songs and their Singers.

"Aliens" ever bright & fair . . . . The Team	The Singer was Irish . . . . R.A. O'Donnell
Just tell them that you saw me — The Oyster in the Hot-Pot	I smote him on the boko . . . . Sid Bishop
The Captain said ——— } . . . Bob Jones	I wonder if you'll miss me sometimes . . Jaffir
(i) Come on Boys	We're all getting older every day . . W.G. Flint
I never lose my temper . . . . R.A. O'Donnell.	One of the boys . . . . Bert Ellis
Solid, substantial & thick . . . Sid Bishop.	Thy Sentinel am I . . . . R.G. Griffiths.
A most ridiculous thing to do . . Crockie.	A warrior bold . . . . Fred Haney
Little by little & bit by bit . . . The Pack.	I feed the hungry . . . . . . Johnnie Milbourn.
They can't diddle me . . . . . Jack Helme.	In days of old . . . . Bob Knipe.
I'm the catch of the season . . Billy Trist.	I don't care what becomes of me . Bert Baytis.
Run. Run you little ones . . . W.G. Flint	I'll cling to you . . . . Dug Sloss.
Sammy . . . . N. Howe.	Some day I'll wander back again . . Jaffir.
The Man behind . . . . R.G. Griffiths.	I fear no foe . . . . Jack Williams.
He's a naughty, naughty boy . . J. Rumjahn.	Never again . . . . E. Ringrose.
I've made up my mind to sail away . Billy Cocks.	The last post . . . . Fred Applebee.

Great missing word competition
——— open to all Hot-Potters. ———

1st Prize . . . . . . Row of houses (heavily mortgaged)

All you have to do is to fill in the name (on next page) you think most suitable & forward same to the Secretary along with P.O. for 5/-.

N.B. Competitors are allowed more than one attempt, but P.O. must accompany each one.
Editor's decision is final.

Fill in the last word!

"Springboks" "All Blacks", Australians
Parkites, Liverpolitans, or Saleians
May be dashing & rare
But they cannot compare
With a team known by name
as the _____

Team Photograph – Aliens First Team Season 1907/08

Back row, left to right: R.J. Adams, E.E. Bond, A.L. Walker, J.W. Hetherington, D.J. Sloss, W.A. Stewart, W. Rochester, J. Wood, F.J. Haney, J.D. Johnstone. *Middle row, left to right*: W. Thomas, A. Davison, J.W.A. Taylor, R.W. Jones, R.T. Robinson. *Standing*: H.Tolson, H.N. Bell. *Front row, left to right*: H.W. Mitchell, E.P. Bywell, F.J. Applebee, J. Fairley.

Team Photograph – Aliens First Team Season 1908/09

Back row, left to right: C.A. Beverley, R.W. Jones, A. Davison, D.J. Sloss, G.A. Bonney, W.A. Stewart, A.G. Ascroft, G.P.S. Brown, A.L. Walker, R.F. Harding. *Middle row, left to right*: H. Tolson, J. Fairley, F.J. Applebee, J.D. Johnstone, J.H. Helme, G.L. Robinson, E.P. Bywell. *Front row, left to right*: C.G. Stein, H.W. Mitchell.

D. P. BOHL B.Sc

Team Photograph – Aliens First Team Season 1910/11

SEFTON
R.U.F.C.

Back row, left to right: L. Stringer, E. Ringrose, R.W. Jones, S.J. Bishop, W.G. Flint, H.N. Ellis, J. Robson. H. Tolson, F.J. Applebee. *Middle row, left to right*: J. Brown, W. Johnstone, D. Sloss, J.D. Johnstone (Captain), A.G. Ascroft, I.R. Williams, J. Fairley. *Front row, left to right*: A.W. Cocks, A. Williamson.

Team Photograph – Aliens First Team Season 1912/13

Back row, left to right: F.J. Applebee, D. Sloss, R.A. O'Donnell, W.J. Trist, J. Milbourn, S.J. Bishop, H.W. Thomas, F. Outhwaite, T. Madoc-Jones, O.E. Bayliss. *Middle row, left to right*: J.W.A. Taylor, J. Williams, H.N. Ellis, R.W. Jones (Captain), W.B. Croxford, J.H. Helme, J. Rumjahn. *Front row, left to right*: A.W. Cocks, H. Bayliss.

A club stalwart of West Derby Hockey Club, Dr. J. Rumjahn was given a unique honour at their AGM in May 1948 when he became the first man to be elected as a Life Member of the club. He had been with the club for over 25 years as both a goalkeeper and later an umpire.

Honorary Secretary Fred J. Applebee –
remembers how the Club came into being

FRED RECALLS IN 1971 – Looking back sometimes it seems only a very short time since, at tea time in our diggings at 9 Huntly Road, off Sheil Road, I looked across the table and said to my pal Joe Fairley, "Well! If I start a new club will you be the first to join?" That is exactly how the club came into being.

F.J. APPLEBEE. J. FAIRLEY.

Fred was born in Slaithwaite, West Riding of Yorkshire in 1883, son of the Alfred C. and Mary Applebee. His father was born in Bishopsgate, London in 1852 and became Church of England Scripture Reader in the Parish of Slaithwaite St James with Lingards.

Fred was a keen cricketer and was

captain of *The Tramps*, he also played for Clubmoor. They had fixtures against Stanley, Birkenhead Vics, Upton, Garston, Liverpool, Liverpool Police, Frodsham and Old Xaverians. We can see many of the Aliens founder members on the cricket scorecards, and especially W. Marr-Orr

D. P. BOHL B.Sc

RUGBY.
KINGSTON v. ST. JOHN'S COLLEGE, BATTERSEA.

Kingston 19 points; St. John's 0.

The London Devonians having scratched their fixture with Kingston for Saturday in consequence of the International at Blackheath, the above match was arranged and played on the Richmond-road ground, which was in fine condition. A very high wind blew from end to end, and this affected the kicking somewhat. The home team was altered from that announced, as Livingstone was ill, his place at half being filled by Evans, while Grout and Richards were absent from the forwards, Bowry and Frecker filling the vacancies. The visitors were a very smart and likely lot of young players, but the Kingston men had the advantage in weight. Having won the toss, the home Captain set his opponents to play against the wind and sun. From the kick off Marriott was compelled to touch down. The ball was returned from the kick-out into touch in Kingston's half, but the home forwards dribbled it back to the College "25," and then from a rush the ball went over the line, and was touched down. On restarting Evans was nearly over, and Edger appeared to have scored, but a touch down was given. The ball was returned to the visitors' territory and scrummages ensued. Simpson continually got the ball out, the visitors tackled well. Edger got well away, but a forward pass spoilt the effort. Vivian, one of the visiting half-backs, was very smart, and getting the ball out, he led up to his side breaking away to the home "25," where they were checked. Then ensued a lot of foot work, in which the homesters got the best of the argument, and the visitors being penalised, a shot at goal was futile and Thomas touched down. On restarting play ruled even for a time in the centre, but Evans made an opening, and the ball being passed across the ground, got to Tarrant, who opened the scoring wide out. Edger took the kick from a difficult angle, and a fine shot just missed scoring. Following this reverse the Collegians, by a fine effort, raced down the ground, but the result was only to force a touch-down. Then Kingston again took up the attack, with the result that Evans got in in about the same spot as the previous try, Edger again took the kick, and by another fine shot, put on the other two points. Shortly after half-time was whistled, and Kingston led by 8 points to nil. Having the wind against them now, the homesters kept the ball close, and rarely gave their opponents a chance of getting it out, as the forwards wheeled the scrums, and broke up smartly. In this way, notwithstanding the plucky defence of the Collegians, they worked their way to the visitors' "25." Here a bout of passing across the front of goal ended in Tarrant scoring behind the posts, but Marriott failed with the kick. Keeping up the pressure it was not long before Lord ran over,

but again no goal resulted from Edger's kick. Nothing daunted by these reverses the Collegians made a fine effort to score, and Vivian dodged cleverly through the home team to be brought down a yard or two outside by Marriott. From the ensuing scrummages the home forwards again asserted themselves, and led by Sherrard, who was in fine form, they worked the ball down the ground and twice the visitors were compelled to touch down. For a time the play ruled pretty even, until Evans, Huggins and Sherrard, by good foot work, got well down. Two marks kick by Lord and Marriott availed but little owing to the high wind. A few minutes before time Bowry got clear with the ball and running strongly, led up to Evans scoring again behind the posts. Lord was entrusted with the kick, and sent the ball sailing over the bar. Playing with plenty of dash right up to the finish, they put in a final effort, and were on the home goal line when the whistle announced the cessation of hostilities. Kingston thus won by two goals and three tries (19 points) to nil. Sides:—Kingston: A. H. Marriott, back; J. W. Edger, A. Kitching, T. N. Lord and P. J. Tarrant, three-quarter backs; W. Simpson and G. Evans, half-backs; S. C. Sherrard (capt.), F. T. Turk, W. J. Blount, J. Huggins, H. Kerrison, W. Colley, A. C. Frecker and C. Bowry, forwards. St. John's College: F. W. Thomas, back; F. Applebee (capt.), W. Garland, H. Evatt and E. Cain, three-quarter backs; A. E. Smith and H. Vivian, half-backs; H. Andrews, H. Audale, S. Bence, W. Clapham, J. Ewan, E. Ingham, S. Godrich, and T. Stewart, forwards. Referee, Mr. A. E. Colley.

OLD XAVERIANS v. CLUBMOOR.
Played at Townsend-lane. Score:—

OLD XAVERIANS

J. M'Kenna, c Partoon b Hastings	3
R. M'Entegart, b Roby	12
H. C. A. Pratt, b Roby	9
T. Charnock, b Hastings	0
W. M'Entegart, c Brown b Hastings	16
T. Lott, b Hastings	7
G. Chamberlain, b Hastings	23
W. Mercer, c Clement, b Hastings	3
T. Corish, c Brennand b Roby	3
F. A. Morton, not out	3
T. J. Bennett, b Roby	1
Extras	3
Total	**84**

CLUBMOOR

H. Brennand, c Pratt b Lott	4
R. K. Campbell, b M'Kenna	3
A. Hastings, b Lott	0
A. Roby, b Lott	7
E. Ward, c Pratt b Mercer	15
T. Clements, b Lott	15
W. M. Orr, c Pratt b M'Kenna	3
F. J. Applebee, not out	9
H. Scaife, b M'Kenna	3
G. Partoon, b M'Kenna	0
Brown, b Lott	1
Extras	6
Total	**67**

Liverpool v New Brighton.

The first meeting of these teams took place at Aigburth this afternoon in bright weather, there being a sparse attendance. The ground was in splendid condition, and with both sides turning out at practically full strength a tight game was anticipated. A late start was made, New Brighton kicking off. T. W. Fletcher replied, and after scrimmaging in the centre Singlehurst placed the home side in an advantageous position. Turner missed a pass, and again the game veered centrewards, Graham, Appleton, Singlehurst, and Parry being prominent for their respective sides. A free kick to Liverpool gained but little ground, Drinkwater gathering well and finding touch. Play again was located in the centre, but nothing of note was done until the Brighton threequarters essayed another bout of passing, which was spoiled by Parry getting in front. A few moments afterwards Liverpool forced a touchdown, A. E. Wood then romping over the opposing line in easy fashion, Fletcher failing to add the other points. New Brighton, facing the bright sun, could make but little headway, Liverpool up to this point holding the monopoly. Lennox, Appleton, and Westrup made a diversion, but Hammill again intervened. C. E. Allen obtained a second try for Liverpool. Half-time—Liverpool 6 points. New Brighton nil.

Thompson, Mavity, and Smith, forwards.
New Brighton v. Ashford House.—At Liscard, 3 30. New Brighton: W. Lennox, L. Drinkwater, J. W. Parry, W. Garland, F. J. Applebee, H. Westrup, A. Fleming, D. Graham, S. Ellaby, E. A. Weir, A. W. Harris, B. Westrup, E. Jenkins, R. D. Nesbitt, and E. A. Barrett.
Liverpool v. Richmond.—At Aigburth; 3 30.

The New Brighton fifteen, profiting by the "tips" they received from Liverpool, gave a very creditable display at Sale last Saturday, and must be counted distinctly unfortunate in having to accept defeat by 11 points to nil. Taking the game as a whole, the Brightonians were little, if anything, behind their opponents, but it was one of those occasions where everything that came in the way of one team was snapped up, whilst the other side could not do the right thing at the crucial moment. A pleasing feature about the encounter was that the Brightonians lasted much better than the East Cheshiremen, which is pretty conclusive proof that, coupled with their enthusiasm, the players are paying due regard to training requirements.

SALE v. NEW BRIGHTON
Rugby Union match at Sale.
New Brighton.—A. M'Ewan, back; F. J. Applebee, W. Garland, J. W. Parry, and L. Drinkwater, three-quarter backs; H. Westrup and A. Fleming, half backs; D. Graham, S. Ellaby, E. A. Weir, J. Briggs, R. D. Nesbitt, A. W. Harris, R. J. Traynor, and B. Westrup, forwards.
WATERLOO.—DARKFIELD ROAD

Garston's First Defeat.

Garston met with their first defeat in an evening match on Monday and Tuesday, when they failed ignominiously against the Tramps.

The result was altogether unexpected, for the team had had a run of exceptional success, and the collapse was certainly not anticipated in this game.

Though short of Shaw and Robinson they put out a fairly strong team, and they were all dismissed for 69, 32 of those being made for the last two wickets.

The Tramps made 147 on Monday evening, the principal partnership being for the second wicket, which was responsible for 60 runs. It was against this total that Garston replied so ineffectually.

Placing two fast, and at times erratic, bowlers on, the Garston batsmen, with three exceptions, were terrorised. Moss and Chamberlain put up 16 runs for the fourth wicket, after Husband. Ubsdell and Cook had returned to the pavilion with five runs to share amongst them.

Then Helsby further improved the situation, treating the bowling with absolute contempt. He hit up 23 in double-quick time, helping himself to 18 in one over from Best.

Credit should be given to the visitors' fielding, which was never slack, and materially assisted the bowlers, no less than seven catches being taken.

RUGBY.
New Brighton v. Broughton Park.—At Liscard. New Brighton: W. Lennox, full-back; L. Drinkwater, A. N. Other, W. Garland, and F. J. Applebee, threequarter-backs; H. Westrup and S. Ellaby, half-backs; D. Graham, S. Ellaby, E. A. Weir, R. D. Nesbitt, W. W. Harris, H. Westrup, E. A. Barrett, and Wade, forwards.

GARSTON v. THE TRAMPS.
Played at the Avenue, Garston, on Monday and Tuesday evenings. Scores:—

TRAMPS.

P. J. Appleby b Husband	19
H. Viner c Law b Helsby	0
S. W. Smith b Ubsdell	26
J. Williamson b Ubsdell	15
E. Owens st Burge b Husband	2
R. Smith b Law	24
H. Catesby c P. Thompson b Law	11
T. Best c Wilson b Law	12
H. Pearson b Wilson	1
A. Davison c Husband b Law	7
F. J. Haney not out	8
Extras	18
Total	**147**

BOWLING ANALYSIS.

	O.	M.	R.	W.
Law	10.1	0	29	4
Helsby	3	1	18	1
Wilson	6	1	15	1
Ubsdell	13	1	23	2
Husband	7	0	36	2

GARSTON.

G. H. Ubsdell c Viner b Best	0
J. Husband c R. Smith b S. Smith	4
T. Moss b S. Smith	15
W. Cook c Viner b Best	1
G. Chamberlain c and b S. Smith	10
W. H. Law c R. Smith b Best	0
P. Thompson c Pearson b S. Smith	4
J. D. Helsby c Pearson b S. Smith	23
A. Burge c Haney b S. Smith	5
A. Wilson not out	5
Extras	4
Total	**69**

BOWLING ANALYSIS.

	O.	M.	R.	W.
S. Smith	11	3	31	6
Best	11	1	34	3

who was to become Sefton President in 1936. In the early years Fred was Captain of St Johns College in Battersea and started his rugby career on Merseyside for New Brighton. He finished his teaching career at Steers St, Anfield.

TWO HEADMASTERS IN ROAD COLLISION.

Serious Condition After Liverpool Accident.

Feb 17 ——— 1932

Associations With Barkisland.

Two Liverpool headmasters, brothers-in-law, were seriously injured in a collision in Liverpool, between a motor-car and a bread van on Friday week. One of them is Mr. Herbert Victor Clark, headmaster of the Florence Melly Open-air School, son of Mr. William Clark, for many years headmaster of Barkisland Endowed School.

M. H. V. Clark.

Mr. Clark was a pupil teacher under the Halifax Education Committee and is well known in the district. The other injured man is Mr. Frederick J. Appleby, who is also connected with Barkisland by his marriage with Miss Whiteley.

It appears that they were going home in a small car when they came into collision with a bread van in trying to avoid a boy at the junction of two roads. The bread van was hurled over on its side and the motor-car was damaged. The driver of the van was not injured.

The two injured men were taken to Walton Hospital and were detained. They underwent operations and were at first reported to be in a very serious condition.

Inquiring at Walton Hospital yesterday we were informed that Mr. Clark was still poorly, but fairly comfortable. Mr. Appleby is in a more serious condition and is reported to be "very poorly."

Paying Off The Penalty

SO Vivian Jenkins thinks a penalty goal at rugby should count only one point. Why stop there? If it were abolished altogether we could do without those tall posts—and look what a saving that would be to all the "poor" little clubs which contain the real amateurs!

It could be a fine handling game, but it wouldn't be *rugby*.

F. J. Applebee.

Huyion, Lancs.

World Sports, June 1956

What a scrum !

THE other day I mentioned a case in which father and son played in the same Southport Rugby XV, but Mr. F. J. Applebee, of Twig-lane, Huyton, goes one better.

He tells me that some years ago Mr. Harry Daulman and his son, Police Constable Cliff Daulman, played together in the Sefton Rugby F.C. 1st team pack.

The "eight" was completed by two other police constables, three clergymen and one "other rank."

Above: Fred spent most of his retirement penning letters to newspapers.

Left: Fred was lucky to escape with his life after being involved in a vehicle accident in 1932.

D. P. BOHL B.Sc

SEFTON
R.U.F.C.

Freddie with class Std VII at Steers St, Anfield,
where he was known as 'Sapper'

BERT WRIGHT VISITED THE LIVERPOOL ASSOCIATION OF SCHOOL MASTERS'
Athletic Festival yesterday. Above, he records some of his impressions of the gathering
and its personalities.

(ALIAS THE ALIENS)

Chairman R.L. Knipe –
Cycle King of 'The Black Anfielders'

OWD BOB, as he was known to Sefton, was born in Carlisle around 1870. Mr Knipe, who resided in Moscow Drive, West Derby was a fine swimmer and was life governor of the Royal Life Saving Society. His other great sporting interest was cycling, and he was treasurer of the Anfield Cycling Club. In his younger days he took a prominent part in road-racing and created a number of records.

During his forty-four years work in Liverpool schools he constantly took a keen interest in school sport, and under his leadership Steers Street held the athletic championship of the Liverpool elementary schools for five years.

A keen member, also, of Liverpool Association of School Masters, Mr Knipe was elected president in 1929. He retired from his headmastership at the end of March 1936, when, at a gathering of old scholars, colleagues, and friends, he received a presentation of a cheque and a set of bowls.

D. P. BOHL B. Sc

Hon member, Vice-President & President Aliens - Sefton L.C.

THE STORY OF A GREAT "TWENTY-FOUR."

R. L. Knipe's Northern Record of 21 Years Ago. Unsuitable Equipment and Moderate Pacing.

R. L. Knipe, the Anfield crack whose remarkable paced "24" of 1902 is described in this article.

ALTHOUGH there are two records on the books which exceed R. L. Knipe's 24-hour ride of 1902 in the matter of mileage, many good judges are of the opinion that equally meritorious is the Anfielder's feat of covering 406½ miles on northern roads in a full day.

T. R. Goodwin (428 miles, 1898) had the assistance of motor pacing, and both he and Hunt (411½ miles, 1897) used a much faster course in the level Fen country, and had the great advantage of well-organized expert pacing. Knipe achieved his performance under several drawbacks, one of the worst of which was his own choosing. Disheartened by a long series of tyre troubles, he handicapped himself by using wired-on detachable tyres with basil leather bands under the tread; the bands robbed the pneumatics of a great portion of their resilience, making the tyres nearly as slow as cushions. Again, being in a race, Knipe could not get the Anfield pacing which would otherwise have been at his service; other competitors had booked up many of the tandems, so Knipe had to rely largely on inexperienced pacers, whose ideas of helping a man along were crude in the extreme.

In all, Knipe had about a dozen tandems, and many of his pacers were not even clubmen. It was arranged that they should do stretches of 20 to 30 miles, but they generally rode as fast as they were able for as far as they could stay, leaving Knipe to hang on as best he could. Thus the Anfielder's ride was exceptional in many respects, and a wonderful exposition of determination and fitness. His only regular tandem pair were the brothers Rushton, of the North Liverpool B.C., who did splendid service. A very well-known couple who assisted in this classic Anfield event were Lionel Martin and the late Vade Walpole, of the Bath Road Club. They went North to pace Prichard, but, not knowing the roads, did no pacing during the night, and when daylight came, after the first 100 miles, and the course ran down into Shropshire, they picked up their man, and, with the omission of a few odd detours, paced him practically all the rest of the way. If Knipe had had pacers of that calibre, he would probably have done something phenomenal.

The event in which Knipe put up his ride was the annual 24-hour race promoted by the Anfield B.C.

The race was then confined to members of the A.B.C., but for the past few years (since 1914) the club has invited members of other Northern clubs to participate. The start took place at 10 p.m. on July 18th, 1902, and the course made Chester the centre of various extensions during the night. The weather was almost ideal. Knipe took the lead at once, being determined to accomplish the magic 400. At 48¾ miles (2 hrs. 35 mins.) he had established a lead of 32 minutes over his nearest rival, and from this point interest in the race was divided between curiosity as to who would be second and third, and anticipation of Knipe beating record. At 98¾ miles he led by 54 minutes, and covered 217 miles in 12 hours (previous Northern record, his own, 214 miles

... so that he had not the incentive of keen competition with another possible winner to induce him to maintain his speed. At Whitchurch corner (314 miles) it was evident that Knipe was riding in such remarkable form that the 24-hour Northern record (his own, 385½ miles) which was thought so excellent the previous year, appeared to be in for a severe shaking, and hopes ran high of the coveted 400 miles being reached. Hereabouts Knipe had a bad time, which necessitated a rest of half an hour at Whitchurch and very careful riding for the next two or three hours, during which the record-breaker was assiduously looked after by F. H. Koenen.

Wem (366½ miles) was left at 7.33 p.m., and here Knipe availed himself of the extension to Welsh Hampton, and reached Whitchurch again (388 miles) at 8.58, having beaten record by 3 miles with an hour and 2 minutes in hand. Continuing, he piled up the enormous total of 406½ miles before time was called, beating Northern record by 22½ miles and M. A. Holbein's national record (in which motors were used for pacing) by 3 miles.

As we have hinted, the race for the places was close: R. E. Prichard was second, with 344½ miles, and E. H. Fox third, with 342 miles.

The record was originally passed by the Northern R.R.A. as 407½ miles, but in the following year it was discovered that the secretary had confused Hodnet Corner with Hodnet village, and supplied wrong

A42

MARCH 15, 1923.

Story of a Great "24."

measurements, which led to a revision in 1903, when the total was amended to 406½. Knipe rode a Shield bicycle, made by the late H. P. Routledge, and he still has the identical mount, on which he has ridden over 50,000 miles. His nominal gear was 81, increased to a height which it would be difficult to calculate by the aforementioned puncture-proof bands. These Knipe describe as "bullet-proof," let alone merely puncture-resisting! The idea was a patent of J. Butler, a fellow-Anfielder, for whom the lapse of years has doubtless brought forgiveness. A leather band was solutioned on the tread of an ordinary roadster tyre, and a strip of rubber stuck on top of it. For Knipe's special benefit (?) two leather bands were *stitched* on to each cover! Users of modern silk and skin tubulars might ponder on the inevitable result in weight, discomfort, and "deadness."

R. Leigh Knipe was born near Carlisle in 1871. He learned to ride, when 10 years old, on a wooden boneshaker; the "ride" consisted of scorching violently down a hill and along the level till the loss of momentum called a halt. About four years later he was allowed a few rides on an Ordinary as a reward for helping a friend to learn. After another interval of three years he managed to secure some riding on another borrowed machine—a solid-tyred safety. In 1891, when at school at Durham, he won the school 10-mile cycle race on the road, riding a borrowed Humber with stuck-on pneumatics, the other competitors being on Ordinaries and solid and cushion-tyred safeties. The first bicycle he really owned was a Bradbury, acquired in 1896, when he had migrated to Liverpool, where he joined the Anfield B.C. in 1897. He rode his first "50" in 1899, doing fastest time—2 hrs. 41 mins. 12 secs.— and from that time figured on scratch in club events.

beating his predecessor's time. Knipe went third, and did 2 hrs. 35 mins. 34 secs., but the last man, J. E. Green, got the record with 2-32-30.

Whit-Monday of that year saw the last Anfield "100" under the old paced conditions. In terrible weather, W. E. Gee was fastest in 6 hrs. 5 mins. 20 secs., Knipe, after several punctures and a fall, being second fastest with 6 hrs. 17 mins. 47 secs.

In 1900 came the first unpaced Anfield "100," in which W. H. Nutt (North Road) was first and fastest in 5 hrs. 38 mins. 47 secs. Knipe did 5 hrs. 42 mins. 48 secs., and a few weeks later secured the Northern record with 5 hrs. 31 mins. 52 secs. In the same year he won the club "24," with 352½ miles. In 1901 he finished in only one club "50," being first and fastest in 2 hrs. 36 mins. 15 secs., but later he beat the Northern 50-mile record with 2 hrs. 27 mins. 36 secs., the 12-hour with 214½ miles, and the 24-hour with 385½ miles.

Nineteen hundred and four saw the formation of the famous Knipe-Irving partnership, which made a considerable upheaval in tandem times. They beat the Liverpool-Edinburgh record (14 hrs. 44 mins.) and the Liverpool-London (11 hrs. 22 mins.).

In 1905 the pair lowered the Edinburgh-York (11 hrs. 35 mins.) and the York-London (10 hrs. 52 mins.) records. Knipe finished his speed career in 1907, when, with E. J. Cody, he beat the Liverpool-Edinburgh tandem record (13 hrs. 23 mins.).

Our subject is still a very enthusiastic cyclist, a regular attendant at Anfield fixtures, and has for many years acted as the club's hon. treasurer. He is a schoolmaster by profession, and before taking up cycling seriously indulged in rowing; hence, when the Bricknell hand gear was introduced, he thought it might suit him, and devoted a great deal of time and trouble to mastering it. He found it of no real assistance, and never raced successfully with it.

H. W. BARTLEET.

SCHOOLBOY ATHLETICS.

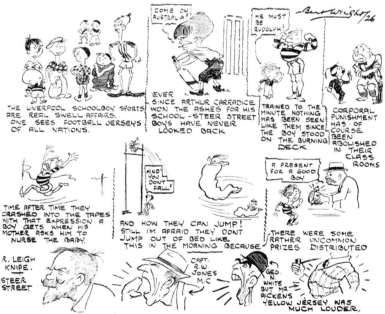

BERT WRIGHT'S CARICATURES AT STANLEY.

D. P. BOHL B.Sc

Sefton RUFC – Committee
Minutes 1920–23

The Committee Minutes 20th January 1921 – W.J.Smith joins committee from Bristol

20.1.21

The vacancy on the committee, caused by the resignation of D.W.F. Bellamy, was filled by the election of W.J. Smith of the Bristol & Gloucestershire County committees, a gentleman who will probably prove to be the most valuable acquisition that the club has ever made.

The secretary proposed that a message be sent to Bellamy, wishing him every success in his new venture — & reminding him that his subscription to the club is overdue. Seconded & carried.

Mr. Dixon read his report of the "Hot Pot" Supper, & presented his balance sheet which showed the handsome profit of £4. 16. 7.
It was agreed that Mr Dixon should make himself responsible for a Hot Pot Supper to be held at the Hare & Hounds on February 19th. Tickets 5/- each. Mr Dixon undertook to make this proposed Hot Pot as big a success as the previous one.

The Secretary reported that the club had

W.J.Smith was Honorary Secretary of Bristol and District Rugby Combination, and sat on the Gloucestershire County Selection and Executive Committees. He played for the Bristol premier team before and after the war.

Report for Season 1920–21

Season 1920-21.

From the point of view of results the past season has been the most unsatisfactory in the history of the club. The first team played 26 matches, won 3, drew 2, & lost 21 scoring 85 points against 337. The second team played 20, won 8, lost 11 & drew 1, scoring 150 points against 276. For the first time in our career we have been able consistently to run a third team, which played practically all its matches away. This team it is pleasing to note was the most successful of our sides. It played 14 games, winning 8 & losing 6, & scored 123 points against 124.

The old difficulties re grounds & dressing rooms are still with us, & I am afraid will continue to be with us until some scheme is developed by means of which we can get a ground of our own. Otherwise the future of the club is bright. We have a larger number of playing members than at any previous date; they are mostly very young

D. P. BOHL B. Sc

to will grow both in size & experience; & I feel confident they will in a few seasons time, be able to hold their own with the best teams in this district. Training & practice are all that are needed.

The thanks of the club are due especially to those older & more experienced players who have turned out so frequently for the 2nd & 3rd teams, & to our latest "acquisition" W.J. Smith, whose advice was not useful in the past season, but not so useful as we hope it will be in the future.

In conclusion I wish to point out to the young members that the future of the club is in their hands, & a little thought on their part will make the working of the club much easier. There are many little "jobs" for which they might volunteer instead of leaving them all in the hands of the officers. This will increase the efficiency of the arrangements, & efficiency of arrangement usually means that an efficient team to put on the field.

WJSmith
30/5/21

RUGBY CODE PLAYERS.

RECOGNISE THE SERVICES OF A LATE OFFICIAL.

Under the auspices of the Bristol and District Rugby Combination a smoking concert was held at the Crown and Dove Hotel last night, when Mr W. J. Smith, the late honorary secretary of the organisation was the recipient of a handsome present. Mr Smith who left Bristol a few months ago to take up an important position at Liverpool was well-known in local Rugby and Cricket circles and there was a large attendance at the concert which was presided over by Mr J. Milburn, president of the Gloucestershire County Rugby Union and Chairman of the Combination. Those present included Messrs E. S. Bostock-Smith (Chairman of the Bristol Rugby Club), J. Oates (secretary Bristol Combination), A. Harris (treasurer, Bristol Combination), E. Seymour-Bell (Clifton R.F.C.) J. Tucker, F. Crooks, F. Feltham (Bristol Rugby Club), C. Browning and J. Feltham (Bristol Referees' Society), and many other gentlemen well-known in Rugby circles. There was an excellent musical programme which was much enjoyed.

Mr Milburn in presenting to Mr Smith a handsome solid silver tea service, said the recipient was worthy in every way of the good wishes of Rugby enthusiasts. He had worked long and well and had played the game as well as worked for it. Every club in Bristol was represented that evening and that was a good sign for he had done all the drudgery work for some years. The fact that the presentation was subscribed for by the members of the local clubs spoke in itself of the appreciation they all had of his services. He was on the County Selection Committee and the County Executive and on those bodies he was missed.

Mr Seymour-Bell, secretary of the Clifton R.F.C. spoke of the work Mr Smith had done and eulogised his services to the Rugby code.

Mr Smith who was received with musical honours, returned thanks for the splendid presentation and reception accorded him. It was a big wrench to leave Bristol. All he had done was a labour of love, and he had received splendid support from everyone. He urged them to keep the Combination going at its high standard. His service with that body had been of extreme happiness.

Rugby Zeal on Merseyside.

Two Merseyside Rugby football clubs have decided to alter their names

Acting on the advice given them by *The Athletic News* last year, the "Aliens" have got rid of their far from pretty title, and for the future will be known as the Sefton F.C., which is much preferable; while the "Cosmopolitans" have determined upon Port Sunlight F.C. as designation.

Athletic News 22 October 1920

A STALWART GOES NORTH.

Mr W. J. Smith, who for some years past has been actively identified with local Rugby, is leaving Bristol in order to take up a lucrative appointment in Liverpool. He goes with the best wishes for his future from every lover of the sport in the city and county. He will be hard to replace. He has been an ideal secretary to the Bristol Combination, combining enthusiasm with tact and wise judgment. For years he has been a member of the Bristol club, and before the war, as last year, played regularly for the premier team. He was the Combination representative, with the President, on the Gloucestershire County Union, and wherever he has worked he has been held in high esteem. Good luck, "Billy"!

CHESTER COLLEGE DEFEAT ALIENS

The match between the Aliens and Chester College, at West Derby, was played in a downpour, the visitors winning by 6 points to 3. Perkins and Walkden got tries for the College in the first half, Walkden just failing with difficult kicks. The Aliens did better in the second half, O'Donnell got a try from a forward rush, and later Outhwaite also appeared to have touched down for the Aliens, but the ruling was otherwise. The Collegians had a well-balanced side, the forwards being capable in the close, Walkden and Sewell deserving mention. Williams (three-quarter) and Bull at scrum half played good games. The Aliens were best represented by O'Donnell, Hutchins, and Outhwaite. The Collegians were three regular players short, and the Aliens had several changes. Kay, their capable and speedy three-quarter, was away with a damaged shoulder, and Younger was missed in the pack.

Brown, Newman, Johnson.

There have been two interesting changes in nomenclature in connection with Merseyside Rugby clubs. Doubtless as the result of the war the club known as the Aliens has resolved to change its name to Sefton, which is a popular choice. The other old team with a new name is Port Sunlight, until this season the Cosmopolitans.

Daily Mail 22 October 1920

Team Photographs –
Sefton RUFC 1920–21

1st team (v Port Sunlight 1921) 26 Mar.
S. H.A. Wareham, E.S. Miller, H.E. Snape, R.A. O'Donnell, D.S. O'Sullivan, J. McIntosh, E. Hoden
M. Cass, A.G. Nazarachi, R. Hemingway, A.L. Stephenson
F. Outhwaite, D. Pereira, H.C.F. Daulman Jun., R.C. Jenkins
A.J. Midd

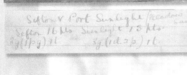

Sefton v Port Sunlight (Reserves).
Sefton 16 pts Sunlight 13 pts
3g (1p.g) 21 3g (1d 2p) 16

2nd team v Bidston 2.4.21
Bidston 20 pts Sefton 11 pts
F. Outhwaite, J.R. Williams (capt), W. Herring, J. McFall, W.J.R. Watts
T.E. Scotson, J.B. Rimmer, K.S. Bradshaw, M. Cass, I.A. Williams
M.J. Crawford, F. Martinez, J.E.C. McGibbon, E.S. Miller,
C.A. Mackenzie

AGM May 20th 1921 –
Proposed County Cup Competition

called immediately

Carried unanimously.

The following members were elected on the sub-committee. R. Hemingway (secretary) W. B. Herring, H. Bayliss, J. E. Lenton & J. A. Williams with power to coopt any further members.

The secretary reported on the proposed county cup competition & stated that he had expressed himself in favour of such a competition. The meeting unanimously endorsed his views on the matter.

It was decided to hold the next general meeting at the Bee Hotel the first week in August.

It was also decided on the proposition of R. Hemingway that the agenda for the meeting should recommend the purchase of an army hut for use as a dressing room.

The meeting terminated with a vote of thanks to

D. P. BOHL B.Sc

The Committee Minutes 29th September 1921 — A.J. Marsh suspended for playing N.U. league

SEFTON R.U.F.C.

the secretary of St Helens O.B. a communication from which the following is an extract:—

"At our general meeting the other evening questions were asked & I was instructed to approach the county committee re A.J. Marsh who was suspended from R.U. games by the committee having played under N.U. auspices, & who is now playing. & has played for Sefton, I am told."

For your information Marsh was not allowed to play for us or for the Varsity by order of the county committee

Oct: 23rd 19.

Dear Sir.

The R.U. Committee have refused Marsh's application for reinstatement

(signed) Chas. Fletcher
Sec.

A.E. Perkins Esq
St. Helens O.B.

Marsh was asked to make a statement as to the facts of the case. He stated

VERN—

The Committee Minutes 29th September 1921 – (continued)

1. That when a youth of 17 he was asked by his sunday school people if he would like a game of football. He replied in the affirmative & turned out for the St. Helens Brook St. Congregational Sunday School Team v some team unknown, played on a N.U. ground under N.U. rules on one occasion. (in 1918)

2. He afterwards applied to join the St. Helens O.B. Club but was told that he was ineligible.

3. He was informed (verbally) by Perkins that he was suspended by the R.U., this being the only notification that he received.

The committee (Sefton) decided that on the facts submitted Marsh could no longer be played in the Sefton team, but they would do their best to procure permission for him to play R.U. football again. They considered that St. Helens O.B. had broken the R.U. rules in playing against him, & they also doubted whether St. Helens had made out the best possible

D. P. BOHL B.Sc

The Committee Minutes 28th April 1922 — Dispute over team called 'Liverpool and District'

SEFTON R.U.F.C.

Committee Meeting held at Hare & Hounds Hotel
28.4.22

Present Messrs Applebee, Cain, Dixon, Hutchings, Linton,
Marshall, Milbourn, Munro, Porter with Mr
W.J. Smith Chairman.

The minutes of previous meeting were read, & confirmed.

Proposed by the Chairman seconded by Mr Marshall
" That the Annual General Meeting be held
at the Victoria Cafe on Friday May 26th."
Carried.

It was decided that the following
should appear on the agenda for the meeting.
Proposed alteration of rule.

1. That nominations for the executive &
committee be sent in writing to the secretary
before the August General meeting each year.
Proposed by S.J. Applebee
Seconded .. W.J. Smith

2. That playing members' subscriptions be paid

WILD

The Committee Minutes 28th April 1922 –
(continued)

on or before December 1st, or within one month of election.

　　　　Proposer H.A. Munro

　　　　Seconder F.S. Porter.

The treasurer reported that he had insufficient cash in hand to meet the expenses due, but that if all outstanding subscriptions materialised, the club would show a profit on the year's working.

　　　Mr. Marshall proposed & Mr. Dixon seconded "That the following letter be sent to playing members whose subscriptions are outstanding"

　　　Dear Sir, At a meeting held on April 28th your committee passed a resolution urgently calling upon all members, whose subscriptions are outstanding to forward same to the Hon Treasurer, J. Millburn 16 5 Moscow Drive, by May 7th at the latest, as there is insufficient cash in hand to meet heavy expenses already overdue.

　　　　　　　　　　　　Carried

The secretary reported that a match advertised as Liverpool & District v Birkenhead & District had been played on the ground of the Waterloo

BALL

D. P. BOHL B.Sc

The Committee Minutes 28th April 1922 — (continued)

SEFTON R.U.F.C.

Club on Thursday April 20th. The players on the Liverpool & District side were chosen from the Liverpool & Waterloo clubs only. Sefton had no official notice of the game.

Mr. Cain proposed & Mr. Hutchings seconded, "That a letter be sent to the County committee asking for an inquiry into the method of selecting the L'pool & District team for the game; if the county authorised the game to be played, & if so whether they allow any club or clubs to select a team & advertise it as a "District" side without consulting all other clubs in that district.

Carried.

Owing to Mr. Hemingway's absence discussion re the finances of the dance held at the Britannia rooms was postponed till the next meeting.

After some informal discussion re nominations for executive & committee the chairman declared the meeting closed.

HODGKINSON

The Committee Minutes 28th April 1922 –
(continued)

Copy of letter sent to Lancs. Football Club.

Sefton F.C.

Robert Leigh Knipe
9/6/22

40 Inigo Rd
Stoneycroft
L'pool
Dale.

Dear Sir,

On Thursday April 20th a match was played on the ground of the Waterloo F.C. under the title Liverpool & District v Birkenhead & District. As far as my committee are aware the Liverpool team was drawn from the Liverpool & Waterloo Clubs only. As the teams which actually turned out could not be considered to represent the full playing strength of either side of the river, it seems desirable that, in the interests of the public, & also to preserve a spirit of good feeling between the different clubs, there should be some definite ruling on the use of a title which is usually connected with representative games. My committee wish me to bring the matter to your notice for they feel that such games should be played only with the consent of the County Club, & after consultation with all the District Clubs.

Yrs faithfully

S. J. Bradburn Esy
Hon. Sec. Lancs. F.C.

F. J. Applebee
Hon. Sec.

HOPKINS

D. P. BOHL B.Sc

Results/Statistics 1921–22

Season 1921-22.

Captain · R. E. Snape   Later N. W. Hutchings.

First Team.

Date	Opponents	Grnd.	Rslt.	For G.	For T.	For Pts.	Agst G.	Agst T.	Agst Pts.
1921 Sept.	Tyldesley								
17	Tyldesley A	A	L	—	—	—	3	6	30
24	Waterloo 'A'	A	L	—	—	—	1(p.g)	5	18
Oct. 1	Old Salfordians	A	L	—	—	—	1	8	29
8	New Brighton 'A'	H	W	1	—	5	—	1	3
15	Bowdon Rangers 'A'	A	L	—	—	—	—	1	3
22	Birkenhead Park 'A'	A	Cancelled by Park. "Ground too wet."						
29	Chester College	A	" "	Chester mid Term Holiday.					
Nov. 5	Liverpool A	H	W	—	2	6	—	—	—
12	Port Sunlight	A	L	—	—	—	3 (1p. 1d.)	4	24
19	Heaton Moor	A	L	—	1	3	2 (1p.)	2	14
26	Preston Grasshoppers	H	L	—	—	—	—	1	3
Dec. 3	Southport	H	Cancelled by Southport who would have had 5 reserves						
10	New Brighton 'A'	A	L	—	2	6	5 (2p)	—	21
17	Kersal	A	L	T	1	8	4	3	29
24	Wigan O.B.	H	L	—	2	6	—	3	9
31 1922	Blead Park 'A'	H	L	—	1	3	2	4	22
Jan. 7	St. Helens O.B.	A	L	—	—	—	2	4	22
14	Liverpool 'A'	A	W	2 (1p.)	1	11	—	—	—

PALMISTRY

Report for Season 1921–22

1921 - 22

The past season's record shows a great improvement on that of the previous one. We were enabled to increase the number of our teams from three to four, & on one occasion we turned out a fifth XV.

The records of the various teams were as follows.

	Played	Won	Drawn	Lost	Pts. for	Pts. agst.
1st team	27	9	–	18	148	331
2nd "	26	7	5	14	113	214
3rd "	19	7	–	12	123	245
4th "	16	5	2	9	138	174
5th "	1	1	–	–	13	11
'A' team	1	–	1	–	3	3

Of their 9 victories, the first team obtained 7 after Xmas, thus showing a very marked improvement during the course of the season.

Several of the younger players have made their places secure in the first XV, & there is much latent ability in the junior sides. Enthusi—

D. P. BOHL B.Sc

Report for Season 1921–22 (continued)

was never at such a high pitch in the history of the club. This is proved by the fact that on several occasions when playing "away" we provided players, referee & linesmen for the home teams;

I wish to draw your attention to the unselfish manner in which the captains of the junior teams have sacrificed their chances of playing for the "first", & have changed mere collections of players into enthusiastic teams; to the sporting action of the reserves who so cheerfully answered the call to fill vacancies in the first team in away matches; & to the action of some of the younger members who voluntarily ran a dance, at their own risk, with the avowed intention of augmenting the ground fund.

The number of playing members at present is 90, & there are 57 honorary members. We have the nucleus of a powerful club, & if all will act up to the Club spirit we can look forward to the future with every confidence.

You will see by the balance sheet

Report for Season 1921–22 (continued)

that we owe the Treasurer the sum of £6.12.3.
This deficit should be cleared before the com-
mencement of another season.

A Watch Competition has been run with
the idea of starting a ground fund. The exact
figures are not yet available, but the result has
been a splendid success. For this, while many
members have worked excellently, we are chiefly
indebted to Mr W.J. Smith who has disposed of
close on £40 worth of tickets.

During the season a hot pot supper was held
at the Hare & Hounds Hotel, over 70 members & friends
being present. The affair showed a profit of £3.17.6.
A Dance was also held at the Britannia Rooms, but
up to the present no balance sheet has been
produced for this.

In conclusion I wish to ask you to consider
very seriously nomination for your officers for the
coming season. The work in the past has fallen
too heavily on the shoulders of the "faithful few"

With efficient officers & a real working
committee the work will be lightened for individuals
& the "running" of the club will be smoother
than ever.

L.J. Applebee
Hon. Sec.

D. P. BOHL B.Sc

AGM Cash Statement 1921–22

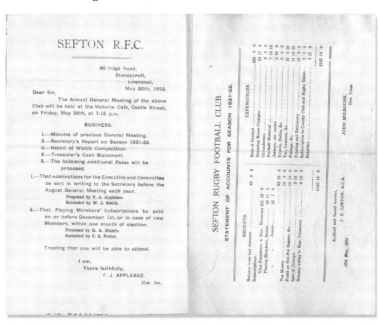

Newspaper Cuttings

KEEN GAME AT WEST DERBY.

Bidston beat Sefton A in a hard-fought game on the latter's ground by a goal and two tries (11 points) to a try (3 points). In the first half Sefton were superior in attack and Perrin scored a try. There would have been more scoring but for some resolute tackling by Parry, the Bidston full-back. In the second half, however, Bidston improved, and tries were scored by Galloway, Price, and Woodward, the latter also converting.

The visiting three-quarters were a better lot than Sefton's in that their handling was much superior and their running stronger, while Price and Poe showed a good understanding. Among the forwards Pavillard, A. Taylor, and Cooper were prominent. Dr. O'Sullivan, at full-back for Sefton, played a sterling game, and in the second half undoubtedly saved his side from defeat. Bayliss gave his rear division the ball on numerous occasions, only to see it lost through faulty handling. The home forwards were outplayed in the loose, but worked hard, especially Perrin and Ledger. During the scrums the ball was rarely brought out cleanly, a general fault of second-class rugger.

Result.—Bidston 11 points, Sefton A 3 points.

Teams.—Sefton A: Dr. O'Sullivan; Thompson Millington, Hudson, Davey; Bayliss, M'Gibbon; Ledger, Perrin, Williams, J. A. Cass, Rimmer, Mackenzie, Martinez, Jenkins. Bidston.—Parry; Burns, Ellam, Woodward, Galloway; Price, Poe; Cooper, Hudson, Pavillard, Williams, Rylls, H. Taylor, A. Taylor, Hinson.

W. B. Croxford

R. Leigh Knipe

Membership Handbook Season 1921–22

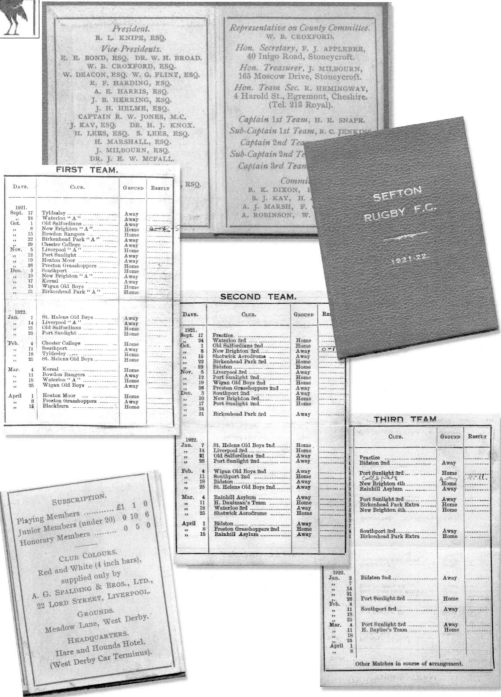

D. P. BOHL B.Sc

The Committee Minutes 9th June 1922 –
Hearlequin F.C. propose 'loose-head'

SEFTON
R.U.F.C.

Committee meeting held at Hare & Hounds Hotel
Friday June 9th 1922

Present Messrs Applebee, Milbourn, Smith, Menoo,
Kay, Croxford, Outhwaite, Marshall, Hutchings,
Robinson, Porter, Bayliss, Cain, with R.L. Mile
in the Chair.

Business transacted.

1. Minutes of previous meeting read, & Confirmed
   on motion of W.J. Smith slended by J.P. Porter.

2. R. Hemingway having submitted a statement
   of accounts concerning dance held at Britannia
   Rooms on March 17th. As he was unable to
   attend the meeting the matter was left over
   until he could be present.

3. The secretary produced the agenda for the
   Annual General meeting of the English Rugby
   Union, with requests from the Hearlequin
   F.C. & Kent County F.C that we should
   support their resolutions regarding "loose-

The Committee Minutes 9th June 1922 –
(continued)

lead" & Sunday Football in France respectively.
Mr Smith intimated his inability to attend
the meeting in question, & Mr Marshall proposed
& Mr Robinson seconded "That the admission
Card to the meeting be forwarded to A. D. Stoop
with instructions to "our" representative to
vote also in favour of the Kent resolution
                                    Carried.

4. The secretary reported that he had given
permission to the Clarendon Publicity Service
of Newcastle on Tyne to print fixture
sheets for next season, & distribute them
in convenient places in the neighbourhood.
No change whatever was to be made on the club,
the only condition being that the Clarendon
Publicity Service have the sole advertising
rights thereon, together with an option for the
following seasons on same conditions
        The secretary's action in the matter was
confirmed.

5. The secretary reported that he had received

The Committee Minutes 9th June 1922 — (continued)

no reply to his letter to the Lancs. F.C., re the L'pool & District match played on April 20th.

Mr. Croxford, the club's representative on the County Committee gave a lengthy account of the "doings" at the General meeting of the County Club, at which the letter was read.

Mr. Smith proposed & Mr. Croxford seconded

"That the secretary be instructed to write to the Lancs. F.C., pointing out to them that common courtesy demands an acknowledgment of the letter, & pressing for the ruling already asked for.

Carried.

It was also agreed that Mr. Croxford should write to the Lancs F.C. challenging the constitution of the meeting.

It was decided to call a meeting of the County committee at the Victoria Café Friday 16th inst at 7.30 p.m.

The Chairman the ~~proper~~ declared the meeting closed

July 28/22

Letter to Lancashire RFU regarding the use of 'District' title in county games

Copy of Letter to Lancs F.C. as instructed at
Committee meeting 9.6.22

Sefton F.C,

40 Irnjo Rd
Stoneycroft
L'pool
20.6.22

Dear Sir,

On a certain date last month I sent to you on
behalf of my Club a communication suggesting the
advisability of the county formulating a rule with
regard to the use of the "District" Title for any R.U.
games in the county.

Up to the present time I have received no
reply to my communication. My committee strongly resent
this, considering they have been treated in a most
discourteous manner, & have instructed me to write
you once again for a reply, as they do not consider
the matter closed, but on the contrary are considering
what further steps to take in the matter.

Yrs faithfully
S.J. Applebee
Hon. Sec.

S.J. Bradburn Esq
Hon. Sec. Lancs F.C.

Reply to Lancashire RFU regarding the use of 'District' title in county games

SEFTON
R.U.F.C.

Dear Sir,

     Your letter of May 6/22 Re the use of the 'District' title after a match played at Waterloo during the past season was brought before my committee at a meeting held in Manchester on May 20th, they consider the matter is a very trivial one, one over which they have no jurisdiction.

     As regards your letter June 30/22 I can only say that your representation was present at the said meeting, I cannot see any reason why he did not convey my Committee's decision to your Committee.

       Yours faithfully
        TJ Bradburn
         Hon. Sec.

General Meeting 18th August 1922 –
Outhwaite leaves for South Africa with gold watch

The minutes of the previous general meeting were read, & confirmed on motion of S. J. Kay seconded by N. W. Hutchings.

Mr. Milbourn presented his balance sheet in connection with the Watch Competition. A balance of £103.2.6 was shown & it was decided to hand over £100 to the trustees, remaining £3.2.6 being placed to the club's account.

The secretary reported that he had taken the grounds in West Derby at a rental of £50 for the season. His action was confirmed on motion of W. B. Crossford seconded by W. J. Smith.
A. Vote of thanks to retiring officers & committee was carried unanimously
The election of Officers & Committee resulted as follows.
President   W. J. Smith
Senior Vice-President.   J. Kay.
Vice Presidents. Messrs Bond, Broad. Crossford. Deacon, Flint, Herring, Helme, Jones. Knox, A. Lees, H. Lees, Marshall, Milbourn, MacFall. Morgan, O'Donnell Runjohn, Stringer, J. W. A. Taylor, J. R. Williams.

D. P. BOHL B.Sc

General Meeting 18th August 1922 – (continued)

SEFTON
R.U.F.C.

J. R. Williams, J. W. Taylor, Fraser, Bate, Myers, Ellis.
Dixon, Rae, Briggs, Lowe, Cain.

Ex President   R. L. Knipe.

Hon. Treas.   J. Milbourn.

"   Sec.   F. J. Applebee

"   Team Sec.   H. A. Munro.

Asst.   "   "   H. Brownbill.

Captain 1st Team   N. W. Hutchings.

"   2nd   "   H. E. Snape.

"   3rd   "   H. Daulman.

"   3rd   "   H. J. Bateman.

Committee:

Messrs. Skey, Porter, Dubourg, Mackenzie, Robinson,
Hemingway, Bayliss.

Mr. Smith proposed that "life membership may
be conferred on members who have rendered exceptional
service to the club"   Carried unanimously

Mr. Croxford proposed that the secretary & J. Outhwaite
be elected life members.   Carried unanimously.

It was decided to place the order for jerseys in

General Meeting 18th August 1922 –
(continued)

the lands of D. Williams, Sun Hall, Kensington

The president on behalf of the members of the
Club made a presentation of a gold watch & chain
to Mr. L. Outhwaite who, prior to his departure to
take up a new post in South Africa.

After several of the older members had
spoken appreciatively of Mr. Outhwaite, as a man
both on & off the field, & after everyone had
wished him the best of luck in his new sphere
of work, Mr Outhwaite replied, touching on the
happy times he had spent with the members
of the Club & expressing his best wishes for the
success of the Club, to which, as a life member
he would always belong.

The secretary announced that practices would be
held each Tuesday & Thursday at 6 p.m & Saturdays
at 3 p.m.

The Chairman then declared the meeting closed

D. P. BOHL B.Sc

F.D. Outhwaite joins Great Brak River Pirates in South Africa

Great Brak River Pirates 1922—23

1923—24

The Committee Minutes 21st September 1922 –
Directive from RU to reduce front row to three

with Messrs Croxford, Marshall & Dr. Dubourg.

    The secretary reported receipt of a communication from the Rugby Union requesting that clubs would play the game with no more than three forwards packed in front row of scrimmage, although the referee had no power to penalise a side which packed 4 in front.

    The chairman then declared the meeting closed.

RJ Smith
6.11.22

Photograph Sefton v Old Salfordians 1922

Sept 1922 at Irlam o'Th Heights

D. P. BOHL B.Sc

Results/Statistics Season 1922–23

SEFTON
R.U.F.C.

1922 - 23.

1922			1st Team.						
			for			agst.			Roll
			G.	T.	Pts	G.	T.	Pts	
16.9	Tyldesley	H	-	1	3	-	5	15	L
23.9	Old Salfordians	A	1	2	11	-	1	3	W
28.9	New Brighton 'A'	H	-	2	6	-	1	3	W
30.9	R.A.F.	A	1(a)	1	7	2	1	13	L
7.10	Rainhill Asylum	A	2	1	13	-	1	3	W
14.10	Prestwich	H	2(d)	5	24	-	-	-	W
21.10	Wigan Old Boys	A	-	-	-	1	4	17	L
28.10	Hoylake	A	-	2	6	-	-	-	W
4.11	Liverpool 'A'	A	-	-	-	-	2	6	L
11.11	Preston Grasshoppers	H	-	-	-	1	1	8	L
18.11	St. Helens G.B.	H	-	-	-	1	1	8	L
25.11	Southport	A	1(p)	1	6	1(p)	-	3	W
2.12	Kersal	H	1(th)	1	6	-	2	6	D
9.12	Wigan Old Boys	H	1(d)	-	4	-	2	6	L
16.12	Rainhill	A	abandoned						—
23.12	Port Sunlight	H	1	5	20	-	-	-	W
30.12	Bidston	A	-	-	-	-	-	6	L
1923									
6.1	St. Helens G.B.	A	-	-	-	3	1	18	L
13.1	L'pool 'A'	H	1	-	5	-	3	9	L
20.1	B'head Park A	A	-	-	-	3	5	30	L
27.1	Port Sunlight	A	-	1	3	1	-	5	L

AGM Cash Statement 17th May 1923

Sefton R.F.C.

40 Inigo Road,
Stoneycroft,
Liverpool,
10/5/23.

Dear Sir,
The Annual General Meeting will be held at the Victoria Cafe, Castle Street, on Thursday 17th inst., at 8 p.m., prompt.

BUSINESS.

1. Minutes of previous General Meeting.
2. Secretary's Report for Season 1922-23.
3. Cash statement.
4. Outstanding subscriptions.

Trusting that you will be able to attend.
I am,
Yours faithfully,
F. J. Applebee,
Hon. Sec.

Sefton Rugby Football Club.

STATEMENT OF ACCOUNTS

For the Season 1922-3

RECEIPTS.	£ s. d.	£ s. d.	EXPENDITURE.	£ s. d.
Collection at Annual Meeting...		4 6 0	Balance from last account	6 12 3
Subscriptions outstanding last season		2 6 6	Rent of Ground	50 0 0
Subscriptions for 1922-23 :			Dressing Room Charges	31 0 0
Vice-Presidents & Hon. Members	24 16 6		Groundsman	11 10 11
Playing Members :-			Football material	9 6 7
Senior	51 2 6		Tea, Lemons, etc.	10 18 7
Junior	20 4 0		Postage	11 18 7
		96 3 0	Printing and Stationery	17 4 2
Tea Money		19 5 0	Subscription to County Club & Rugby Union	2 2 0
Entertainments, etc.		35 14 2	Sundries	1 8 3
Sundry Receipts		7 15 8	Postlethwaite Fund	5 0 0
Postlethwaite Fund		5 0 0	Balance	13 9 0
		£170 10 4		£170 10 4

Audited and found correct.
J. E. LINTON, A.C.A.

JOHN MILBOURN,
Hon. Treasurer.

GROUND FUND.

TRUSTEES' ACCOUNT.

1922.	£ s. d.		£ s. d.
Aug. 19 To Amount received from Hon. Treasurer	100 0 0	By Cash, purchase of £126 War Savings Certificate	100 16 0
Proceeds of Auction at Hot-Pot Supper & WhistDrive	1 1 0	Balance in hand	0 12 0
Bank Interest	0 7 0		
	£101 8 0		£101 8 0

Audited and found correct and the Securities examined.
J. E. LINTON, A.C.A.

W. J. SMITH, } Trustees.
H. A. MUNRO, }

D. P. BOHL B.Sc

Newspaper Cuttings

Dr. F. H. Anderson in South Africa.

Dr. F. H. Anderson, ex-captain of Manchester University and Lancashire County Rugby XV., has lost very little time in making his mark in South African Rugby football circles.

Soon after his return to that country he led his club—the Wasps Wanderers of Pietermaritzburg—to victory in the final of the Murray Cup; and the Blue Riband of Natal Rugby. That was on September 24, 1921, the last Saturday of that season.

On May 6 Dr. Anderson played in a Natal trial match for the Rest of Natal v. Combined Durban. Durban won by 18 points to 12 (thanks to superior place-kicking), but so greatly did the Doctor impress that he was not merely selected to partner W. H. Townsend, the Springbok half-back, but he was actually, on his first selection for Natal, appointed captain of the team in succession to H. W. Taylor, the South African cricket captain, who has now retired from active participation in Rugby football.

The distinction which has been accorded Dr. Anderson will be understood better when it is explained that the Natal team selected contains no fewer than five members of the South African side which visited New Zealand last year, and of those five one is a former Natal captain.

The Natal team was due to sail from Durban on May 19 for the purpose of playing three Currie Cup matches in the Cape Province, their opponents being the Border, the Eastern Province, and the Western Province.

To play these three matches the team will have to travel over 2,400 miles, and will be away from Natal 13 days.

* * *

Old Public Schoolboy Keenness.

In this final article of the season it may not be inappropriate to touch upon the work of some of the junior clubs that are apt to be overlooked during the busy football period. Sefton were the last of the Merseyside clubs to finish their season. They concluded, as they began, with a defeat at the hands of Tyldesley, in a game played in such an admirable sporting spirit that only one free kick was given in the match and that for a scrummage infringement. The Sefton season has not been quite satisfying from the point of view of results. The first team won only seven and lost twenty-two of the thirty-one matches played, and had an adverse balance of 182 points. The best work, indeed, was done by the fourth team, who had thirteen victories against nine defeats.

Four teams have been run regularly and a fifth when grounds have been available, so that the club is by no means short of playing members, but injuries have sadly upset the smooth working of the first team, and the difficulties that have had to be faced may be gathered from the fact that of the fifteen players in the first match of the season only two were available for the last match.

A feature of the Sefton club is the youthfulness of its playing membership, a membership that has included during the season representatives of such schools as Ampleforth, Rossall, St. Bees, Liverpool College, The Mount (Chesterfield), Blackrock, Birkenhead, Glasgow High, Whitgift, Denstone, Kingswood, Giggleswick, Merchant Taylors', King William's, Lancaster Grammar School, and others, and of the Universities of Oxford, Liverpool, and Manchester. With players from so many great Rugger schools steadily gaining in experience the future seems bright enough, especially as they are under the eye of a keen, practical, and enthusiastic committee.

Wigan Old Boys v. Sefton.
Wiganers' Fifth Win.

The Old Boys entertained their old friends from Liverpool, and although the game did not reach the usual high standard of play, there were several smart movements, but a strong cross-wind somewhat interfered with accurate handling and kicking. A remarkable feature of the game was that all 17 points were scored in the first half. Teams:—

Old Boys: A. R. Hoggins, S. H. Garner, V. Bradshaw, N. K. Smith, J. A. Owens, H. Sawbridge, J. Walkden, P. Wild, F. Atherton, J. Hodgkinson, J. Newble, F. Booth, A. E. Saunders, R. T. Ball, and C. Arrowsmith.

Sefton: W. D. Herring, H. J. Thompson, S. Hitchings, C. G. H. Webley, E. O. Duborg, C. A. Redhead, N. W. Hutchings, W. N. Laker, H. S. Damsell, C. H. Mackenzie, J. C. H. Danlman, T. F. Scotson, H. Brownhill, W. H. Dobourg, and F. H. Dalton.

Atherton was soon to the front with a good kick to touch. Following the line out, Bradshaw was off at rare speed, but the move broke down. Sefton went back with a rush, but Sawbridge relieved. The Wigan forwards were getting the ball with Saunders strong in the loose. A clever bout of passing by Sefton looked dangerous for the home side, but the line was saved. A free kick to Sefton further harassed the Wiganers, but Walkden got the ball away. Arrowsmith and Smith got off on their own account, but without the desired result, the Sefton full-back playing a sound game. The visitors again handled the ball nicely, but failed to get over. The Wiganers now had a look in, but smart tackling upset their intentions, the visitors driving back hard, narrowly missing with a drop at goal. The home forwards worked the ball down, Saunders breaking away, and Smith, getting hold, raced over for the Wiganers' first try, Hoggins failing with the kick. From the re-start the visiting forwards went with a rush, but Bradshaw picked up, and was only stopped by heavy tackling, appearing to be somewhat shaken up as the result. Garner was looking dangerous when bundled into touch. Following forward work, Booth rushed over for the second try, the place kick again failing. Shortly afterwards Hoggins got in a high kick, and following up at top speed, charged down the reply of his vis-a-vis, and dribbled the ball over for a smart try. Bradshaw went through with a brilliant burst, and handing over beautifully to Smith, he scored his second try, Hoggins narrowly missing the goal. The Sefton forwards got to work, and in stopping a rush Sawbridge got a nasty knock on the nose, he having to receive the trainer's attention. The visitors' continued to have more of the game, and got close to the Wigan line, but Newble kicked out. Half-time found the home team 17 points ahead.

On the resumption, Sefton tried a forward rush, which Sawbridge stopped by finding touch, the line out enabling the home team to open out the game. Bradshaw and Smith indulged in a very smart re-passing movement, but Sefton stopped this and counter-attacking with vigour, nearly scored. The home defence was hard put to it. Play getting back, Owen was pushed into touch when close up. Smith came near with a strong effort, but the Sefton backs defended well, the full-back relieving with a powerful kick. Ball was laid out with leg trouble, the game having to be stopped. The Sefton forwards were smart in the loose, putting the Wiganers again on the defensive. Hoggins carried the ball up, and giving the "dummy," nearly got over. No further score resulted. Result:—

Wigan Old Boys .... 17 points.
Sefton .... Nil.

Wigan Examiner 24/10/22

Sefton's Last Match.

Sefton were the first of the Liverpool clubs to open the Rugby season on Merseyside, and they are the last to complete their programme. They are due to visit Tyldesley next Saturday, and, though they are not likely to emulate the feats of Sale and Workington, the only clubs that have won on the Well-street ground since football was resumed after the war, they are assured a warm welcome and a good sporting game.

Though they are given the credit by every club that meets them of playing clean and wholesome and usually clever football, the Tyldesley club have lost the whole of their Merseyside connection with the exception of Sefton, who, it has to be admitted, are not quite good enough for them. Since the war Tyldesley have met and have beaten Birkenhead Park, Liverpool, Waterloo, New Brighton, Port Sunlight, and Sefton, but each of the first five clubs have dropped their fixtures.

Port Sunlight are the latest of the Merseyside clubs to decline matches, their explanation being, it is understood, that they are giving up long-distance games. And yet the Cheshire club have arranged with the Old Salfordians and Manchester Y.M.C.A.! It would be interesting to learn the real reason for the ostracism of an undeniably clever side by the clubs of Merseyside.

OPENING GAME ON MERSEYSIDE.

SEFTON'S HARD FIGHT.

By V. A. S. Beanland.

In opening their programme against Tyldesley, at West Derby, on Saturday, and, incidentally, leading the way in the new season's Merseyside "Rugger," which does not begin in earnest until this week-end, Sefton faced as heavy a problem as they are likely to be called upon to tackle during the next few months. They faced it bravely, and made a good fight up to a point, but they were no match either in speed or skill or condition for a very well-balanced and capable opposition. Tyldesley won by 5 tries, scored by Hodgson (3), Smith and Hindley, to 1 try, by S. Brown, the St. Helens Old Boys, Lancashire, and North forward, who is helping Sefton in a match or two, and the margin fairly accurately represents the difference between the teams.

Sefton had one piece of very bad luck during the second half, when H. C. G. Webley and F. Porter, trying to field a high ball, collided with such force that the former had his eye cut open and the latter's nose was so badly damaged that he could take no further part in the game. It was during the absence of those two players that Tyldesley scored a couple of their tries, though the visitors were at that time playing with such confidence that they would probably have beaten down the defence in any case. Confidence was one of the essentials Sefton lacked. They did not quite believe in themselves, and failed to finish at least two very promising movements by hesitancy when the opposition appeared to have been beaten. Possibly the knowledge that they lacked speed in part explained this wavering when the goal-line was in sight, but a clear weakness in attack was exposed.

Where Tyldesley Excelled.

The Tyldesley men were the more experienced and more adaptable side. Their forwards were stronger in the scrummages and at the line-out, and in the open J. Anderson was allowed so much latitude that he was continually opening out the game for his backs. As a consequence Nichol and Lawson at half-back, and a lively three-quarter line had quite a merry afternoon of attacking work, and Fearnley, at full-back, had little opportunity to show the powers that have commended him to some members of the Lancashire Selection Committee.

But Sefton will not be discouraged in falling before a side they could hardly have expected to hold. The forwards, some of whom are rather raw, would soon be developed if a man like Brown, who stood out from the whole field, were able regularly to take charge of them, and there is some good material behind the scrummage. Webley, an old Cheltenham Town boy, played a capital game at stand-off half-back. N. W. Hutchings, if a little short of speed, was sound at centre, and W. D. Herring is a full-back of promise. On a few occasions W. B. Croxford, playing on the left wing, showed his old qualities, but the pace of other days had gone. H. J. Thompson, on the right wing, is very young, and was too inexperienced successfully to face so smart a winger as Hodgson, who gave one of his cleverest displays. Match practice will remedy some defects in the home team's play, and Sefton should do fairly well with a playing membership of over a hundred, but at present they cannot hope to do more than make a fight with a side of Tyldesley's quality. Teams:—

Sefton.—W. D. Herring, full-back; H. J. Thompson, N. W. Hutchings, H. S. Hutchings and W. B. Croxford, three-quarter backs; H. C. G. Webley and H. W. Scotson, half-backs; J. V. Stephens, S. Brown, F. Porter, H. S. Damsell, J. C. H. Danlman, S. Kay, W. H. Scott and Chadwick, forwards.

Tyldesley.—F. Fearnley, full-back; J. Hodgson, A. S. Hindley, James Quinn and S. R. Kenyon, three-quarter backs; W. C. Nichol and F. Lawson, half-backs; J. Anderson, W. E. Dowling, R. Carr, John Quinn, W. Dutton, J. Leyland, J. Lewis and G. Smith, forwards.

PRESENTATION TO SEFTON PLAYER.

At the annual meeting of the Sefton R.F.C., Mr. F. Outhwaite, a long-service member of the club who has frequently appeared in Lancashire trial games, was the recipient of a gold watch and chain from the officers and members of the club, on the occasion of his departure to take up an appointment in South Africa. The presentation was made by the new club president, Mr. W. J. Smith, who as senior vice-president succeeds Mr. R. Leigh Knipe, who has held the position for the allotted span of two years.

Sefton will as last year field four fifteens, N. Hutchings, who was the Liverpool District full back in 1920, and who played last year with Ebbw Vale, will lead the first team. Practices will be held on Tuesday and Thursday evenings and Saturday afternoons, from August 22nd to September 16th. The match season opens on the latter date, when Tyldesley visit West Derby.

Cartoon from Wigan Examiner

Former player Cec Adams recalls – I remember playing against Wigan Old Boys, always a tough match. A remark from the scrum, "Some b*stard has bitten me!" A Welsh voice replied, "I haven't got my teeth in!", 'twas Taffy Evans, a front row forward, aged but of great experience from South Wales.

When we played Kendal this was always a good match – a highlight of the season. Good fun in the local after the match. We had at the time a beautiful Welsh tenor who sang lovely sentimental songs – such as 'Good Night Ladies' etc. It was a great picture to see tough Sefton bods dropping tears into their beers by the time he had finished his repertoire.

WIGAN OLD BOYS V. SEFTON.

D. P. BOHL B.Sc

Membership Handbook 1922–23

SEFTON
R.U.F.C.

President :
W. J. SMITH.

Ex-President :
R. L. KNIPE.

Senior Vice-President :
J. KAY.

Vice-Presidents :

F. A. Bate, E. E. Bond, J. T. Briggs, Dr. W. H. Broad, A. E. Cain, W. B. Croxford, W. Deacon, C. K. Dixon, H. N. Ellis, W. G. Flint, C. F. Fraser, J. B. Herring, J. H. Helme, R. W. Jones, Dr. H. J. Knox, S. Lees, W. Lowe, H. Marshall, Dr. Dubourg, J. Milbourn, H. J. Morgan, E. R. Myers, R. A. O'Donnell, A. Rae, Dr. J. Rumjahn, L. Stringer, J. W. Taylor, J. W. A. Taylor, I. R. Williams, J. R. Williams, R. K. Mackenzie.

County Representative :
W. B. CROXFORD.
Hon. Secretary : F. J. APPLEBEE, 40, Inigo Road, Stoneycroft.
Hon. Team Sec. : H. A. MUNRO, 5. Cook Street, Liverpool. Phone Bank 524.
Asst. Team Sec. : H. BROWNBILL, 37, Alverstone Road, Egremont.
Hon. Treasurer : J. MILBOURN. 165, Moscow Drive, Stoneycroft.
Captain 1st Team :
N. W. HUTCHINGS.
Captain 2nd Team :
S. J. KAY.
Captains 3rd Teams :
H. F. P. BAYLISS.
H. F. BATEMAN.
Committee :
J. F. Dalton, W. H. Dubourg, R. Hemingway, R. K. Dixon, C. H. Mackenzie, F. S. Porter, A. Robinson.

Members Name *Lily Applebee*

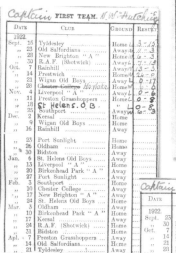

Captain FIRST TEAM. *N. W. Hutchings*

Date	Club	Ground	Result
1922.			
Sept. 16	Tyldesley	Home L	3 . 12
,, 23	Old Salfordians	Away	11 . 3
,, 28	New Brighton "A"	Home	6 . 3
,, 30	R.A.F. (Shotwick)	Away L	7 . 13
Oct. 7	Rainhill	Away	13 . 3
,, 14	Prestwich	Home W	24 . 0
,, 21	Wigan Old Boys	Away L	0 . 17
,, 28	Chester College *Hoylake*	Home W	
Nov. 4	Liverpool "A"	Away L	0 . 6
,, 11	Preston Grasshoppers	Home L	0 . 6
,, 18	St Helens O.B.	,,	0 . 8
,, 25	Southport	Away W	8 . 3
Dec. 2	Kersal	Home	
,, 9	Wigan Old Boys	Home	
,, 16	Rainhill	Away	
,, 23	Port Sunlight	Home	
,, 26	Oldham	Home	
,, 30	Bidston	Away	
Jan. 6	St. Helens Old Boys	Away	
,, 13	Liverpool "A"	Home	
,, 20	Birkenhead Park "A"	Away	
,, 27	Port Sunlight	Away	
Feb. 3	Southport	Home	
,, 10	Chester College	Away	
,, 17	New Brighton "A"	Away	
,, 24	St. Helens Old Boys	Home	
Mar. 3	Oldham	Away	
,, 10	Birkenhead Park "A"	Home	
,, 17	Kersal	Away	
,, 24	R.A.F. (Shotwick)	Away	
,, 31	Bidston	Home	
Apl. 7	Preston Grasshoppers	Away	
,, 14	Old Salfordians	Home	
,, 21	Tyldesley	Away	

Captain SECOND TEAM. *Stan J. Kay.*

Date	Club	Ground	Result
1922.			
Sept. 23	Old Salfordians 2nd	Home	8 . 0
,, 30	R.A.F. (Shotwick) 2nd	Home W	3 . 0
Oct. 7	Hoylake	Home D	14 . 14
,, 14	Prestwich 2nd	Away	41 . 0
,, 21	Wigan Old Boys 2nd	Home D	0 . 0
,, 28	Hoylake	Away W	15 . 3
Nov. 4	Liverpool 2nd	Home	
,, 11	Preston Grasshoppers 2nd	Away	
,, 18	New Brighton 3rd	Away	
,, 25	Southport 2nd	Home	
Dec. 2			
,, 9	Wigan Old Boys 2nd	Away	
,, 16	L'pool University 2nd	Home	
,, 23	Port Sunlight 2nd	Away	
,, 30	Bidston 2nd	Home	
1923.			
Jan. 6	St. Helens Old Boys 2nd	Home	
,, 13	Liverpool 3rd	Away	
,, 20	Birkenhead Park 3rd	Home	
,, 27	Port Sunlight 2nd	Home	
Feb. 3	Southport 2nd	Away	
,, 10	Hoylake	Home	
,, 17	New Brighton 3rd	Home	
,, 24	St. Helens Old Boys 2nd	Away	
Mar. 3	L'pool University 2nd	Away	
,, 10	Birkenhead Park 3rd	Away	
,, 17	Hoylake	Home	
,, 24	R.A.F.		
,, 31			
Apl. 7			
,, 14			

SUBSCRIPTION.

Playing Member's	£1	1	0
Junior Member's (under 20)	0	10	6
Honorary Member's	0	5	0

CLUB COLOURS.
Jersey : Red and White Hoops, Navy Knickers.
Stockings : Red and White Rings.
Supplied only by :
D. WILLIAMS, Sun Hall Buildings, 269, Kensington.

GROUNDS :
Meadow Lane, West Derby.

HEADQUARTERS :
Hare and Hounds Hotel.
(West Derby Car Terminus).

*Lily Applebee
40. Inigo Rd*

5th team

et 28	St Helens	A	L	9-12
ov 4	Hoylake	A	L	3-5
ec 9	St Helens	H	L	3-30
,, 16	St Edwards	A	L	- 18
,, 27	Collegians	H	W	15-9
,, 30		H	L	21-34
,, 24	Bidston	A	W	14-12

Sefton
Rugby F.C.
1922-23

Team Photographs 1922–23

Back Row. J. J. Applebee R. L. Knife, R. Pharshall, J. J. McCormick, W. B. Croxford, W. R. Baker.
J. D. Taylor, H. Browned, H. W. Jones.
seated E. R. Mawdsley, H. C. J. Gebb, J. L. Dalton, H. E. Snape, W. J. Snell, W. D. Herring.
C. R. Hashbage, J. L. Finish, R. A. Tobych. (R. W. Hutching captain)
In front T. L. Acoton K. S. Bradshaw, C. L. Redhead absent

2nd team 1922–23.
J. Morrissey H. A. Munro.
W. H. Scott. A. L. Foggo. T. Mailleye, D. R. Chideock, R. K. Dixon, W. F. Arrowsmith
J. Crawford. E. Hartley.
D. Simpson, F. King, E. A. Martinez. A. J. Kay, J. A. Williams G. C. Ledger

D. P. BOHL B. Sc

Report for Season 1922–23

SEFTON
R.U.F.C.

Season 1922-23.

The past season, which opened in such promising
fashion ended from a "results" point of view, in
comparative failure. We were enabled to run
four teams regularly, & on occasions, five. The
results were as follows.

	won	drawn	lost	For	Agst
1st	7	2	22	131	313
2nd	12	3	13	203	259
B	3	2	23	158	350
C.	13	2	9	244	274
Extra	2	—	5	65	121

The seven victories of the first team
were obtained in the first half of the season, at
the end of which the balance of points was in
our favour (106 – 97). Later, the team was so severely
hit by illness, injury, & by the fact that several
of our more prominent members had to leave the
city, that in the final match v Tyldesley, only
two of our players were available of those who
figured in the opening game. This fact
naturally weakened all the other teams.

The future, however, is full of promise. We

Report for Season 1922–23 (continued)

have several young players who should go far in the game, & if they will devote a little more time to training, & above all, to combination, we shall have little to fear from the teams we shall meet next season.

The balance sheet is before you, & altho' we have something above £13 in hand, that balance would have been materially increased had the Entertainments' Committee received the whole-hearted backing they deserved.

I wish to ask the younger members in particular to do what is in their power to lighten the work of the Club's Officials, particularly the Team Secretaries & Entertainments' Committee, & not to look upon the club merely as an instrument enabling them to fill what would otherwise be a blank Saturday afternoon.

In conclusion I wish to thank most heartily the captains of the junior teams, those men who have so loyally turned out at extremely short notice for the distant matches, & the very small number of men who have put in necessary work at the ground, thus cut-

ting down ground expenses. The names of all these should be emblazoned in letters of gold in the club's dressing rooms, but I am afraid the finances would not stand it.

D. P. BOHL B.Sc

Sefton RUFC –
Committee Minutes 1923–25

General Meeting 17th August 1923–
Lord Sefton forbids football on his playing fields

Team Sec.   H. A. Munro.
Asst. Team Sec.   H. Brownbill

Capt. 1st XV   H. C. G. Webley
Vice-Capt 1st XV   J. H. Morrissey

Capt. 2nd XV   I. S. Porter
Vice-Capt. 2nd XV   G. Martinez

Capts. 3rd XV.s   H. S. Bateman
                     J. A. Williams
Auditor.   J. E. Linton.
Committee   S. J. Kay, W. H. Dubourg, C. H. Mackenzie
            N. W. Hutchings, S. King, H. S. P. Bayliss,
            C. A. Redhead.

The secretary reported that Lord Sefton's agent
had forbidden the sub-letting of any grounds
for the purpose of football, & consequently the
club was without a ground. Numerous efforts
had been made to secure a pitch but up
to the time of the meeting success had not
been achieved. Several alternative grounds

The Committee Minutes 17th September 1923 –
the club pleads with Lord Sefton's decision

The secretary reported that all attempts to secure a ground had failed, in spite of great efforts which had been put forth by Mr. Knife. There was still open an offer for the use of the Stanley Athletic Grounds for Saturdays only at a rental of £50. This was felt to be excessive as the ground would accommodate one pitch only.

The Committee did not definitely turn this offer down, but it was felt that if we were forced to apply for the ground we should make a smaller offer.

The chairman proposed, & the Committee passed unanimously, a vote of thanks to Mr. Knife for his great efforts to procure a ground.

Messrs Dubourg & Mackenzie left the meeting to interview Lord Sefton's agent. On their return they reported that he was still away, but they had seen his assistant, who assured them that on his return, certain facts would be brought before him, & these facts would probably cause his decision re the letting of the club's old grounds to be reversed. The meeting broke up in a more optimistic frame of mind than when it assembled.

Sefton Pantomime 3rd May 1924

SEFTON
R.U.F.C.

Report for Season 1923–24

The treasurer reported that there was a deficit on season's working but if outstanding sub-materialised the balance sheet would show a surplus.

Members present volunteered to try to obtain all outstanding subscriptions.

The meeting then terminated.

W Smith
13/8/24

Secretary's Report for Season 1923-24.

The Season 1923-24 has shown some improvement on previous one. The results are as follows

	Played	Won	Drawn	Lost	Pts for	Agst
1st	32	8	4	20	119	412
2nd	28	15	–	13	276	189
3rd	49	20	5	24	477	497
Extra	6	3	–	3	95	100

The 2nd team record is easily the best in the club since the war, & is very creditable especially as the 1st four games were lost.

Of the 3rd teams losses, three were

D. P. BOHL B.Sc

Report for Season 1923–24 (continued)

SEFTON
R.U.F.C.

against 2ⁿᵈ team opponents, & 1 was against 1ˢᵗ team opponents.

It is to be regretted that on several occasions our teams have turned out short handed, the result being that we have often suffered reverses where victories should have been obtained. The club has, however, had its glorious days, the most note-worthy being on the occasions of the 1ˢᵗ team's victories over R.A.F. & St. Helens Q.B, the games V Tyldesley & Turners; the 2ⁿᵈ team's victories over Wigan Q.B. 2ⁿᵈ Old Birkonians 2ⁿᵈ; over R.A.F 2ⁿᵈ (with 12 players) & their remarkable performance on the Preston ground when with 11 men, they scored 3 tries against the Hoppers' 2 goals; & the victory of the 3ʳᵈ team at Preston, where, with 11 men they scored 23 points against the 5 obtained by a full & heavy XV of the Grasshoppers.

We have now in our ranks players fit for any club in the district, & with a little more consideration from certain members of the club, the results next season should show a further improvement.

With regard to finance the balance sheet

Report for Season 1923–24 (continued)

at present shows a deficit of £17, but when outstanding subscriptions are paid, it will show a surplus.

Several members of the club have made laudable efforts to increase the ground fund. Mr. Marshall led the way with his excellent toffee-scheme, the members generally made the national sweep a huge success. The Hot Pots showed a profit, + the "Scrummagers" are out to beat the record. The Rummage Sale will also bring a little grist to the mill, but the Scrummagers show + the Rummage Sale will not be financial successes without the whole hearted support of the majority of the members.

In conclusion I should like each member to ask himself the question "Have I done my whack for the Club this season?". If the answer is in the affirmative, do just a bit more, + if in the negative — well — finish in style.

J. Applebee

D. P. BOHL B.Sc

Results/Statistics Season 1923–24

1923 -24

First Team			For G.	T.	Pts	Agst G.	T.	Pts	
Sep. 15	Tyldesley	away	–	–	–	5	10	55	L
" 29	Prestwich	"	1	1	8	1	–	5	W
Oct 6	Old Salfordians	Home	–	–	–	–	2	6	L
" 13	St Helens OB.	"	–	1	3	–	–	–	W
" 20	New Brighton A Away		–	–	4	2	22		L
" 27	Wigan OB.	away	–	–	2	4	22		L
Nov. 3	L'pool	"	–	1	3	4	1	21	L
" 10	Preston G'hoppers	"	–	–	2	2	16		L
" 17	Old Birkonians	Home	–	–	1	2	11		L
" 24	Hoylake	Home	2	2	15	–	–	–	W
Dec. 8	Furness	Away	–	–	3	6	33		L
" 15	B'ston	Home	–	2	6	1	–	5	W
" 22	Southport	"	–	1	3	–	1	3	D
" 26	Hoylake	Away	1	1	8	–	1	3	W
" 29	Cammell Lairds		–	2	6	2	6		D
Jan 5	Port Sunlight	"	–	–	–	–	3	9	L
" 12	Southport	"	–	1	3	–	–	–	W
" 19	R.A.F	"	–	1	3	–	1	3	D
" 26	Port Sunlight	Home	–	1	3	2	–	8	L
Feb. 2	L'pool 'A'	"	–	1	3	1	–	5	L
" 9	St Helens OB.	away	–	1	3	3	2	21	L
" 16	Old Birkonians	"	–	2	6	3	6	33	L

BALL

Newspaper Cuttings

ANOTHER WIN FOR PORT SUNLIGHT.

SEFTON DEFEATED AWAY.

BRILLIANT KICKING BY HAGMAN.

(By "Herbitus.")

In a very stubborn struggle Port Sunlight, minus five of their regular team, were able to defeat Sefton at West Derby, on Saturday, Hagman notching all the points for the Southenders, his judicious kicking all through the game being a marked feature of the contest. Sefton were very unfortunate to lose the services of Kidd in the first few minutes of the game, the clever threequarter twisting his ankle, which will necessitate his not being able to play for some weeks. In the first half Port Sunlight monopolised the play and came very near scoring on many occasions, their backs being cool, quick, and very clever, and played with good understanding, the mistakes being very few, and when mistakes were made they were quick to retrieve them. The first real test of the game came when Morisson, with a Herculean effort, almost forced himself through, to be followed soon after by a masterly effort on the part of Bimpson, who failed in his attempt by inches. The crowning part of the first half, however, was the brilliant footwork of Hagman, who not only scored a try after a free kick taken by himself, but also converted against a powerful wind. The penalty kick, in which he also was successful in guiding over, was a piece of fine judgment on his part, and he was heartily applauded for his success. No doubt Sefton were badly handicapped by the loss of Kidd, but they could not get going at all, Bradshaw, at times, making poor use of the many opportunities he had behind the scrum. The fear was that the local forwards would not be able to withstand the weight of the opposing pack, but that fear soon became groundless, although there were some anxious moments towards the finish in the many scrummages that were formed near Port Sunlight's line. They may not have got possession so frequently at the scrums, but at the line outs, and in their strong rushes and dribbles, Port Sunlight were very effective. Sefton, in the second half, played with great determination, and on more than one occasion Munce should have made better use of the opportunities afforded him, Webley and Morrisey giving him some very useful passes. Herringe was very conspicuous in his clever kicking, and at times he was so badly pressed that he was compelled to touch down. It was an excellent game all through, Mr. H. Schofield (New Brighton) handling the play in a very able manner. Teams:—

Port Sunlight.—A. Hallam; J. S. Gilyead, R. J. Segger, H. Hagman, A. Bimpson; W. Smith (capt.), J. Sutherland; H. J. Smith, L. A. Griffiths, A. Morisson, W. R. Greatbanks, C. M. Irvine, G. A. Toft, P. Roberts, C. B. Clarke.

Sefton.—W. D. Herringe; C. H. Munce, H. S. Kidd, W. Webley, J. Taylor; K. Bradshaw, J. Morrisey; A. White, J. R. Taylor, H. McKenzie, W. Bulmer, W. Prentice, T. Wicks, J. McCormick, T. Jones.

Port Sunlight won the toss and chose to play against the wind, a stiff breeze blowing across the ground at the time. The visitors were penalised in the first few minutes for offside. Port Sunlight were early in attack, Segger, from a neat pass by W. Smith, gaining ground in a solo run, finding touch in the home half. Bradshaw snapped up from a scrum, but was quickly tackled by Gilyead and well held, Morisson shortly afterwards dribbling into the home 25. Offside against Port Sunlight enabled the home team to gain a little ground, Taylor, in attempting to break away, being forced into touch. Munce and Kidd effected a neat movement, the last-named, in an effort to cut through, coming in contact with Hagman, and twisting his ankle, which necessitated his retirement from the game. The visitors further pressed, the game being mostly in the home half, Bimpson finding touch with a neat kick. Webley was again prominent in a movement on the left wing, but his effort was not a complete success, Bimpson kicking to touch after a splendid tackle. Sutherland stopped a dangerous rush of the home forwards, following which Toft carried the game in Sefton's half with a useful dribble. Good work on the part of Sutherland, Morisson, and Gilyead enabled the visitors to force the play, the game at this period being in the proximity of the home 25, several scrums forming close to the line. Herringe was prominent in a long kick, Hagman returning, play again ruling for a time in Sefton's half. Webley coming to the rescue with a huge punt to touch. Sefton were penalised, Hagman taking the kick, the ball going dead. From the drop out J. Taylor snapped up the ball and was

well away, but was tackled by W. Smith and brought down. Further pressure on the part of the home team resulted in Hallam effecting a great save by falling upon the ball, the visiting full-back afterwards finding touch with a long kick. Then Port Sunlight forwards indulged in some good work, spreading across the field, Toft making great efforts to force himself through, W. Smith, a few moments later, nearly getting over, being tackled by Herringe close to the line, the full back, in attempting to gather soon afterwards, being tackled by Toft, who, along with Morisson, made a grand attempt to break down the home defence, Herringe having a particularly warm time of it, but stood the test well. Port Sunlight were having most of the game, and for a while the ball was hovering dangerously near the home line, Bimpson grounding a few inches short. From the ensuing five yards' scrum Sefton came away, being penalised for offside. Hagman took the kick from the 25 line, and following up was able to tackle Herringe just on the point of clearing, the home full back fumbling, leaving HAGMAN with a grand opportunity of scoring which he was quick to take advantage of, the same player converting. This reverse seemed to wake the home players up a little, and for a time play was confined in the visitors' half, Taylor and Webley being very conspicuous in some neat exchanges. Toft was again prominent in a good dribble, Herringe clearing with a judicious kick. The full back soon afterwards being well beaten after some brilliant passing by Sutherland,

W. Smith and Bimpson, Munce coming to the rescue and saving the situation by kicking to touch. Sefton's defence continued to have a warm time of it, and after Hagman had picked up the ball he got nicely away, handing to Bimpson, and the last-named, still travelling, looked all over a try-getter, but Herringe was not to be caught napping again, making a wonderful tackle, and clearing when hard pressed. Sutherland quickly following, forcing the home full back to touch down. Sefton broke away, Hallam relieving, and after further pressure on the part of the visitors, Webley made a fine clearance with a long kick to touch. From the line out the visiting "threes" indulged in some fine passing, Hagman took the ball on the bounce, and handed on to Segger, who passed to Gilyead, the winger, in his effort to race through, going into touch. Sefton were again penalised, and from the kick HAGMAN scored a beautiful penalty goal. Following the kick-off Port Sunlight were quickly in the home half, Gilyead making a fine attempt to get through, Herringe bringing off another great save with a timely tackle and transferring play to the visitors' half, where play ruled until the sound of the whistle for half-time, the visitors leading by 8 points to nil.

On resuming Port Sunlight were the first to show prominence, Morisson gathering very smartly and handing to Bimpson almost on the touch line, Munce bundling the winger into touch. After Webley had made some ground from the line out he was able to give to Munce in a splendid position, but the winger, in his excitement, seemed to lose control of himself, and was quickly tackled by Sutherland and brought down, Hallam gathering from a forward rush soon afterwards and sending to touch. Sefton were now having far more of the game than their opponents, and for a time the visiting defence was sorely tested, Morrisey and Munce in particular indulging in some pretty passing, the latter again experiencing very hard luck after a brilliant solo run, offside against Sefton easily the pressure. Several times Sefton tried to get their passing going, and after Taylor had received from the scrum he was able to send Webley away with an excellent pass, but the latter had not gone far, however, before he was tackled by Hagman, and well held. Another fine movement on the part of the visiting forwards ended in Greatbanks narrowly dribbling through, Herringe smartly picking up, and with a huge punt finding touch well up. Another round of passing on the part of Munce, Webley, and Taylor saw the former in possession, but he was handicapped for room, and ran into touch. By easy stages the visitors again assumed the aggressive, and following some fine exchanges on the part of Seggar and Gilyead the latter was tackled by Morrisey and well held. Hagman, a few moments later, saving a certain try by tackling Taylor close to the line. Port Sunlight were penalised for offside. Morrisey took the kick, Hagman catching, and running well in transferred to Seggar, the last named tapping the ball over Herringe's head, Port Sunlight being pulled up for offside when a try seemed certain. Following another brilliant forward rush Sutherland gathered very smartly effecting a fine pass to Hagman, the latter knocking on and spoiling another glorious opportunity. From this Sefton attacked strongly, Munce being particularly prominent in another solo run, Morisson bundling him into touch close to the visitors' line. Sefton continued in their attack, and following a fine forward rush WEBLEY

crossed over after a grand attempt on the part of W. Smith to avert the disaster, the visiting captain receiving a nasty kick on the chest forcing him to drop the ball. Morrisey failed to convert. From the kick off Sefton were soon again in the visiting half Gilyead kicking to touch when hard pressed, Hallam directly following returning a long kick from Herringe, the ball dropping into touch in the home half. Aided by the wind, Port Sunlight put on a little pressure, Herringe having great difficulty in keeping his line from being penetrated after another rush by the visiting forwards, Griffiths being very prominent. Hagman was next seen in a fine run, Munce effecting relief, the latter player, along with Herringe, forcing play in Port Sunlight's 25 by some neat passing. W. Smith and Sutherland initiated some fine movements behind the scrums, from which Port Sunlight gained considerable ground, Bimpson having very hard lines when in a good position, Taylor making a timely tackle and saving the situation, Webley transferring play again in the visiting half with a huge punt, McKenzie narrowly missing dribbling through, Hallam saving, kicking to touch. Port Sunlight broke away, Herringe saving under great difficulties, Gilyead making a sensational run towards the finish, Herringe having to touch down to save his line, the whistle sounding for full time, leaving Port Sunlight the victors by 2 goals (1 penalty), 8 points, to 1 try, 3 points.

COMMENTS.

With Morisson back in the forwards Port Sunlight played brilliant football, H. J. Smith leading a good pack, who were dangerous right through the game, opening out the play in brilliant fashion. Sefton's forwards were never really dangerous, always being held in check, McKenzie and Taylor being the pick of the line. The home threequarters were seen to better advantage in the the second half, Munce and Webley giving the best displays. Bradshaw and Morrisey, behind the scrum, did not work with that cohesion as is necessary to the initiation of good movements, and were frequently tackled before being able to get the ball away. Herringe, at full back, was very sound, and in defence was in direct contrast to the weakness of the other backs, his one mistake, however, in fumbling the penalty kick, costing his side a goal. The visiting defence was sound in every department, W. Smith and Sutherland both being excellent defenders. Of the threequarters Hagman was in every way the best on the field, and seldom made a mistake, and was ably assisted by Bimpson on the wing. Hallam, at full-back, was very safe, his tackling and kicking being very effective.

The Committee Minutes 26th January 1925 — Tour to the Isle of Man Arranged

SEFTON R.U.F.C.

The following were elected members of the club.

	Proposed by	Seconded by.
Rev. J. O. Nicholas	W. H. Scott.	J. Wood
" F. J. MacBride	J. Wood	F. Gibbs.
R. Murray	H. J. Gilman	F. J. Appleton.
E. Humphreys.	W. D. Sherring	J. K. Humphreys.

The secretary reported that he had, as requested at last general meeting arranged a "tour" at Easter.

Three games will be played in the Isle of Man. as follows. Good Friday Mona.

Easter Saturday Castletown

" Monday Onchan Rangers.

The above clubs agree to allow Sefton half gross gate in their respective matches.

Mr. Forsyth reported progress with regard to the dance.

He had out, over 400 tickets & was hoping that he would have very few returned.

The matter of "alcoholic refreshment" was discussed.

Mr. Milbourn proposed & Mr. King seconded

"That there be no alcoholic refreshment whatever"

The Committee Minutes 4th May 1925 –
Isle of Man Tour a Great Success

Committee Meeting held at Hare & Hounds Hotel.
May 4th 1925.

Present. Messrs Milbourn (chairman) Bayliss, Applebee,
Arrowsmith, King. Williams, Kay. Lockier, Cawthra, Webley,
+ Mackenzie afterwards joined by Messrs Knibb,
J.W.A. Taylor & W.B. Croseford.

The Minutes of the Previous Meeting were read
& confirmed.

The Treasurer reported that after receiving £25
from the "Sweep" a/c, & paying all dues, he
had about £10 in hand. There were a few
subs outstanding & an effort would be made to
get them in before the general meeting.

It was decided to hold the general meeting at
the Victoria Café on Monday 25th inst. or Fri.
29th inst.

The committee were deeply grieved to hear
of the sudden death of "Dick" Illingworth,

HODGKINSON

D. P. BOHL B.Sc

The Committee Minutes 4th May 1925 — (continued)

Possibly the most enthusiastic of our younger honorary members.

It was decided to send to his parents a message of sympathy from the members of the club, & also a wreath for the funeral.

Mr. Mackenzie reported that the Tour in the Isle of Man had been a great success. One match had been won & two lost. The tour had resulted in upwards of £6 being added to the ground fund. The Isle of Man clubs were anxious for the tour to be repeated next year, & all players who had taken part were anxious to go again.

The meeting then terminated

Report for Season 1924–25

Season 1924-1925. Secretary's Report.

It is with profound sorrow that I have to chronicle the untimely death of two of our members, T. W. White, an excellent forward of the 1st team, & "Dick" Illingworth the most enthusiastic of our young honorary members. Their places in the club will be hard to fill.

The past season has been a record one in several ways. For the first time five teams have turned out regularly & altogether 115 games have been played. The Ground fund has been substantially increased, the club has at last run a dance which has showed a considerable profit, the "sweep" has broken the record & a most successful & enjoyable Easter Tour took place in the Isle of Man.

Although the First Team Results did not show a great amount of success, I think we can look back on the season as a very satisfactory one. The Team Records are as follows.

	Played	Won	Drawn	Lost	Pts for	Pts agst.
1st	28	6	2	20	133	324
2nd	24	10	1	13	163	238

D. P. BOHL B.Sc

Report for Season 1924–25 (continued)

SEFTON
R.U.F.C.

	Played	Won	Drawn	Lost	Pts for	Pts agst
3rd (Bateman's)	23	10	–	13	183	239
3rd (King's)	21	11	2	8	267	156
Extra (Dubourg's)	14	5	1	8	114	167
'A' team	5	1	–	4	23	70
Total	115	43	6	66	883	1194

I should like to mention particularly the efforts that have been put forth on behalf of the club by the team secretary & captains of teams, the club treasurer & his able assistant.

It has been a matter of regret that the 1st team captain has only been able to take charge of his team on few occasions, for apart from his well known playing abilities his presence has, upon the remainder of the team, an inspiring effect which no one else can create.

The Ground Difficulty is still with us & it behoves each member of the club to be always on the look out for a suitable pitch, & to report to the committee immediately.

The fixture list for next season is much as usual, no new teams appearing, but in order to shorten the season I have omitted Rainhill & Cammell Lairds.

Results/Statistics Season 1924–25

First Team. 1924-25.

Date	Opponent	Venue	For			agst			Result
Sept. 20	Old Salfordians	away	–	–	–	3	1	16	L
,, 27	Prestwich	home	–	2	6	–	1	3	W
Oct. 4	Dick-Kerrs	home	6	5	45	–	–	–	W
,, 18	Wigan Old Boys	home	–	–	–	3	9		L
,, 25	Old Salfordians	home	–	1	3	–	2	6	L
Nov. 1	Liverpool 2.	away	–	1	3	–	1	3	D
,, 8	Bidston	away	1	–	5	–	1	3	W
,, 15	Cammell Lairds	home	1	2	11	–	–	–	W
,, 22	Blead Park 2	away	–	–	–	1	4	17	L
,, 29	Prestwich	away	–	–	–	1	1	6	L
Dec. 6	St Helens QB	home	2	–	7	–	4	12	L
,, 13	Old Birkonians	away	–	–	–	1	5	20	L
,, 20	Southport	home	–	–	–	3	5	30	L
,, 26	Warrington	away	–	–	–	1	4	17	L
,, 27	Hoylake	home	1	–	5	1	1	8	L
Jan. 3	Preston Grasshoppers	home	–	–	–	–	1	3	L
,, 10	Port Sunlight	away	1	–	4	2	3	17	L
,, 17	St. Helens QB	,,	1	3		3	4	27	L
,, 24	Blead Park 2	,,	–	1	3	2	3	17	L
,, 31	Liverpool	home	–	1	3	–	–	–	W
Feb. 7	Preston Grasshoppers	away	1	–	3	–	1	3	D
,, 14	Southport	,,	–	–	–	2	1	13	L

D. P. BOHL B.Sc

Newspaper Cuttings

Vice-President Ex-Chief Inspector R. Nelson with his Golf Trophies 1924

SEFTON LOSE AT WARRINGTON.

There was a surprise result to the visit of Sefton to Warrington yesterday. Sefton found themselves unable to withstand the vigorous tactics of the home men, and were defeated by 17 points to nil. Occasionally, owing to the weakness of the Sefton defence, Warrington were presented with openings of which they took full advantage. The visitors' forwards played a splendid game, their footwork being strong, and they gained a fair amount of possession from the scrimmage.

A dribble by the Warrington forwards was followed by a breakaway by Connor, and after short passing Gibbs scored a try in the corner. Carruthers added a second, while Connor put Warrington further ahead. In the second half Connor again scored, and Creighton finished up the scoring with a try, which Healey improved.

Result: Warrington 17 pts., Sefton nil.

There were some lakes, but Sefton had left their fishing rods at home.

A Ground Fund.

Eight players reported fit in 1919, and a fresh start was made. The old name no longer seemed suitable, and the present name—Sefton—was adopted. First team results have not been very thrilling, there having been a sad lack of weight and height, but there are now signs that these defects will shortly be remedied, and with a playing membership of about 120, and a general level of ability through the five teams which the club now puts regularly in the field, the outlook is bright. N. W. Hutchings, the captain of the side, has been missing most of the season for business reasons, and his absence has been badly felt. Of the present side, Arrowsmith, in the centre, and Sorenson forward, are the most promising. Foggo, the stand-off half, is a splendid kick with very good hands, who only needs resolution to make him a very fine player.

The club is in a sound financial position, and with the knowledge that the need for a permanent ground is the greatest of the present handicaps, a start has been made with a ground fund, to which, thanks to the energies of the treasurer, Mr. J. Milbourn, and the president, Mr W. J. Smith, the old Bristol and Gloucestershire forward, substantial contributions have already been made. A club dance held at the Embassy Rooms on Tuesday last, at which over 300 members and friends were present, should result in a further addition to the fund.

Old players of the club still take a very active part in club legislation. R. A. O'Donnell, the Lancashire forward, is very keenly interested in the St. Edward's Club; F. P. Arthur, a founder and secretary of Hoylake, still plays, and F. Outhwaite, who was reserve for the Lancashire scrum in 1921, was chosen for the Western Province S.A. trials last year, but stood down to give younger men a chance. With an enthusiastic body of young players, and the steadying influence of an imposing group of vice-presidents, not the least honoured of whom is Mr. R. K. Mackenzie, the founder of the Watsonians, there are signs of an advance in the near future.

SEFTON 15 Pts., HOYLAKE 0.

Sefton's third win of the season, at West Derby, on Saturday, against the Hoylake team, was very welcome, and though the visitors were a trifle unlucky not to score the home side was full value for a victory by 2 goals (1 dropped) and 2 tries (16 pts.) to nil. A rearranged side saw C. A. Redhead at full-back in place of W. D. Herring, who went to right-wing three-quarter. There was not much to choose between the respective packs. Sefton forwards holding the advantage in the loose.

Sefton's first try came through a solo dribble by J. Finnigan, whose effort was unconverted by H. C. G. Webley. T. W. White, who played a splendid game forward and kept the Sefton pack moving, registered the next two tries, one before the interval which Finnigan failed to convert, and another after fifty-five minutes' play. Finnigan on this occasion adding the goal points. Redhead had followed up very close to his forwards and seizing his chance he dropped a splendid goal. Sefton kept up the pressure mainly throug their forwards. A. A. Lyons, H. Hulme, and W. O. Williams put in some good work for Hoylake, who held a slight superiority behind the scrum. Redhead played well for Sefton at full-back.

Liverpool Post 26 November 1923

CAMMELL LAIRDS 6 Pts., SEFTON 6 Pts.

The Sefton teams were seen to good advantage in their week-end games. The first team, against Cammell Lairds at Rock Ferry, encountered a stiff opposition, and both sides made the most of their opportunities. Cammell Lairds displayed good bustling forward tactics, and against two tries by Sefton eventually forced a draw. Sefton II. met Higher Elementary School Old Boys at West Derby. In the first half Gibbs and Humphreys scored tries for the home team, and late in the game Robinson completed the victory with a try which made the score: Sefton II, 9 pts., H.E.S.O.B. nil.

Sefton B, 24 pts., H.E.S.O.B. II nil.

Liverpool Post 31 December 1923

SEFTON WIN AT SOUTHPORT.

The ground at Victoria Park was heavy after the snow, and a high standard of play could not be expected. The only score was a try by Bradshaw for Sefton after fifteen minutes, Finnigan took the kick but was beaten by the conditions. He made a gallant effort, but Gibbs stopped with his hand the ball in its flight. Sefton who had been the more aggressive, continued to exert pressure, and Pennell, for Southport, again proved his worth as a resourceful full-back.

There was, on the whole, nothing much to choose between the teams, whose handling was indifferent as much through the state of the ball as anything else. Both sets of forwards showed promising iniative but finished badly. For Southport, W. L. Smith, C. E. Gibbs, Houghton, and Guest were as prominent as any, while for Sefton W. H. Prentice, White, and Wickes were noteworthy.

Liverpool Post 14 January 1924

R.A.F. 3 Pts., SEFTON 3 Pts.

Sefton were the visitors at Shotwick, where a hard and fast game ended with the scores level at three points each. All the scoring was done in the first half. Kidd was prominent early on, and Munce, who came in at stand-off half, was also good. R.A.F. were the first to score, Cocks, their full back, handing off several men before he scored a try at the corner, the kick failing. Munce started the movement which enabled Sefton to equalise, Mackenzie accepting a pass from Jones and crossing the R.A.F. line, Webley's kick failing.

Both sides attacked strongly in the second half, but no further score resulted. Mackenzie was the best of the Sefton forwards, though all played well, the back division being good at times. The R.A.F. forwards were good, and the three-quarters handled well.

Sefton A 27 pts., R.A.F. II. nil.
Sefton B 8 pts., Hoylake B 3 pts.
Sefton C 6 pts., New Brighton Extra 3 pts.

Castletown v. Sefton.

Liverpool Club on Tour.

The Sefton (Liverpool) touring team, who were defeated by Mona yesterday, visited Castletown to-day to oppose the new club, and as the Association team had scratched their match with St. George's, the home side was strengthened by the inclusion of Preston at full-back. The match attracted considerable interest in the Southside, and there was quite a decent turn-up to witness this exhibition of the handling code by an English side.

In the first half, Murphy and Henchy scored tries for Castletown, and Henchy improved one of the tries, Castletown leading by eight points to nil at the interval.

Murphy scored three more tries in the second half, Allen improving one of them. The game was fast and open, and was greatly enjoyed by the spectators, Castletown playing fine football. Result:—

Castletown, 2 goals, 3 tries (19 pts.).
Sefton: Nil.

Easter Tour to the Isle of Man 1925

mackenzie & half Darnell at Onchan

Easter 1925

v. mona. Easter 1925

allen. at Onchan

Former player Cec Adams recalls, "They were great days, especially the Isle of Man Easter Tours when we played five matches in four days (i.e. two matches in one day). Tough boys then! Members of the Club were drawn from the Royal Liver Insurance Company, teachers, Liverpool College...and sundry comedians."

D. P. BOHL B.Sc

Membership Handbook Season 1924–25

SEFTON
RUGBY
FOOTBALL CLUB.

Season 1924-25.

President :
J. KAY, B.A.

Past Presidents.
J. G. LEGGE.
R. L. KNIPE.
W. J. SMITH.

Senior Vice-President :
J. W. A. TAYLOR.

Vice-Presidents :

A. G. Ascroft.	S. Lees.
F. A. Bate.	W. Lowe.
J. T. Briggs.	R. K. McKenzie.
Dr. W. H. Broad.	H. Marshall.
F. Burrell.	J. Milbourn.
A. E. Cain.	E. R. Myers.
W. B. Croxford.	R. Nelson.
C. K. Dixon.	R. A. O'Donnell.
Dr. Dubourg.	Dr. J. Rumjahn.
H. B. Ellis.	T. Scotson.
H. N. Ellis.	H. L. Scholfield.
W. G. Flint.	H. E. Snape.
Dr. W. Howell Evans.	L. Stringer.
J. B. Herring.	J. W. Taylor.
J. H Helme.	I. R. Williams.
R. W. Jones.	J. R. Williams.
Dr. H. J. Knox.	

County Representative :
W. B. CROXFORD.

Hon. Secretary :
F. J. APPLEBEE,
40, Inigo Road, Stoneycroft.

Hon. Treasurer.
J. MILBOURN,
165, Moscow Drive, Stoneycrof
and Victoria Cafe, Castle St.

Asst. Hon. Treasurer.
H. F. P. BAYLISS,
21 Undercliff Road, Stoneycroft

Hon. Team. Sec.
A. N. LOCKIER,
9 Osterley Gardens, Aintree,
or 32 Whitechapel.
Tel. Royal 3101.

Capt. 1st XV N. W. Hutchings
V. Capt. „   R. A. Forsyth
Capt 2nd XV   S. G. Bacon
V. Capt. „   R. Hemingway
Capt. 3rd XVs H. F. Bateman
              F. King.

Hon. Auditor.
J. E. LINTON, A.C.A.

Committee :
H. S. Damsell, W. H. Dubourg,
W. D. Herring, S. J. Kay,
H S. Kidd, F. S. Porter,
        H. C. G. Webley.

Hon. Life Members.
F. J. Applebee. F. Outhwaite.

FIRST TEAM

Date	Name of Club.	Ground	Sefton G.	T.	P.	Opponents G.	T.	P.
1924								
Sep. 20	Old Salfordians	A.						
27	Prestwich	H.						
Oct. 4	Dick-Kerrs	H.						
11	Hoylake	A.						
18	Wigan Old Boys	H.						
25	Old Salfordians	H.						
Nov. 1	Liverpool 2	A.						
8	Bidston	A.						
15	Cammell Lairds	H.						
22	B'head Park 2	A.						
29	Prestwich	A.						
Dec. 6	St. Helens Old Boys	H.						
13	Old Birkonians	H.						
20	Southport	H.						
26	Warrington	A.						
26								
27	Hoylake	H						
1925								
Jan. 3	Preston G'shoppers	H						
10	Port Sunlight	A.						
17	St. Helens O B.	A.						
24	B'head Park 2	A.						
31	Liverpool 2	H						
Feb. 7	Preston G'shoppers	A.						
14	Southport	A.						
21	Bidston	H						
28	Cammel Lairds	A						
Mar. 7	Wigan Old Boys	A						
14								
21	Old Birkonians	H.						
28	Dick Kerr's	A.						
Apr. 4	Rainhill	A.						
11								
13	Warrington	H.						
18	Port Sunlight	H						

General Meeting 22nd May 1925 –
The Secretary to have a Telephone Installed

The minutes of previous meeting were read & confirmed

The secretary's report on season 1924·25 was adopted on motion of Mr. Croxford seconded by Mr. Bayliss.

The Treasurer submitted a provisional balance sheet which showed a balance of £23 in hand. Complete balance sheet to be shown at next meeting. The Secretary reported the stages by which the ground fund had been increased by approximately £100 during the past season.

Mr. Smith proposed (from the chair), & Mr. Croxford seconded

"That a telephone be installed at the secretary's house"

The meeting agreed that this was a necessary evil; the treasurer estimated the cost at about £10 per annum; & the meeting passed the resolution unanimously.

Several Club Photographs being left over, tw

AGM 21st August 1925 –
Sefton Supports Inauguration of a Lancashire Cup

SEFTON
R.U.F.C.

After a protracted discussion a resolution proposed by N.W. Hutchings seconded by E.G. Robinson "That the Sefton Club support the effort to inaugurate a Rugby Union Cup Competition in Lancashire" was passed by a large majority.

Mr. Croxford obliged by selling a few proofs of photos of previous seasons teams, & the meeting then terminated.

*AGM
Cash Statement
Season 1924–25*

Team Photographs – First Team 1924–25

Back row, left to right: J.E. Dixon, A.L. Foggo, W.K. Arrowsmith, J.R. Taylor, H.S. Damsell, A.N. Lockier, L. Sorenson, W.E. Howard. *Front row, left to right*: F.J. Applebee, Rev. J.O. Nicholas, T.F. Scotson, H.G.C. Webley, N.W. Hutchings (Captain), C.H. McKenzie, G.E. Nelson, C. Jones, H. Brownbill.

Team Photographs – Second Team 1924–25

Back row, left to right: J. Rutter, D. Simpson, F. Rhodes, B. Leask, H.E. Wickes, S.G. Bacon, S.H. Chadwick, G.A. Clubbe. *Front row, left to right*: F.M. O'Hara, R. Huntington, H.J. Thompson, F.C. Cawthra (Captain), G.E. Nelson, J.B. Dodd, A.L. Foggo.

D. P. BOHL B.Sc

Team Photographs – Third Team 1924–25

Back row, left to right: K.H. Trevitt, D.R. Lloyd, W.R. Harper, J. Rutter, F.A. Chadwick, C.E. Shoobridge, E.R. Humphreys, T.K. Humphreys, *Middle row, left to right*: F.J. Applebee, C.H.S. Basnett, E.G. Robinson, J.C. McGrath, T.J. Fitzpatrick, H.F. Bateman (Captain), B.P. Lloyd, J.A. Williams, J.H. Bagot. *Front row, left to right*: A. Addis, C. Ferguson.

Team Photographs – Extra Team 1924–25

Back row, left to right: J.A. Warrington, J.G. Kelly, C.H. Cook, S.G. Bacon, A.W. Pottier, A.S. Thomas, S. Blankstone, R.Murray. *Front row, left to right*: H. Bayliss, J.E. Smith, J.S. Blakiston, F.H. Gough, W.H. Dubourg (Captain), J.F. Moore, R.C. Hughes, H.J. Gilman, F.J. Applebee.

v . Hoppers .

V . Grasshoppers .

D. P. BOHL B.Sc

Hare and Hounds Hotel, West Derby Village

Prentice & Mackenzie

& Lockier

The Hare & Hounds

The Hare and Hounds and
the back yard in 2002

Former player Cec Adams recalls, "I remember playing down Meadow Lane ground and changing behind the pub in the square – cold water in zinc tubs after the match, sometimes the groundsman chucked in a couple of buckets of hot water. Alex Lockier, the team secretary for years, was always in trouble with his firm for too many telephone calls on Saturday mornings."

(ALIAS THE ALIENS)

Bert Brownbill recalls from his retirement in Norfolk in 1980 – "In those bad old days of the early twenties the name of the game was a struggle for existence for we had no ground and no cash but only our unbounded enthusiasm for the game and fielded five XVs nearly every Saturday. It was my duty as Team Secretary to notify at least 75 members as to who, where and when they were playing the following Saturday and 'crying off' from any of them was a rarity. We had two primitive pitches in separate fields down Rose Lane beyond the Police Station and as we had no pavilion we changed at the Hare and Hounds some distance away. The two visiting teams and the two home teams changed in a small back parlour of the pub. There were no showers, no hot water, no towels or soap, just small zinc foot-baths and a hose pipe attached to a cold water tap in the stable yard."

Bert used to coin the phrase "SEFTON UBER ALLES."

D. P. BOHL B.Sc

Sefton RUFC – 1925–52

Ye Hotte Potte 1st December 1926 –
Fred Applebee retires as Secretary of Club

The menu was kindly produced by Mrs Sue Totty, the daughter of Sefton Captain W.E.Howard, who is the

PHOTO OF SEFTON TEAM BEING TAKEN AFTER THE BATTLE OF PORT SUNLIGHT.

SEFTON'S "GUNGA DIN"

EXTRA

SEFTON

"EMINWAYS 'OBOS OUT FOR EXERCISE"

"SLATS"

'BARD SMIFF' (COMPLETE WITH FACE FUNGUS)

ALEC. SAT. 11·30 'CRY-OFF' CROSS-WORD ARTIST

CROX.

'OWD BOB"

reference to 'Will' on the front of the document. The Hot Pot venue was The Victoria Café in Castle Street, Liverpool and fondly referred to as 'Maison Milbourn', the other home of Club Treasurer John Milbourn.

Note the subtle Coat of Arms on the front of the menu, an apple and a bee to represent Freddie.

D. P. BOHL B.Sc

Menu

Hors d'Oeuvre de studs conical

SOUP
A la Hare et Hounds
ou
Creme de Mud West Derby

FISH
Eel de la scrum avec Sauce de linament

ENTREE
Grasshopper de Preston a l'undervest

JOINT
Ear de Prestwich au Palmer

LEGUME
Herbes de Meadow Lane

SWEETS
Perhaps

CAFE
Doubtful

WINES
BEER
MORE BEER
STILL MORE BEER

Cocktails de Mackenzie (Censor permitting)

SEFTON R.F.C

SOCIAL EVENING

HELD AT

THE VICTORIA CAFÉ

WEDNESDAY
1st December, 1926

On the occasion of a presentation made by the members of the club to **Mr F. J. APPLEBEE**, the retiring Hon. Secretary, as a token of the affection and esteem in which he is held and in recognition of the invaluable services he has rendered to the club during his twenty years of office.

Artistes

During the evening the following outrages will be perpetrated. You are respectfully requested not to throw your boots, empties or false teeth at the offenders, as some of them are due to play on Saturday.

Mr. CLIFF JONES will warble. Gentlemen please refrain from eating audibly during this item; Seftonians Must.

G. NEVILLE WHITE has the joker up his sleeve.

BIG FRANCIS will render "The Refrain from Spitting."

"Framed" facetiousness by Arthur. Banjo banging by Billy.

H. L. sweetly sings sonorous sonnets (simultaneous sipping to be suppressed.)

BILL SMITH in his special "Flower Song" (not out of "Carmen.")

If the premises are big enough BILLY TRIST will oblige.

At the piano—a slight impression of a dog digging, by Douggie.

WARNING.
The man who is responsible for the gross libels, on the cover of this document played for the "Aliens" when we had a real team, and is an ex-light weight champion.

Some items of **Club News**
from an Unreliable Source

The Hon. Treasurer is pleased to report that all playing members subs. were duly paid at the beginning of the season.

All the honorary members have paid twice.

The "Hobo" XV. has been discontinued owing to all the players signing professional papers.

A well known Rugby League Club has offered to buy the 1st XV. en bloc, after seeing the match against the "Park".

There was a tremendous boom in the mineral water trade in the I.O.M. during the Sefton Tour last Easter.

A prominent member of the 1st XV. has been suspended for cannibalism.

Mr. L. A. WILSON has got a new job; he now tells the bed-time story for the Children's Corner of the B.B.C.

Mr. PAISLEY is getting quite proficient at Snap.

Mr. LESLIE HARRISON is to be the new President of the "Pussyfoot League."

Acquisition of new ground in 1929 –
H.C. Adams remembers

IN 1928 MR A.N. LOCKIER discovered the present ground and the proposed land was surveyed, it covered an area of over 10 acres and was 'fairly flat, well drained, and about two thirds having excellent turf, the remaining third recently under cultivation'. The value of the land was put at £1300.

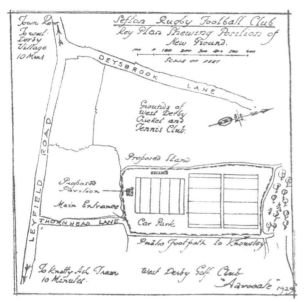

Former player Cec Adams recalls, "I have fond memories of the club such as the £700 loaned from the England Rugby Union for us to buy the Leyfield Road Ground, arranged mainly through the good efforts of W.B.Croxford. Quite a lot of money in the days.

"When we moved from Meadow Lane all bods were asked to get the new ground ready. The work of levelling the new ground and erecting the clubhouse was mainly carried out by dedicated members - some may have been Shanghai-ed. I think the posts for the clubhouse were borrowed or stolen.

"The final bath completed was rather rough concrete - no tiling at first - present day players would not put up with such conditions!"

Ground Levelling 1929

SPADEWORK
DIGGING IN PEACE IN SEFTON MEADOWS

"COME A-DIGGING, Writer?"

D. P. BOHL B. Sc

SEFTON
R.U.F.C.

"A-digging, Reader?"

"Yes, and you shall see youth is not all tennis and motoring in the summer."

"That is no conviction of mine, Reader. Let me but see the real life, and I am happy to come even a-digging."

So the faithful pair hied to one of Sefton's fair meadows, where the green grass grows all around, but for one patch where earth had been taken off to the depth of maybe three feet, where the clay was laid bare, and where the waste was being used to fill adjacent hollows.

A rugger ground was being made, and considerable levelling was necessary if three full-sized pitches were to be accommodated, together with room for sprinting, jumping, and other adjuncts concomitant with "keeping fit".

Reader conducted Writer about the ten acres, and explained the Great Scheme. The Great Scheme was, as usual, very simple. It depended mainly on the continued interest and practical endeavour of those most intimately concerned.

Of that interest and practical endeavour, Writer perceived the signs on returning to the site of excavation. A team of young men and men middle-aged, not all of them brawny, were throwing earth into tubs on rails, vigorously, silently, enthusiastically, all ferociously intent on their work.

They were members of the club, men to whom a spade was no familiar companion, yet were happy to get down to bedrock, call a spade a spade and apply it accordingly, for the sake of their sport.

The work to be done had been neatly adjusted. Lest the unaccustomed labour of much digging should pall, as even voluntary labour will, there were different teams for each evening, and it was astonishing what a dozen fresh men could accomplish.

True, they worked twice as feverishly as the steady everyday navvy would work, and accordingly exhausted themselves in half the time; but therein lay the virtue of the next night's team continuing the work. They worked

hard by easy stages, as it were, felt no loss, and kept the advantages.

"The height of human achievement," said Writer sententiously, "is what others will do for one, plus what one will do for oneself."

At which Reader, having changed into an old suit, took up a spade and laid into the earth. Writer, though normally an onlooker was not one to be idle while his friends worked. He also took up a spade. This digging was infectious.

A spade is a beautiful tool to wield, especially when it is bright and sharp. It cuts into the loam clean and deep, at pressure of the foot. There's a heave, a swing, a clod floats unerringly through the air, the tub fills and the poetry of the spade may grip one very forcibly.

> That simple tool
> Evoked by Tubal Cain to cleave the sod
> Of Eden, man's first dwelling,
> And his last.

Among the diggers were men developing their first blisters, their first segs of the spade. There were men, too, who had dug for their lives; men with holes in their bodies big enough to hold a fist - men of forty years and thereabouts.

Here the birds created the only sound above. The twittering swallows alone cleft the evening air. Only the sun flashed with blinding brilliance, and the thunder had gone before.

The facetious fellow - the fellow with the fund of fun and flowing eloquence - was there, happily: but this was digging in peace, dear peace.

The Great Scheme was splendid, thought Writer.

BLE

Annual Carnival 5th July 1930

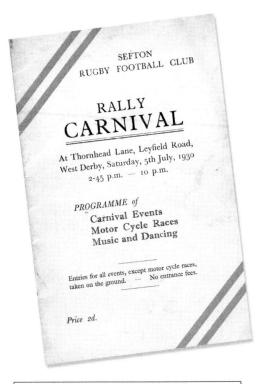

Officials of the Carnival

Chairman MR. W. J. SMITH.
Hon. Treasurer MR. J. C. PARKINSON.
Hon. Secretary MR. S.G. CHRISTIAN.

Stewards-

Chief Stewards-Messrs. F. J. APPLEBEE and W.B. CROXFORD

Pay Gates and Tickets MESSRS. J. W. BARKER, J. S. BLAKESTON, J.W. BROWN, L. F. PARLE.

Car Park MR. F. L. PAISLEY.

Pavilion MESSRS. D. R. LLOYD, R. A. LEES.

Programmes MR. A. FORREST.

Carnival Events (ring)- Messrs. R. L. KNIPE, H. MARSHALL.

Result Board-C.J. BULMER.

Treasurer's Stewards MESSRS. T. F. SCOTSON, J. E. BERNER.

Patrol MESSRS. T. J. LLEWELLYN, K. TREVITT, J. McCAULEY J.HILL, A. S. BUDGE.

Mock Rugby Match-Mr. F. L. PAISLEY.

Ankle Competition - Judges - MESSRS. A.G. CLARK, GEO. WHITEFIELD.

Steward. Mr A. FORREST.

Baby Show-Judges-Mrs. G. BUIE, S.R.N., R.S.I., Miss BARTLETT, S.R.N., R.S.I

Stewards Miss D. E. HUGHES, MRS. W B. CROXFORD.

Badges-MR. .B.ROBINSON.

Runners BOY SCOUTS, 244th COMPANY.

Time Table

2-30 p.m.

Band Performance commences.
2-45 p.m.
Official Opening Ceremony by
SIR J. SANDEMAN ALLEN, M.P.
3-0 p.m.
Gymnastic Display by the boys of Steers St. Cl. School
(Mr. F. G. NEWSON, I/C).
Toddlers' Race (under 7). 50 yds. handicap, by size.
V. C. Race (boy competing runs 30 yds., picks up partner
chosen for him and returns to starting point).
Thread the Needle Race (Lady and Gentleman).
Lady runs 60 yds. with thread and needle to
gentleman, who threads needle and then
runs back to starting point.
Skipping Rope Race (Girls). 60 yds., handicap by size.
Egg and Spoon Race (Boys and Girls). Open, scratch.
Three-Legged Race (boys)-Committee reserves the right to
handicap if it seems desirable.
Chariot Race (teams of 6 boys).
3-30 p.m.
BABY SHOW (in marquee).
Class 1, under 12 mths. 1st Prize, 10⁻, 2nd 7/6.
Class 2, over 12 mths and under 2 yrs. 1st Prize 10!-, 2nd 7:6.
Special Prize for Best Girl in either Class, Tuscan China Set
presented by the Everton China Market.
4-0 p.m.
MOCK RUGBY MATCH, Ladies V. Mere Males. Teams-
The Ladies Miss Fortune, Miss Fitt, Miss Chance, Miss
X. Omer, Miss H. I. Flyer, Mrs. Middlemiss, Miss Happ.
Mere Males A. R. Abbit, S. P. Rinter, A. Sloper, T. Roddenon,
A. S. Winger, A. P. Usher, M. A. Lingerer.
Referee Mr. Will Tootle (Warbler's Union).

Played under Catch-as-Catch Can Rules Biting Barred.
4-20 p.m.
Biscuit and Balloon Race (Lady and Gentleman) Over 16.
Gentleman runs to Lady, who feeds him with biscuit,
which must be eaten. Gentleman then inflates balloon,
which lady ties and both return to starting point.
Gentleman's hands are tied behind his back throughout.

TIME TABLE-contd.
Sack Race (boys) under 14.
Three-legged Race (Girls) The Committee reserves the right
to handicap.
Married Couples Race. Husband, with cigarette in mouth and
hands in trousers pockets, runs 50 yds. to wife, who lights the
cigarette. Wife links arm with husband, and the happy pair
make their best time back to starting point.
Sack Race (boys between 14 and 40).
Three-Legged Race (Boy and Girl pairs) open handicap.
Sack Race (boys over 40).
4-50 p.m.
GYMNASTIC DISPLAY by Boys of Steers St. Cl. School.
5-0 p.m. 5-30 p.m.
Tea Interval. Band.
5-30 p.m. 7-30 p.m.

MOTOR CYCLE RACES.
Preceded at 5-20 p.m. by Grand Parade of Competitors, all riding two laps.
(Organised by the Liverpool Motor Club, under permit of the A.C.U.
(Cheshire Centre). All events (standing start) 4 laps, approximately 1 mile

Classes-
1. Up to   350 c.c. No spikes in tyres.
2. Up to   350 c.c. Spiked tyres.
3 Up to   500 c.c. No Spikes in tyres.
4. Up to   500 c.c. Spiked tyres.
5. Up to   600 c.c. Sidecars. No spikes.

(For order of events, heats and riders, see enclosed special slip).

7-30 p.m.
BLINDFOLD DRIVING (Cars) (entry on ground). Driver, having been shown position of his car and of two canes representing entrance of his garage, is then blindfolded and required to get his car into the garage. Musical Chairs-for Lady pillion Riders.
7-45 p.m.
Ankle Competition. 1st Prize, pair Silk Stockings; 2nd Prize, Box of Chocolates.
7-45 p. m.
Dancing on the Green.
10-0 p.m.
National Anthem. Carnival Closes.

Sefton R.U.F.C.
Terms of Membership
Playing Members (senior) £1 1s. 0d. per annum.
(junior) 10/6 per annum.
Honorary Members, 5/- per annum.
A small covered Stand will be erected for the opening of the 1930-31 season, for which the following annual charges, to include honorary membership, will be made.

Gentlemen 10/6.   Ladies 5/-

During the season, 1929-30, five teams were regularly run, with the following results.

	P.	W.	L.	D.	Pts. For	Pts. Agst.
1st	32	22	7	7	336	131
2nd	29	20	9	9	328	166
3rd	29	19	10	10	307	192
4th	22	19	3	3	347	112
5th	19	7	11	11	141	232

Acknowledgement.
The Sefton R.F.C. desires to acknowledge, with thanks, assistance and/or gifts received from

The Liverpool Motor Club and its Officials.
Mr. Ossie Wade and the Stanley Speedway Ltd.
Messrs. Cadbury Bros.
The Imperial Tobacco Co.
Everton China Market (Mr. G. T. James).
Jack Sharp.
Messrs. Aird & Anderson.
The Service Guild and their Advertisers in this Programme.

Officials for Motor Cycle Races

Stewards:
MR. G. A. JONES (A.C.U.)

MR. W. B. CROXFORD (President, Sefton Rugby Club)
MAJOR D. E. M. DOUGLAS-MORRIS (President, Liverpool Motor Club)

Judge
MR. W. J. SMITH (Chairman, Sefton Rugby Club)

Starter
MR. L. H. LUMBY

Timekeeper
A.C.U. Official.

Chief Marshal
G.C.M. WOOD.

Marshals and Line Judges
MR. PARRY and Members of N. Liverpool M.C.

Secretary of the Meeting and Clerk of the Courrse
MR. S. W. PHILLPOTT, F.I.M.T.

Refreshments

by Mr. J. H. BALMER, 93 Errol Street, St. Michael's.
HIGH TEAS   AFTERNOON TEAS
at fixed charges or a la carte.
ICES AND MINERALS.

All Goods Guaranteed First Quality.

Aigburth Silver Prize Band
(Bandmaster MR. H. WEARING).

Afternoon Programme-2-30 5-30.
MARCH "Utopia" Clark
OVERTURE "Spirit of Youth" Greenwood
WALTZ "Casino Tange" Gungl
SELECTION "The Desert Song" Romberg
PIECE "A Day with the Huntsmen" Rimmer
SELECTION "The Pirates of Penzance" Sullivan
WALTZ "The Blue Danube" Strauss
PIECE " In a Monastery Garden" Ketelby
SELECTION "Gems from the Operas" Rimmer
PIECE "Four Indian Love Lyrics " Woodfood Finden
MORCEAU "Bells of Ouseley" Ord Hume
MARCH "Deeds of Daring" Rimmer

Evening Programme-**DANCE MUSIC**
7-45-10-0.
A selection of popular Waltzes and Fox Trots.

Side Shows
(Members and Friends in Charge)

Coconut Shies. J. B. Dodd.
Houp-La. W. Dane.
Marching Toff.-A. Spencer.
Knocking the Lady out of Bed.-H. Mooney
Bowling for a Pig. H. J. Thompson.
Deck Quoits.-T. C. Gosling.
Darts and Rings. G. E. Nelson.
Wheel of Fortune.-J. L. D. Lewis.
Treasure Hunt.-Miss E. Wilcox.
Competition Stall. Miss M. Carter.
Crazy Kitchen. S. Dudley Ward.
Goal Scoring.-H. F. Orford.
Through the Bars. D. Alexander.
Aunt Sally. L. Harrison.
Clay Pipes.-D. S. Leghorn.
Lucky Coin.-Miss H. Jonathan.
Balls and Buckets.-A. S. Roberts.
Name Cards.-J. Birchall.
Lucky Dips.-Miss D. Roberts.
Putting Green.-J. B. Herring.
Bursting the Balloon.-P. E. Cryan.
Fortune Teller.-Mrs. Birchall.
Money for Nothing.-Mrs. Croxford.
Nigger's Head.-E. G. McLean.
On the Clothes Line.-W. H. N. Blake.
Coconut Stall (Sales) -Miss Comrie.
Sweet Stall.-Miss Parkinson.

Membership and Inquirees – Mr. H. F. P. Bayliss

D. P. BOHL B. Sc

Cartoon of Honorable Secretary J.F. Moore 1935

Popular Species of Secretary Bird

Chairman R.L.Knipe killed on the East Lancs, late 1930s

Treasurer John Milbourn 1935 – 'Vagabond Chief'

FORMER LIVERPOOL HEAD MASTER

MR. R. L. KNIPE FATALLY HURT IN ACCIDENT

Mr. R. Leigh Knipe, former head master of Steers Street Council School, Liverpool, and a well-known Liverpool sportsman, died in Whiston Infirmary yesterday, from injuries received in an accident on the East Lancashire Road a few days ago.

He was cycling to Warrington to attend swimming tests in connection with the Royal Life Saving Society, and was thrown heavily from his machine, receiving a fractured skull.

Mr. Knipe, who resided in Moscow Drive, West Derby, was a fine swimmer

and was a life governor of the Royal Life Saving Society. His other great sporting interest was cycling, and he was treasurer of Anfield Cycling Club. In his younger days he took a prominent part in road-racing and created a number of cycling records. During his forty-four years' work in Liverpool

MR. R. L. KNIPE.

schools he constantly took a keen interest in schoolboy sport, and under his leadership Steers Street held the athletic championship of the Liverpool elementary schools for five years.

A keen member, also, of the Liverpool Association of Schoolmasters, Mr. Knipe was elected president for 1929. He retired from his headmastership at the end of March, 1936, when, at a gathering of old scholars, colleagues, and friends, he received a presentation of a cheque and a set of bowls.

The "Vagabond Chief"

John Milbourn, chairman of the Vagabonds' Lawn Tennis Club and treasurer of the West Derby and District Lawn Tennis Tournament, is a well-known character in sporting circles throughout the city. He is the donor of the John Milbourn Tennis Trophy for open singles at West Derby, and, with Mr. H. Richardson, the secretary, does sterling work in organising the tournament. John has been connected with the Vagabonds since 1912, when he was an enthusiastic playing member, and since then he has turned his hand to many ventures in the cause of charity. He is the chairman of Aughton Parish Council, and is equally well known in the Ormskirk district.

D. P. BOHL B. Sc

World War Two 1939–1945 – Sefton becomes a Heavy Anti-Aircraft Gun Site

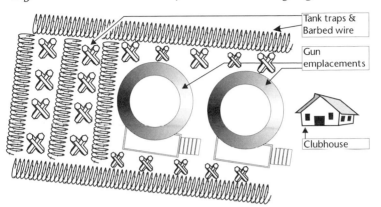

Tank traps & Barbed wire

Gun emplacements

Clubhouse

The ground at Sefton was requisitioned by the Army and two large concrete bunkers were built for the Royal Artillery to site their heavy anti aircraft guns.

Looking at Geoff Daley's map above I would hazard a guess that they were probably the large 5.25 inch variety, as the smaller 3.7 inch gun was usually wheel mounted.

The large concrete structure housed hydraulic equipment to move the heavy equipment inside the gunpit, steps led down to it. The steps inside led up to the actual gun mounting and a combined slope and steps led down to a semi-sunken chamber for the power room.

The original doors were steel and inside the chamber, some 4 metres high, a ventilation shaft running up to the roof, and an access to the gunpit.
Expense catridge lockers ring the structure, and a massive gun mount sits in the deep gun pit.

(ALIAS THE ALIENS)

Dame Bert Brownbill – Theatre Actor

HIS ROLES:

As Nurse Merryweather at the Empire, Liverpool just after WW2

As Barmaid Busy 'B' at the Prince of Wales Theatre

In *Little Old King Cole* in 1961

Cast as Stanley Holloway role of Doolittle for the provincial tour of *My Fair Lady* following its colossal West End run in 1964

Understudying Nellie Wallace as Widow Twankey in *Aladdin* in 1964

D. P. BOHL B.Sc

Former players Lt. Col W. K. Arrowsmith and Capt. K. E. T. Bark – WW2 Casualties 1945

SEFTON R.U.F.C.

Survived Many Campaigns

Loses Life In An Accident

In the midst of the peace celebrations news has reached Liverpool of the death, in a motor accident in Western Europe, of a Liverpool officer who had a distinguished record of service in several campaigns, extending over 5½ years.

He was Lieut.-Colonel W. Kingsley Arrowsmith, of the Royal Artillery, husband of Mrs. Marjorie Arrowsmith, of 17 Linnet Lane, Liverpool, and son of the late Rev. William and Mrs. Arrowsmith. Lieutenant-Colonel Arrowsmith, who was 39, was in the reserve of officers when war broke out. He had served in North Africa, Sicily, Italy, and also in Western Europe.

Lt.-Col. Arrowsmith.

He was awarded the M.B.E. recently and had been mentioned in despatches.

Lieut.-Colonel Arrowsmith, who was educated at Kingswood School, near Bath, was a member of the Sefton Cricket Club, and used to play for Liverpool Rugby Football Club. His father was a well-known Methodist minister in Liverpool.

Captain W. K. Arrowsmith

LOCAL "RUGGER" PLAYER

CAPTAIN K. E. T. BARK KILLED IN BURMA

Captain Kenneth Eric T. Bark, R.A., son of Mrs. Violet Taylor-Bark and the late Mr. Reginald Taylor-Bark, formerly of 4 Alexandra Drive, Sefton Park, Liverpool, was killed in action in Burma on May 18, 1945. He was a member of Sefton and Liverpool Rugby Clubs, Liverpool Cricket Club, and an old boy of Ruthin Grammar School.

He was 26, and was formerly on the staff of Messrs. Tate and Lyle, Liverpool.

Captain Bark.

A letter from his battery commander states that he was wounded when operating on the west bank of the Irrawaddy as forward observation officer to one of the companies of Gurkhas which had got behind the Japanese lines. An example of the estimation in which he was held by the Gurkha troops is that owing to his wounds they refused to allow him to travel by Jeep ambulance, and volunteered to carry him over the hills to the base. His sister, Joen, is in India with the F.A.N.Y., and his mother is working with the American Red Cross in London.

Captain Bark had been with his unit of the Royal Artillery, which includes many Liverpool men, since its formation in 1939.

The Halton Trojans play American Baseball at Sefton 1947–48

The 'Old Man of Baseball' Norm Wells recalls Sefton hosting American Baseball as early as 1947–48. A group of demobbed servicemen formed a baseball team in 1946 and started to meet in The Halton Castle in West Derby Village. The favourite ale at the time was Higson's Trojan Beer, the bar-

1948 Liverpool Trojans (many thanks to the Trojans for the photograph)

maid referring to them as 'The Trojans' in the back room, so they named themselves The 'Halton Trojans'. The pub manager was elected as team manager and an American ex-Liverpool Giant professional player, Eddie O'Melia was asked to be player/coach.

The Trojans fielded two teams, the first team had their diamond at the top of the field, the second team playing on the now Melwood Training Ground of Liverpool FC. This was origi-nally a farmer's field and was taken over as a sports ground in the 1920s by St Francis Xavier's College until it was bought by Liverpool Football Club in 1951.

Fixtures continued into the late 50s against teams such as Liverpool Robins, Bootle Athletic, BAT, The Nalgo Cubs, Stoneycroft, Liverpool Dockers and Caled-onian who the great Dixie Dean played for.

D. P. BOHL B.Sc

Sefton (8) Vs Southport (9) – Played on 19th March 1949

SEFTON
R.U.F.C.

Sefton (0) Vs Oldershaw (11) – 3rd April 1948

Sefton (21) Vs Liverpool Collegiate (0) at the now Bill Shankly Field 4th March 1950

THIS FAMOUS PATCH of green grass on the corner of Eaton Road and Barnfield Drive, West Derby was nearly sold off by the City Council for a housing development in the 80s. However it was saved by the endeavours of the late Nessie Shankly, the wife of Liverpool legend and Manager Bill Shankly who used cast his critical eye on the kids playing footy there during his spare time.

D. P. BOHL B.Sc

Results/Statistics 1948–49

1st XV Fixtures and Results 1948-1949. Scorers.

Date 1948	Versus	Att.	Rslt.	For G.	For T.	For PTS.	Against G.	Against T.	Against PTS.	Tries	Goals
18 Sept.	Southport	H	LOST	-	1	3			44	W.E.C.	—
25. "	Old Instonians	A	LOST	-	-	0			36	—	—
2. Oct.	Collegiate. O.B.	H	WON	5(6P)	1	22	1(P)	1	6	W.E.C A.DAV. J.S.	J.P.W.S (3P)
9. "	Hoylake.	H	LOST	-	1	3			20	C.W.	
16. -	Hightown	A	WON	1	1	8			6	W.E.C. D.JEN. W.E.C.	
23. -	Old Wirralians	H	LOST	-	1	3	1(P) 3		12	A.DALY.	—
30. -	Orrell	A.	LOST	1	-	5			56	W.E.C.	J.S.
6. Nov.	Port Sunlight	H.	DRAW	1(P)	-	3	1(P)	-	3	—	J.P.W.
13. "	Old Newtonians	A	LOST.	-	-	0	-	1	3	—	
20. -	Old Rockferrians.	H	LOST.	-	1	3	2(1P) 2		14	A.DALY	—
27. -	Old Caldeians	A	LOST.	-	2	6	3	2	21	C.T., A.McGu.	—
4. Dec.	Wrexham.	A.	LOST.	-	1	3	2(P) 3		17	W.Ro.	—
11. -	Warrington.	A.	LOST	1(P) 1		6	2	3	19	W.E.C.	J.P.W.
18. -	Orrell	H	LOST	-	-	0	1	4	17	—	

P.14   WON 2   DRAWN. 1.   LOST 11.   65   274

J.P.W. 7.
W.E.C. _ 5 _____ 1
A.DALY. 2.
J.S. _ 1 _____ 1
A.DAV, C.W.
D.JEN. C.T. } 6
A.McGu. W.Ro.
(coach.)
[14]   [9]

(ALIAS THE ALIENS)

Team Photograph Season 1931–32 at Port Sunlight

Back row, left to right: Mr Lewis, G. Cliffe, M. Paisley, M. Phillips, L. Wilson, L. Harrison, P. Riddle, C. Dean. *Middle row, left to right*: K. Trevitt, L. Lewis, G. Bulmer, E. Winter (Captain), J.C. Parkinson, W.H.N. Blake, T.C. Gosling, A. Lockier. *Front row, left to right*: H. Mooney, R. Orford.

Team Photograph Season 1932–33

Back row, left to right: Ref. F. Cliffe, L.A. Wilson, F.L. Paisley, C.E. Dean, M. Philips, J. Birchall, T.J. Llewellyn. *Middle row, left to right*: K. Jones, D. Riddell, A.L. Stephens (Captain), J.C. Parkinson, M.W. Blake. *Front row, left to right*: E. Winter, H. Mooney, G. Bulmer, A.H. Holbert.

NOTE: Charles Dean remembers his Chester College Days 1929
http://www.chester.ac.uk/alumni/2000/1929.html

D. P. BOHL B.Sc

Team Photograph Season 1935–36

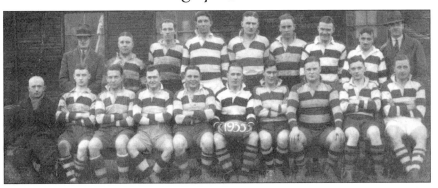

Back row, left to right: J.F. Moore, G. Bulmer, E. Woodcock, A.L. Hulme, E.A. Howarth, F. Whyte, L. Clarke, H. Carr, L. Harrison. *Front row, left to right*: F.J. Applebee, Not Known, F.D. Alder, W.H. Blake, J.C. Parkinson, E. Winter (Captain), H. Wilkinson, B. Wall, W.H. Calvert, A. Machin.

Team Photograph Season 1948–49
Tribute to Dr Cyril Taylor

Back row, left to right: B. Wall, D. Lancaster, W.E. Caldecott, R.G. Wright, J. Christian, C. Whitfield, B. Barry, A. Daly, C. Taylor. *Front row, left to right*: A. O'Hagen, A.D. Wright, A. McGuffog, J.P. Williams (Captain), J.H. Daybell, D. Baines, L. Skinner.

Dr Cyril Taylor

Liverpool Labour Party leader Gideon Ben-Tovim writes in December 2000 "There are some people with so much energy, so much vitality, with such strength of personality that it is almost impossible to think that they are no longer with us - nor is it possible to do justice to their lives in a few words. Cyril Taylor was such a person, a man of extraordinary drive, a medical visionary, a life-long socialist, a unique individual with enormous charm, warmth and commitment. He was one of this city's finest citizens, making a profound mark on the lives of many". Dr Cyril Taylor - a life of commitment: http://www.duncansociety.org.uk/pages/alife.htm

---

(ALIAS THE ALIENS)

Team Photograph – 'A' Team Season 1948–49

Team Photograph Season 1949–50 at Bill Shankly Field

Back row, left to right: B. Barry, J. McGrail, E. Firth, W.E. Caldecott, L. Griffiths, N. Griffiths, W. Williamson, J. Oakley, J. Daybell. *Front row, left to right*: L. McLoughlin, S. Holden, J. Boland, J.P. Williams (Captain), J. Wren, A. O'Hagen, R.T. Edge.

D. P. BOHL B.Sc

Team Photograph Season 1950–51

Back row, left to right: J. Tiernon, D. Richman, B. Barry, J.N. Griffiths (Captain), F.L. Griffiths, C. Whitfield, D. Taylor, E.T. Johnson, A. Moloney. *Front row, left to right*: R.T. Edge, A. McMillan, A. O'Hagen, J. McGrail, L.J. Smith, A. McGuffog.

Team Photograph Season 1950–51

Back row, left to right: C.V. Windsor, R.T. Edge, C. Whitfield, J.P. Williams, B. Barry, J.N. Griffiths, E. Rawlins, J. Parr. *Front row, left to right*: A. McMillan, A. Moloney, D. Taylor, A. O'Hagen, A.D. Wright, W.T. Robbins, J. McGrail.

Sefton RUFC – 1952–1972

Reopening of the ground December 1952 – The Councillor kicks off

THE GROUND WAS REQUISITIONED as a heavy anti-aircraft gun-site and it remained requisitioned until long after the war. It was found possible after the war ended to secure enough space for one playing pitch, this is the area now occupied by both bottom pitches, and a number of pre-war players worked hard to make it fit for play in the 1946-47 season. Despite the handicap of a ground, which from a playing point of view had been rendered almost impossible by the requisitioning, and the invasion of the pavilion by 'squatters', the efforts of the old players and of the new ones who joined them helped to keep the club alive.

After prolonged negotiations with the war department it was found possible to start work on restoring the ground and pavilion in September 1951, and by December 1952 the ground was reopened on the thirteenth of that month by Councillor Hedley A. Williams (deputising for the Lord Mayor of the City, Alderman A. Morrow), a game being played against Davenport RUFC (now Stockport RUFC) to mark the occasion.

Councillor Kicks Off

Councillor Hedley A. Williams, deputising for the Lord Mayor, kicks off for the match between Sefton Rugby Union Football Club and Davenport R.U.F.C., to commemorate the restoration of the ground and pavilion at Thornhead Lane, Leyfield Road, West Derby.

Liverpool Evening Express
13 December 1952

Chairman Barney Wall Introduces the Ceremony

THE TOWN HALL, LIVERPOOL

THE REOPENING of the Sefton Rugby Ground in Thornhead Lane is not only an occasion for the Club itself but is an encouragement to the sporting life of the city as a whole. The Sefton Club have for the past 50 years been worthy exponents of the art of rugby in this city and the handicap under which they have been training since the war, deprived of their ground, must have been very great. It says much for the enthusiasm of the players and supporters that they have kept going and I hope that now their ground has been restored once again, they will enter upon an era of continued prosperity.

Lord Mayor

Barney Wall was the star of Everton Swimming Club's water polo team and played at the Harold Davies baths in Dovecot. He was apparently a ruthless player under the water and was coached by former Sefton Captain Ernie Winter.

(ALIAS THE ALIENS)

Lancashire RFU President Mr J.H. Roberts performs the official
opening ceremony.

PRESIDENT OF THE LANCASHIRE RUGBY FOOTBALL UNION

IT WAS WITH VERY GREAT PLEASURE that I learned that the reconditioning of the Sefton Club's ground at West Derby had been completed, for as an Officer of the Lancashire County Union, I had been well aware of the difficulties under which the club had laboured since the war. Such difficulties might well have broken both the heart and endurance of those who have been responsible for the club's affairs.

Those who carried out negotiations with the various Government Departments concerned after the de-requisitioning of the ground, those responsible for the rehabilitation planning, and not least those who managed to keep sides running when poor facilities, mutilated pitches, and the presence of squatters in the pavilion made the acquisition of new blood unlikely, are all to be much congratulated on the success of their efforts. On my own behalf and on that of the County Union I wish the club calmer waters ahead and greater playing success, and I am pleased on such an occasion as this to be associated with the Lord Mayor of the City in which the club's ground lies.

J.H. Roberts

D. P. BOHL B.Sc

A great day for Sefton

BY W. B. CROXFORD

DURING the war, Liverpool, and indeed the whole of Merseyside, had good reason to thank the vigilance and accuracy of the A.A. gunners who were stationed on the Sefton R.U.F.C's ground at Thornhead Lane, West Derby.

But when peace came the club found itself in possession of an estate from which all fencing had disappeared and which very much resembled a battlefield.

In possession is not quite correct, because it took a long time to get even a part of the ground derequisitioned, and when that part was freed members had to remove much angle iron, set in hundreds of underground concrete blocks, before they could play on it.

To add to the difficulties, squatters took possession of the pavilion and had to be compressed by movable partitions before the players could find room to change.

The reconditioning of the once fine first team pitch, pitted with deep gun emplacements, and with levels varying many feet through protective mounds thrown up, was a job beyond the scope of the most enthusiastic amateurs.

But negotiations on compensation with various Government departments dragged on for five years and a settlement allowing the work to go on was not reached until eighteen months ago.

LORD MAYOR'S VISIT

Now the main part of rehabilitation has been completed and the club has arranged a morning reopening match with Davenport, old opponents, on December 13, after which the team will go to the Lancashire v. Yorkshire match at Blundellsands in the afternoon.

The Lord Mayor of Liverpool (Alderman A. Morrow), who will not be a stranger to the ground, as he opened one of the pre-war carnivals there, will speak and later kick off, and Mr J. H. Roberts (president of the Lancashire County R.U.), who will be supported by other county officers and club representatives will re-open the re-conditioned portion of the ground.

The game which follows and to which admission is by souvenir programme which can be obtained through members or at the gates on the day, and for which both the Lord Mayor and Mr Roberts have written forewords, will be refereed by Mr S. S. C. Meikle.

The club, which is the only open one between Aigburth and Blundellsands, did much before the war for the game in the schools by loaning its grounds in mid-week and on Saturday mornings.

Heavy winter use will not be advisable for some time, but the club is anxious that the ground shall not be quite out of use during the close season, though what form of summer sport should be encouraged has not yet been decided.

Schools Rugby

Councillor Kicks Off For Sefton

Sefton R.U. Football Club (Founded 1907) ground at Thornhead-lane, was officially opened this morning by Councillor Hedley Williams, who also kicked off in the match between Sefton 1st XV and Davenport R.U.F.C. visitors from the Stockport district, this afternoon.

The game ended with 11pts each.

The first 15 minutes play was very even but provided plenty of thrills.

COUNCILLOR Hedley Williams, deputising for the Lord Mayor of Liverpool (Alderman A. Morrow), kicking-off at the re-opening of the Sefton R.F.C. ground, Thornhead-lane, West Derby.

Both full-backs, B. Wilton (Sefton) and B. Walker stemming forward rushes.

Sefton gained the lead through Peter Maloney, the scrum-half, who broke through to register an unconverted try. Davenport equalised with a penalty kick by P. H. Smith, fly-half.

Sefton three-quarters were now getting more of the ball, and J. N. Griffiths, their captain, at left-centre, broke away to score a try which he also converted—to gain their second lead.

Five minutes before the interval P. H. Smith scored his second penalty.

H.T. Sefton 8pts. Davenport 6pts.

On resuming, M. D. Marshall, the visitors' right-wing three-quarters, crossed for a try, which he easily converted. J. M. Griffiths missed an easy penalty kick at goal for Sefton.

E. Green, with a fine run, crossed for a try, Griffiths failing to convert.

NORTHUMBERLAND

GUN SITE TO PITCH
Sefton R.F.C. Open Their
Reconstructed Ground

On a green and pleasant pitch where, during the war, A.A. guns blazed in defence of Liverpool, Sefton Rugby Club this morning celebrated the reconstruction of their ground and pavilion by holding Davenport to an 11-11 draw in a most entertaining game.

It was a notable occasion for the go-ahead Thornhead Lane club, who have only now finished the transformation of their ground from gun site into rugby pitch, and celebrities were present to mark it.

Mr. R. H. Roberts, president of the Lancashire County Union, was there to wish the team success, and Mr. Hedley Williams, West Derby's councillor, came to pledge his aid to the club and to kick off.

This Sefton headquarters obviously has great potentialities and may yet have a county future. Appropriately both sides played some very good Rugby. For Sefton scrum half Moloney slipped over early for a try and then stand-off McGrail dummied through to put Griffiths in for a try, which the latter converted.

Before half-time M. Smith landed two great penalties from half way for Davenport and converted a try by Marshall.

Sefton were not done, however, and a movement in which all the backs handled saw Green score the equalising try.

Liverpool Echo
13 December 1952

New Ground Plans

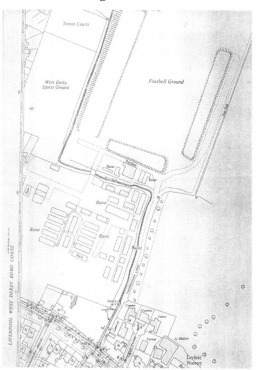

The buildings marked as 'Ruins' on the map were probably barracks
for the Royal Artillery gun crews

Sefton v Davenport – Background to the fixture

OUR OPPONENTS

The Davenport Rugby Union Football Club was formed in 1923 and are
one of the best known sides in the Manchester Area. They have a very
fine ground in Davenport, just outside Stockport, and visiting teams
are always assured of an enjoyable game and a hearty welcome.
The fixtures between Sefton and Davenport only started last season
and we have already met them this season when Sefton won. We
expect they will be all out to reverse this result, and are looking
forward to an excellent game.

Opposing teams, and officials, face the camera.

D. P. BOHL B.Sc

Sefton Vs Davenport — The Teams

Sefton Vs Davenport, 1952 — reopening of the ground

PROGRAMME OF THE MATCH

SEFTON R.U.F.C.		DAVENPORT R.U.F.C.	
(Colours : Red and White)		*(Colours : Red, White and Green)*	
Full Back	B. WILTON	*Full Back*	B. WALKER
Left Wing Threequarter	S. HOLDEN	*Left Wing Threequarter*	R. J. CAPPER
Left Centre Threequarter	J. N. GRIFFITHS (*Capt.*)	*Left Centre Threequarter*	F. WOMBY
Right Centre Threequarter	T. CAMPION	*Right Centre Threequarter*	A. F. KOENEN (*Capt.*)
Right Wing Threequarter	E. GREEN	*Right Wing Threequarter*	M. D. MARSHALL
Fly-half	J. McGRAIL	*Fly-half*	P. H. SMITH
Scrum-half	P. MOLONEY	*Scrum-half*	M. K. SMITH
Prop Forward	B. BARRY	*Prop Forward*	K. YOUD
Hooker	D. TAYLOR	*Hooker*	P. W. SUTHERLAND
Prop Forward	C. WHITFIELD	*Prop Forward*	C. H. GEARY
Lock	E. RAWLINS	*Lock*	W. D. GRAY
Lock	B. J. McAREE	*Lock*	R. N. CUSS
Wing Forward	D. LANCASTER	*Wing Forward*	R. FARLEY
No. Eight	P. McCORMACK	*No. Eight*	C. O. GIBBONS
Wing Forward	J. BATTISTE	*Wing Forward*	D. R. POYNTON

Referee : Mr. S. S. C. MEIKLE (Waterloo, Lancashire and England)

Sefton v Davenport – The Programme

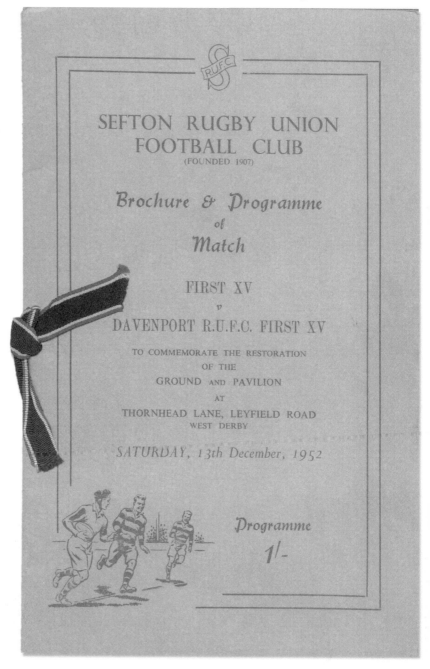

SEFTON RUGBY UNION
FOOTBALL CLUB
(FOUNDED 1907)

Brochure & Programme

of

Match

FIRST XV

v

DAVENPORT R.U.F.C. FIRST XV

TO COMMEMORATE THE RESTORATION
OF THE
GROUND AND PAVILION
AT
THORNHEAD LANE, LEYFIELD ROAD
WEST DERBY

SATURDAY, 13th December, 1952

Programme

1/-

D. P. BOHL B.Sc

Sefton v Davenport — Match Report

SEFTON
R.U.F.C.

It's just like home for Sefton once again

By DEREK JEWELL

SEFTON 11, DAVENPORT 11

ON a morning of mist and mellow chilliness Sefton Rugby Club celebrated on Saturday the years of negotiation and the months of hard work well and willingly done which have enabled them once again to call the ground at Thornhead Lane, West Derby, their home.

To demonstrate that their hospitality is of the finest they allowed Davenport to share the points in a most entertaining game, scoring a goal and two tries to their guests' goal and two penalty goals. But this was one Saturday when the play was not the thing—or not the only thing.

For this was an occasion—one that recalled this progressive club's forty-five years' history and a reminder of that tradition of voluntary and faithful service without which Rugby Union in this country would sicken and die.

During the war the Sefton pitches became a maze of A.A. gun-pits and concrete blocks. In 1946 the guns had gone, but the morass remained and squatters had taken over the pavilion. Now the transformation is complete—the pitch green, smooth, in perfect condition, the pavilion bright, handsome and with amenities many more senior clubs would envy. All the club may say proudly, our own work.

The ground, in fact, looks full of possibility. With covered accommodation it could easily become a county venue, for it has great holding capacity. And, out of season, it looks made for athletics.

CEREMONY IN BRIEF

Cause for celebration, indeed, and to mark it on Saturday there was ceremony—brief as ceremony should be. Lancashire County Union president, Mr R. H. Roberts, came to toast success, and West Derby's Councillor Hedley Williams, deputising for the Lord Mayor, was there to add his good wishes and kick-off in a game refereed by former Lancashire and England player, S. S. C. Meikle.

And so to the Rugby. It appeared likely at first that Sefton might extend hospitality too far, for the first fifteen minutes was all Davenport.

The Smith twins at half were wreaking fraternal devilry. Womby at centre was looking ever-dangerous, and Farley and Poynton in the pack were foraging successfully. It needed all the sternness of McAree, McGrail and Rawlins in defence to preserve the Sefton line.

But they did it, and while we were waiting for a Davenport score, Sefton suddenly whipped play to the other end and were leading — through scrum half Moloney who wriggled his way over for a try after a quick heel. Davenport were undismayed, and soon scrum half M. Smith, whose service had glorious length and accuracy, demonstrated that this was not his sole accomplishment by kicking a soaring penalty from 50 yards.

Sefton got ahead again when stand-off McGrail carved out the opening for Sefton captain Griffiths to go over, a try which Griffiths himself converted. Then, just on half-time, M. Smith clipped the margin with a second splendid penalty from halfway.

The second half opened like the first—but this time Davenport's pressure was rewarded. It was noticeable that the Sefton forwards were not so well together now, and solid Davenport scrumming put them in a position from which Koenen, their captain, sent winger Marshall on a dazzling run through the Sefton defence and in by the posts. The punctilious Smith inevitably converted and Sefton were three down.

LESSONS WERE HERE

Thus it remained, for all the strivings of McGrail and Griffiths, until near the end. Again the stand-off made the opening and the ball slid through the threes for right wing Green to pound over in the corner.

The end came, fittingly, with the scores still level and one felt that there had been lessons here even for the more illustrious, particularly the intelligent throwing of the wings into the line-outs—but then it was time for history again.

Into the clubhouse to see the ox-horn trophy for which Sefton and Kersal battle each year, to note from the handsome programme that at the end of the club's first year of existence (they were called "The Aliens" in 1907) their assets were one ball and two jerseys, and to meet the men of Rugby, past and present, among them Mr Jack Parkinson—son of that Jack Parkinson, who played the other ball game for Liverpool and England at centre forward—who in his scrum half days once kicked a fabulous round dozen goals in one match.

This was sportsmen's talk, rich, redolent, memorable and who cared if the minutes were flying and there were appointments to be kept—for Sefton were home again.

Liverpool Daily Post
15 December 1952

Sefton Tour to Ireland 1953

Back row, left to right: Barney Wall, Fred Telfer, Jimmy McGrail, Eddie Johnson, Caddy McCormack, J.Holden, Barney Barry, Jack Daybell, Brian McAree, Les Wilkinson, Gordon McAree, Fred Barry, guest, guest, guest, Tom Daley, Walter Callender, Irish Courier. *Front row, left to right*: Derek Taylor, guest, J.J.Jones, Bernard Wright, Mick Moloney, Peter Moloney, guest, S.Holden, J.F.Moore

Newspaper Cuttings 1950s

WEDNESDAY, APRIL 8, 1953.

BOHS. GOOD WIN OVER SEFTON.

Bohemians 9
Sefton 8

At Thomond Park on Saturday, Bohemians defeated Sefton (Liverpool) by a try and two pen. goals (9 pts.) to a goal and a pen. goal (8 pts.).

Bohemians were rather lucky to emerge winners against this fine English side and no one will deny Sefton the fact that a draw would have been a fair result. However, full credit must go to Bohemians for the grand way in which they withstood the fierce Sefton rushes in the closing minutes of the game.

A high wind made handling rather difficult, but both sides made light of this handicap, and some bright football resulted.

Sefton had a very competent back division, of whom Bellwood, McGrail and Wright caught the eye. Forward they were well served by D. Taylor, B. McAree and McCormack.

On the Bohemian side, S. Connolly, making one of his rare appearances for the home side, was outstanding and kicked two fine penalty goals. Of the backs, McCarthy, English and O. Liddy were most dangerous.

Bohemians took the lead after ten minutes when Connolly kicked a fine penalty goal. The same player added to this some minutes later when a Sefton player was caught off-side. Just on half-time a grand movement by the home side saw Liddy cross far out. Connolly failed to convert.

Sefton made a great come-back in the second period and we saw a well-taken try by McGrail, McCormack adding the points. Ten minutes from time McCormack kicked a fine penalty. Sefton now attacked furiously but the final whistle saw Bohemians victors by the narrowest of margins.

During the dinner which followed the game it was decided that the fixture between the two clubs become an annual one. The President of the Bohemian Club has presented a trophy—The Swillinger Trophy—which is now in the hands of skilled craftsmen.

Limerick Chronicle, Saturday, April 11th, 1953.

* * *

Bohemians On Top In Bright Game

Bohemians, 9 Pts.; Sefton (Liverpool), 8 Pts.

In a holiday friendly at Thomond Park, Limerick, on Saturday, Bohemians staged a come-back after their inglorious defeat in the Munster Cup by defeating Sefton (Liverpool) by 9-8, in a game that provided some some fine open play.

In the first half the home side had the support of the wind and they controlled matters in the tight and loose and forward rushes.

Bohemians opened the scoring when Liddy broke through to touch down near the posts. Shortly afterwards, Connolly landed a fine penalty from near the touch-line, a feat he repeated just before the short whistle. On the change-over, Sefton became more prominent and some hectic forward rushes brought them into Bohemian territory time and again. McCormac, for Sefton, kicked a penalty and McGrail, having upset the home defence with a successful dummy-movement, grounded far out, McCormac adding the extra points.

Prominent for Bohemians were—back English, McCarthy and Liddy, and forwards Connolly, Dinneen and Geary. Sefton were best served by Wright, McGral, Wellwood and forwards Holden, Gill, Taylor and McCormac.

D. P. BOHL B.Sc

Ex-Player and WW2 Spitfire Pilot
W.E.Caldecott killed 1958

At Investiture

Flight-Lieut William Edward Caldecott, R.A.F., of 14 Swanside Avenue, Stoneycroft, Liverpool, who to-day attended an investiture at Buckingham Palace where he received the A.F.C. from the Queen. A Spitfire pilot during the war, Flight-Lieut. Caldecott rejoined the R.A.F. in 1949 and is serving in Northern Ireland.

Sefton Vice-Captain and forward in the late 1940s. He became Squadron Leader but was killed, along with his co-pilot on 9th October 1958 as a result of a crash. Buried at South Cerney on 11th October 1958. A grand fellow!

Cartoon 1958

THE LIVERPOOL ECHO, SATURDAY, APRIL 26, 1958

(ALIAS THE ALIENS)

The Monk in the Red Beret —
Sefton Captain Peter Moloney 1958

Daily Express Saturday July 12 1958

THE MONK IN THE RED BERET
BY DONALD SEAMAN

GOING TO CHURCH tomorrow? From the blazing heat of the great paratroop base in Cyprus, piled high with all the accoutrement of war, I bring you the story of parachutist-extraordinary Peter Desmond Moloney. I think it may help you, whatever your denomination, when you and the family face once more that awkward Sunday question which nags secretly at so many of us.

Second Lieutenant Peter Moloney is unique among the many varied types who wear the Red Beret. He was formerly a Trappist monk, and went direct from the monastery to National Service in the Army. Think of that for a moment. Two years in silent Order, two years of devout service to God, two years of rising at 2 a.m. for prayer, and then, still shaven bald, straight to the tender mercies of a parade ground sergeant major.

TRANSFORMED

I FOUND PETER MOLONEY in the grinding heat of a Cyprus summer evening lying ill in his tent with suspected dysentery. As I walked in he was reading a book, *Saint Bernard and his Monks,* by Theodore Maynard.

"You see," said this remarkable young man. "I am still a monk at heart." His once shaven head was now covered with hair of crew-cut length. On his broad chest the identity discs of the soldier replaced the crucifix he used to wear. It was hard to imagine anyone less like the traditional monk. His was the appearance of a tough parachutist, but his words were the words of the dedicated priest. "I thought and I still think," he said, "that the finest thing any man can do is devote his life to the love, the knowledge and service of God."

D. P. BOHL B.Sc

VOLUNTEER

THEN HE TOLD ME how he came to join the paratroops. In 1953 he was a student at Liverpool University, a brilliant linguist and the university's champion debater. He volunteered to spend his holidays helping to build Santa Maria, the Trappist abbey at Nunraw, south of Edinburgh. He knew at once that this was his calling, went to the guest master and told him: "I believe I have a vocation to enter the service of God."

"After one month as a postulant I took the habit and became a novice," he said. "I had been a novitiate for 20 months and was entirely happy when I was called one day to the Lord Abbott. The Lord Abbott said gently to me that he thought my vocation lay elsewhere, outside the service of God. I had to leave the abbey! I was heartbroken at the thought. 'My Lord Abbott,' I asked, 'what can I do out there? How can I now face the outside world?' He said to me simply: 'Go in peace, my son, and remember Vaughan's crossing.' "

There in the tent, ill as he was, Moloney's face lit up at the memory. "I didn't know what he meant," he confessed with a broad grin, "and I had to look up the reference after I left the monastery. Now I commend it to all. Remember Vaughan's crossing! "

WITH A GUN

I ASKED: "How can you reconcile your religious teaching with your duties as a parachutist? Suppose you were told to take a gun in your hand and use it on your fellow-men?"

(ALIAS THE ALIENS)

"That's it," he said. "Vaughan's crossing! It is, in fact, a reference to the celebrated Jesuit, Father Vaughan, who, when he first became a Jesuit, was asked by his friends how he felt about it."

His reply was: "It doesn't matter what I do, if it's the will of God. I would not have minded if I had become a crossing sweeper! But if I had become a crossing sweeper I would have swept my crossing so well that people would have come from miles around to see Vaughan's crossing."

"When I entered the Army I thought: 'If it's God's will that I shall be a soldier for two years. I consider it my duty to be as good a soldier as possible, and in the best possible regiment.' That is why," he pointed to the faded red beret, "I am wearing that."

PRAYERS

WHEN NEXT I saw Moloney he was still sick and thought he was alone. He was kneeling by his 'bed', his blankets on the sand. He was praying, just as he would have done at home in Liverpool. I can tell you one thing: Second Lieutenant Peter Moloney is a very happy man.

Going to church tomorrow?

JANUARY 2003 PETER MOLONEY WRITES:

IT IS GOOD TO NOTE that, half a century on from this 'Monk in the Red Beret' article's first appearance in the *Sunday Express*, the members and supporters of Sefton RUFC remain as savvy, sophisticated and cultured as ever! Since its appearance on the website some informed Seftonians have informed me that my mistaken attribution of my Lord Abbott's aphorism to the Jesuit Father Vaughan should have been to the famous Redemptorist convert and Hymnologist Father Edward Vaughan.

They are probably correct. If not, and anyone knows of Vaughan Franciscans, Dominicans, or Carthusians keep it until next season. Happy New Year!

Cartoon 1959

LIVERPOOL ECHO AND EVENING EXPRESS, SATURDAY, FEBRUARY 20TH 1959

Cartoon 1960

THE LIVERPOOL ECHO AND EVENING EXPRESS, SATURDAY, NOVEMBER 5, 1960

(ALIAS THE ALIENS)

Pitch Vandalism 1962

THE HACKED POSTS

SMASHED WINDOWS

SENSELESS WRECKING

Vandalism of the most senseless kind has been hitting Sefton Rugby Club at their West Derby headquarters. Three times in the past months their pavilion has been broken into and subjected to wrecking, and on Saturday the first members to arrive at the club found that a set of the goalposts on the first team pitch had been chopped down about a yard above the ground. To put up new posts – as they are set in concrete and expensive in themselves – will be a considerable financial blow to the club. Such wrecking, which must be viciously premeditated, is poor reward indeed, for a club who have been in favour of the movement for helping and encouraging youth in Rugby. Sefton did, however, have one ray of light at the weekend. Their first team went away and beat Orrell 15–12 after trailing 13–8 at half time – only the second side to beat the doughty Orrell men (highly successful once more and conquerors of St Helens, too) at home this season.

pavilion break-ins, of which there have been three lately. Fences and walls have been damaged.

HELPS YOUNGSTERS

The irony of the wanton damage is that the club has given every possible encouragement to youngsters participating in the R.U game or wishing to do so. The ground has been loaned repeatedly for such events as county schoolboy trials, under-15 inter-city matches, and junior schoolboy sevens. The annual match between the teams representing Liverpool and Birkenhead grammar schools is due to be played there a week today, the 13th, kick-off at 5 p.m. Recently the club have been considering the running of a colts' team, which would cater for the boys leaving school, until the time they were ready for inclusion in normal squads.

HAVOC AT SEFTON RFC GROUND

One of the worst reported cases of wanton vandalism occurred last Saturday, at the ground of Sefton RUFC. When the groundsman arrived to prepare the pitches for the afternoon games, he found that both the posts at one end of the first team ground had been chopped off three feet above ground. This could hardly have been the work of small boys, as the 40ft. posts, deeply embedded in concrete, are strong and substantial. Rather did the cuts suggest a forester's axe. The cost of replacement, removing the old bed, and resetting may amount to £40, no small amount for a small amateur club already hard hit by

D. P. BOHL B.Sc

Diamond Jubilee Dinner 10th November 1967

SEFTON
R.U.F.C.

Menu

Cream Germiny
or
Consommé Printanier

•

Suprême of Sole Bonne Femme

•

Fillet of Beef Bourguignonne
Tomatoes Nicoise
Cauliflower Polonaise
Petit Pois à la Francaise
Berny and Gaujrette Potatoes

•

Meringue Chantilly
or
Cheese and Biscuits

•

Coffee

Toast List

————

LOYAL TOAST
The President - Sefton R.U.F.C.

SEFTON AND FOUNDER MEMBERS
D. BAINES, ESQ.

Reply - W. B. CROXFORD, ESQ.
Captain Sefton R.U.F.C. 1911-12-13-14

LANCASHIRE RUGBY FOOTBALL UNION
J. C. PARKINSON, ESQ.
Captain Sefton R.U.F.C. 1930-31-33-34-36-37

Reply - L. MORTLOCK, ESQ.
President Lancashire R.F.U.

GUESTS
L. M. C. SCOTT, ESQ. - Captain Sefton R.U.F.C.
Reply - J. HEATON, ESQ. - Waterloo and England

Tomorrow at the Strand Hotel, Sefton Rugby Football Club celebrate their Diamond Jubilee.

Among the guests will be representatives from many clubs in the North West who have long-standing fixture arrangements with Sefton.

The Sefton club emerged from one originally called The Aliens, which was formed in 1907. The reason for that rather uncommon name was that most of the members were alien to Liverpool. They comprised of a great number of rugby-playing schoolmasters who were working in the city. Not surprisingly they did not even possess their own ground. All the early fixtures, therefore, were played on their opponents' grounds. Eventually they played at Clubmoor cricket ground. They had several homes before they moved in 1929 to their excellent premises at Leyfield Road, West Derby.

Freddie Applebee, one of the few surviving founder members will not, unhappily, be able to attend the dinner, but W.B.Croxford, who has done so much for rugby on Merseyside (and particularly for schoolboy rugby) is to be present and so is the President of the Lancashire Rugby Union.

(ALIAS THE ALIENS)

Newpaper Cuttings 1960s

Severely handicapped for weight

SEFTON 8 pts., ORRELL 14 pts.

At West Derby on Saturday in extremely difficult conditions, Orrell beat Sefton by a goal and three tries to a goal and a try. The two sides gave an excellent display, and it was largely due to efforts of Orrell's heavy but capable pack, with a total weight of some 120 stones, that the margin was as much as six points.

With early possession from the set-scrums, Orrell were soon well inside the home half, but good Sefton covering prevented an early score. After 15 minutes, however, Wilkinson quickly followed up a cross-kick to touch-down for an unconverted try on the right.

Play was fairly even for a period, and apart from seeing little of the ball from the set-scrums, Sefton pack held their own in loose play and line-out.

SUDDEN SWITCH

After 30 minutes, a m o v e sparked off by Bailey led to a clever inter-passing movement between Donnelly and Kelly, which the latter finished with a try on the right. Raynor converted, to give Sefton the lead.

Minutes later, Orrell regained the lead when Wilkinson dribbled over for a try. Hurst converted.

Half-time: Sefton 5 pts., Orrell 8 pts.

The sides changed over without an interval. Sefton pressed for several minutes, but good Orrell tackling and strong forward play in critical line-outs kept the visitors' line clear.

A sudden switch took play to the Sefton goal-line and from a line-out the weight of the Orrell pack took the ball over the line for Hankey to touch down for an unconverted try.

With continued supremacy in the set-scrums, Orrell were soon on the attack again, and from another line-out near the Sefton goal-line Bibby went over for another push-over try, backed up by the tremendous weight of the visitors' pack.

Minutes later, Kelly intercepted an Orrell pass and ran on strongly to add an unconverted try.

Although severely handicapped for weight, the home pack played extremely well, and in Maloney had probably the most hard-working forward on the field.

Tomorrow, Sefton first are away to another fine side, St. Helens Recs. The second teams meet at Leyfield Road. Kick-off 2.45 p.m.

Opponents retained trophy

KERSAL 17 pts., SEFTON 3.

At Altrincham, on Saturday, Kersal defeated Sefton by a margin of 14 points, which equalled the West Derby side's winning margin earlier in the season. The Horns Trophy, for which the two clubs compete each year, therefore remains in the hands of the Manchester club, both sides having scored 23 points.

It must have been extremely difficult for both the referee and the players to keep in touch with the game, as visibility on the ground was never more than 30 yards and often less, although the tops of the goal posts could be seen from the touch-line. The fog made it impossible for spectators on the pavilion side to follow the game and information of the scores was passed by message from the players near enough to see what had happened.

During the very short periods when play was visible it could be seen that the Sefton pack, with three late changes, were having a hard time and that the home side's method of giving the ball plenty of boot was more likely to pay off on the heavy ground than the Sefton efforts of orthodox passing with the very greasy ball.

Kersal were first to score with a try by prop forward Jeffrey, which we were informed was converted by right-wing Massey. A few minutes later, Sefton prop forward Raynor reduced the lead with a penalty goal.

Massey added a penalty goal for Kersal and scrum-half Sanson added an unconverted try before half-time.

Half-time: Kersal 11 points, Sefton 3.

A short view of the game saw Sefton with a chance of scoring when left-wing Kelly was near, and then scrum-half Stevens was almost over, but a kick cleared the home line to put Kersal on the attack again somewhere in the fog on the far side.

A message was passed across that Kersal left-wing Appleton had crossed for an unconverted try and after another long wait, more information that the same player had scored again was communicated to the spectators. This try was also not converted.

Tomorrow, Sefton 1st have a scratch fixture with New Brighton 2nd, at Reeds Lane, Leasowe. Kick-off 2-45 p.m.

Killed In Car Crash

Liverpool Man In Hong Kong

Mr. Jack Kelly, 27 years-old Liverpool-born engineer, was killed today when his car plunged over a flyover in Hong Kong.

Mr. Kelly, a bachelor, has lived with his parents, Mr. and Mrs. George Kelly, of 34 Wilbraham Street, Kirkdale, before he left to take up a four-year post with the Hong Kong Telephone Company two years ago.

Second eldest of a family of eight, he was educated at St. Anthony's R.C. School, Newsham Street, Liverpool, and De La Salle Grammar School.

He was formerly employed as an engineer with Liverpool Leeds Street.

A playing member of Sefton Rugby Club, Mr. Kelly was due to return to Liverpool February, 1964.

Sefton:

P. Moloney
McMath
Donnelly
Kelly
Briley
Edwards
B Moloney
Robins
Raynor
S. Wick
Stacey
Davies
Scott
Snape

Orrell:

Hurst
Wilkinson
Lloyd
Riker
Miller
Williams
Taylor
Johnston
Robinson
Bibby
Sutton
G. Huxley
Mason
Hankey
W. Huxley

In the Bath at Sefton, 1971

Tailpiece or Glimpse of the future?

(ALIAS THE ALIENS)

Tributes to W.B. Croxford 23rd November 1971

A TRIBUTE TO MR RUGBY UNION

THE DEATH OCCURRED in Newsham General Hospital, Liverpool, yesterday of Mr W.B. Croxford, one of the best known figures in Merseyside Rugby Union for more than 50 years.

Mr Croxford wrote on rugby for the *Daily Post and Echo* for 37 years, but he was also widely known as an administrator in the game and, in earlier years, as a player.

Mr Croxford, who was 88, won Lancashire county honours as wing three-quarter. He was one of the founders of Sefton Ruby Club in 1907 and was club captain from 1911–14. After his retirement as a player, he became a county selector and was chairman of Lancashire Schools' Selection Committee. Mr Croxford, who lived at Lyndhurst, Leyfield Road, West Derby. Liverpool, was headmaster of Barlows Lane County School, Aintree, until his retirement. On Saturday Sefton, who are at home to Wrexham, will observe a minute's silence before the kick-off in tribute to Mr Croxford.

TRIBUTE

HARRY FRY, a former England international and Past President of Lancashire rugby writes: W.B. Croxford was one of the great men of Lancashire rugby. Educated and trained in the game at Denstone, he played for Lancashire as a wing three-quarter before the First World War. I knew him first when I was an up and coming fly-half or centre three-quarter at Liverpool College and he advised me – wise man as he was – to go back to my original position as a wing forward – advice which paid me handsomely. He was a great student of the game, particularly with regard to schoolboys, for whom he did tremendous work. He was always at hand to bring to the notice of the county selection committee any young players who showed promise.

He attended Caldy Sevens every year, always affording Sefton a

D. P. BOHL B.Sc

pronounced feature in the press. Never admitting as to his age, he would reply, "You work it out I had a trial for Surrey in 1890! "

It has been said that his wife was a rugby widow from the day he got married.

SEFTON
R.U.F.C.

To the right is a photograph of Walter Bernard Croxford playing for the Aliens in season 1912/13.

Born in London 1883 and educated at St Chads College, Denstone, Uttoxeter he was a prolific scorer for the Aliens, crossing for 14 tries in the aforementioned season:-

Also 12 tries in the last season before the First World War in which he was Captain and County Rep (see charts below).

Sefton RVFC – 1972–2002

Founder Member Fred Applebee passes away 1974

Our ref GNB/CS

David Appleby Esq.,

Huyton with Roby.   16th July, 1974

Dear David,

  Please accept our sincere condolences upon the recent loss of your Father.

  You will know the great reverence in which his Name is held at Sefton, as befits the Founder Member of the Club. Without him there would be no Sefton Rugby Club and there can be no higher tribute than that.

  Our thoughts are very much with you at this time.

           Yours sincerely,

ROBY, LIVERPOOL

18 July 1974

Dear George

  Very many Thanks for your kind letter re my father.

  I think dad would say that he wrote the first few chapters in the book of Sefton Rugby but that the club its self is more important than any one member how ever long & faithfull his service to the club

  I am glad to be able to tell you how proud he was of the dedicated servants who followed him and I know that he was very proud of the work you and the other committee members are doing at this time/ yours very sincerely
                    David Applebee

Committee 1970s

SEFTON
R.U.F.C.

Jack Wilson, on the left (County cap for Staffordshire)
and Les Wilkinson

Alf Hughes left, who donated the £100 for the first team player of
the year trophy, and 'Old Tom' Fallon (pulling a face at drinking Tartan
Bitter) who used to run the baths after the game.

(ALIAS THE ALIENS)

Bill Williamson
(County caps for
Cumberland and
Westmoreland)

Tom Donnelly and Tom Donnelly, snr

The late Ron Langshaw recalled "Tom Donnelly junior was in my opinion the greatest player to grace the turf at Sefton. He led by example! His kit, when others couldn't care less about their appearance, was always in pristine condition, even down to his boot laces. He was always 100% effort, he never played dirty but if an opponent did, they suffered with a tackle later (within the rules) that made them think about re-offending again, if they recovered."

Former Captain, Bill Collins
dies, 1976

Rugby Union

Fund-raising match will be at Sefton

by Paul Fourdrinier

SEFTON are organising a special fund-raising match for Sunday, April 25, in memory of stalwart member Bill Collins who died recently. He lived in Hooton and was club captain for the season 1970-71.

The match will be between a Select XV chosen by Sefton, and a Wilf Murphy XV composed of Merseyside players.

Sefton's method of selection has been to write to Mersey and West Lancashire clubs on the same fixtures circuit, asking them to nominate a player for a certain position, such as scrum half or wing forward.

Among those whom Sefton have invited to take part are Port Sunlight, Wallasey, Old Instonians, Warrington, St Edward's Old Boys, Liverpool Collegiate Old Boys, Ormskirk, Hoylake, St. Mary's Old Boys and Tyldesley.

Liverpool, who are at home to Cheltenham tomorrow, are hoping there will be no repetition of the late cancellation last season by Cheltenham on the basis that injuries and 'flu prevented them from raising a reasonable team to travel to Merseyside.

Gloucestershire played their county championship final against Eastern Counties at nearby Gloucester on the same afternoon.

Gloucester are again in this year's final which is tomorrow, but they are playing "away" on Middlesex territory.

Liverpool try out an interesting combination at half back. Mark Pye who is becoming a useful utility player, is at stand-off, partnering scrum half Dermot Cullen.

A former St Edward's College, Liverpool, pupil where he was prominent in schools rugby circles, Pye has frequently acted as deputy full back and in the three quarters for Liverpool this season, when injuries have depleted their first 15 ranks.

Bernard Clarke, who also plays for Liverpool University, is being rested and taking his place at wing forward and also making his debut will be John Hardy, who has been playing well lately in the junior side.

Liverpool: I. Hennican (captain), R. Webb, T. McGillicuddy, D. Colford, M. Kirwan, M. Pye, D. Cullen, Humphreys, P. Dodswell, J. Crellin, M. Loudon, P. Rushton, G. Thomas, J. Hardy, J. Pickering.

Rugby man dies

BILL COLLINS, aged 36, who was a Sefton Rugby Union Club player for nearly twenty years and captain during the 1970-71 season died yesterday in Clatterbridge Hospital. He had been ill for several weeks and had had a serious operation last year.

D. P. BOHL B. Sc

Prototype Club Blazer Badge

The design for this badge came about as the result of a competition run by teacher Bryan McDonagh at his school in Calderstones. Pupils of the class were invited to submit their entries.

The Clubhouse gets Extended 1980

The main clubhouse was extended at the front to allow a dance floor, bench seating and two large shuttered windows for viewing the games.

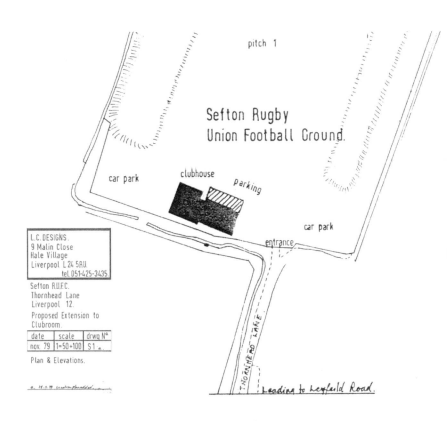

D. P. BOHL B.Sc

Tributes to Cyril Carr 1983

TRIBUTE TO CYRIL

PLAYERS OBSERVED a minute's silence, before Sefton lost 8-10 to Manchester YMCA, for the late Lord Mayor of Liverpool, Alderman Cyril Carr, who died recently during his office. He played for Sefton at scrum half or wing forward from 1946 to 1950.

Vincent Keetley got a penalty for Manchester, John Orme got a try for Sefton and Keith Westcott added another one but Ian Morley failed with both conversion attempts. Keetley got his second penalty for Manchester with Peter McLoughlin their centre getting a try.

Harold Bateman – Sefton 75th Anniversary 15th April 1983

AMONG THE SPECIAL GUESTS at Sefton RU Club's 75th Anniversary dinner this evening will be 93 year-old Harold Bateman, of West Derby, Liverpool who first played for the club 70 years ago.

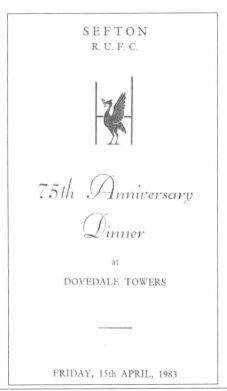

SEFTON
R. U. F. C.

75th Anniversary

Dinner

at

DOVEDALE TOWERS

FRIDAY, 15th APRIL, 1983

Player of the Year Trophy 1983– Dovedale Towers

Season	Winner
1977/78	A.J. Murray
1978/79	D. Lee
1979/80	T. Kinloch
1980/81	K.T. Westcott
1981/82	J. Orme
1982/83	W.F. Jones
1983/84	K.L. Sweetin
1984/85	I. Morley
1985/86	A.M. Pennington
1986/87	R. Cunliffe
1987/88	G.C. Walsh
1988/89	D. Neary
1989/90	K.T. Westcott
1990/91	C. Breen
1991/92	P. Evangelides
1992/93	S.P. Jeans
1993/94	M. Tyms
1994/95	D. Keegan
1995/96	J. Farrington-Rogers
1996/97	A. Sheehan
1997/98	S. Teale
1998/99	W. Osborne
1999/00	P. McBride
2000/01	A. Walsh
2001/02	B. Gardner

The Player of the Year Award was inaugurated by a £100 donation by Alf Hughes.

D. P. BOHL B.Sc

Mike Ledsham – The Fastest Head in West 1983

FASTEST HEAD IN THE WEST

THE FASTEST HEAD IN THE WEST - that's marathon running Michael Ledsham. For the athletic 26 year-old headmaster of Rice Lane County Primary School Walton, has raised £200 during his first marathon run. Michael - who was supported by his parents and pupils completed the recent Mersey Marathon in four hours and 20 minutes, despite suffering a painful thigh injury.

Sefton Rugby Club player Michael, from Prescott, who is married with two children, said: "I had never attempted a marathon before - and though I was promising myself about six or seven miles from the end that I'd never do it again - I can't wait to have another go." A cheque for £200 was donated to Mersey Marathon organiser Mr Derek Johnson at the school today in aid of the Alder Hey Children's Hospital Scanner appeal

Striding ahead of his pupils, Michael on his way to present the cheque to charity.

Japanese Referee visits Sefton on his British Tour 1983

THERE was an Oriental touch to the rugby union clash this week between Sefton and St. Edward's Old Boys for the referee was Katsuhiko Igmai, of Japan, who was officiating at his first match on his British tour. To mark the occasion he was presented with a plaque by host club captain Billy Jones.

There was an Oriental touch in the rugby union clash this week between Sefton and St Edward's Old Boys for the referee was Katsuhiko Igmai of Japan, who was officiating at his first match on his British tour. To mark the occasion he was presented with a plaque by host club captain Billy Jones.

Liverpool Cup Winners 15th April 1984

Sefton R.U.F.C.
May 1984 Liverpool Cup Winners
Played at Liverpool RUFC Ground Aigburth

A.G.Daley President
P.Flaherty Club & 1st Team Captain
R.Langshaw Club Chairman

D. P. BOHL B.Sc

SEFTON
R.U.F.C.

WELCOME TO TODAY'S final of the Liverpool Cup Competition. This will be the fifth year of the cup with previous winners being the Polytechnic, Birchfield and the Police, who are the current holders and will be going for a hat-trick of wins today.

It is not the first appearance of Sefton either, as they were finalists in 1981, losing to Birchfield in that game. They retain seven of the side that appeared in that final and also have two players who have given outstanding service to the club in Bill Jones and Alan Pennington. Both have over 500 appearances.

The Police, as ever, have an experienced side who did remarkably well in the Lancashire Cup, reaching the fourth round and only losing to Vale of Lune in extra time. Their most difficult round so far in the competition was the narrow 9–8 win against Warrington. We look forward to an excellent game involving all fifteen players.

Liverpool Cup Final

15th April 1984
Kick Off 2.30 p.m.

POLICE		SEFTON
A. Donker	15	J. Stitt
M. Reeves	14	R. Wockenforth
P. Sayle	13	P. Flaherty
P. Hill	12	M. Grieves
W. Harris	11	J. Manning
A. Done	10	I. Morley
S. Walker	9	A. Murray
G. Carroll	1	A. Pennington
M. Blundell	2	D. Fields
C. Evans	3	J. McEvoy
W. Bolan	4	K. Westcott
G. Howells	5	J. Nye
P. Jones	6	J. White
V. Barker	7	K. Sweetin
P. Atherton (Cpt.)	8	W. Jones
K. White	16	R. Spencer
P. Roberts	17	P. Evangelides

REFEREE: Mr. J. Heaney, Liverpool Soc.

Scoreline:
SEFTON 26 MERSEYSIDE POLICE 3

(ALIAS THE ALIENS)

Sefton v Kersal – 5th December 1987

A MESSAGE FROM THE PRESIDENT

Today, for Sefton's first sponsored game, we welcome Kersal R.F.C. This is one of our longest-standing fixtures and one of special significance to our two clubs since the first XV's play for "the horns". The original horns were a fine pair of bull's horns but these unfortunately went the way of so many moveable items in rugby clubs and have now been replaced by a splendid pair of antelope horns.

Traditionally the horns are won by the side having the highest aggregate score of two games in the season but, due to disruption by league fixtures, we were unable to find a mutually convenient date for a second game in this season. So, custody of the horns rests on the result of today's game!

A further bond is drawn between Kersal and Sefton by a former Sefton player who holds the Rugby Football Union record for the longest away trip. He achieved this by going to play at Kersal twenty-seven years ago and has not returned yet.

Whilst league games have become important fixtures for us as with most clubs we, at Sefton, regard our long-standing "friendly" fixtures, such as today's as being what rugby football is all about.

Naturally I hope that Sefton retains the horns on this occasion but in the true spirit of the game, may the best team win.

Bernard Houghton

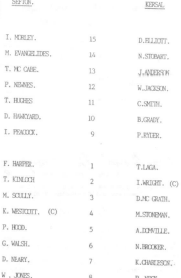

SEFTON.		KERSAL
I. MORLEY.	15	D.ELLIOTT.
M. EVANGELIDES.	14	N.STOBART.
T. MC CABE.	13	J.ANDERSON
P. NEWNES.	12	W.JACKSON.
T. HUGHES	11	C.SMITH.
D. HAWKYARD.	10	B.GRADY.
I. PEACOCK.	9	P.RYDER.
F. HARPER.	1	T.LAGA.
T. KINLOCH	2	I.WRIGHT. (C)
M. SCULLY.	3	D.MC GRATH.
K. WESTCOTT. (C)	4	M.STONEMAN.
P. HOOD.	5	A.DOMVILLE.
G. WALSH.	6	N.BROOKER.
D. NEARY.	7	K.CHARLESON.
W . JONES.	8	P. NECK.

REFEREE.
MR. F. HOWARD.
LIVERPOOL AND DISTRICT
REFEREES SOCIETY.

D. P. BOHL B.Sc

Hillsborough Disaster Fund Raiser May 1989

SEFTON R.U.F.C.

The organisers of this event would like to take this opportunity on behalf of the Hillsborough Disaster Fund to thank all the individuals and companies who have sponsored this event (a full list of sponsors will be available on the day).

We would like to thank the Sefton RLFC for the use of the club and facilities and special thanks to all the players of Sefton and Liverpool Polytechnic for agreeing to play the game and to all the volunteers without whose help this event would not take place.

Sefton RLFC would like to take this opportunity to welcome you to our club. As a sporting club we see ourselves as part of the Merseyside Community. Therefore we would like to extend an invitation to anybody, anywhere in Merseyside who plays rugby or who has ever wanted to play rugby.

If interested ring Alan Pennington on 051-228 9092. All ages, all abilities welcome.

We can assure you of a welcome as it is our belief that rugby is not the sole domain of the public school but is open to all.

ADMISSION: £1-00 each
£2-00 per family

SEFTON R.U.F.C.

PRESENTS A

CHARITY MATCH

IN AID OF

THE HILLSBOROUGH DISASTER FUND

SEFTON R.U.F.C. V **LIVERPOOL POLYTECHNIC**

ON

SUNDAY 14th MAY 1989 . KICK OFF -12.30 pm

TO BE HELD AT THE GROUND OF : SEFTON R.U.F.C , THORNHEAD LANE,
LEYFIELD ROAD , WEST DERBY L12

On the 15th April the City of Liverpool was stunned into shocked disbelief at the deaths of 95 of its people. As we have since observed, the grief and mourning has not been confined to the relatives and friends of the victims.

Although we cannot change the past by preventing the tragedy occuring we can influence the future by showing our love and respect not only to the berieved but also to our city. What the last few weeks has shown to the world is the Liverpool that is real and not one made up to sell newspapers or to fill newsreel.

To this end SEFTON R.U.F.C. wish to pay their respscts by making Sunday 14th May a day of rememberence and fundraising.

We will be playing a fun game of rugby,in full fancy dress,with Liverpool Polytechnic. Kick off will be at 12.30 pm. The players have also arranged many other events for the day culminating with the presentation of a cheque to one of the visiting dignitaries.

Please give your support so that we may make this day a great success.

THIS EVENT IS TO BE SPONSORED BY LIVERPOOL CITY COUNCIL AND LOCAL INDUSTRY.

ALL MONIES RECEIVED WILL BE GIVEN TO THE HILLSBOROUGH DISASTER FUND.

IN ADDITION TO THE CHARITY MATCH VARIOUS OTHER ATTRACTIONS WILL ALSO TAKE PLACE. THESE WILL INCLUDE......

TUG OF WAR CONTEST
SACK RACES
THROWING THE WELLIE
EGG AND SPOON RACES
THE YARD OF ALE CONTEST
THE BOAT RACE
THE MOP RACE
HAMBURGER AND HOT DOG STAND
PLUS MANY OTHER EVENTS.....

A FULL DETAILED LIST OF EVENTS WILL BE AVAILABLE ON THE DAY.

(ALIAS THE ALIENS)

Sefton 10 v Merseyside Police 20 – Lancs Plate Final 11th April 1993

PANNELL KERR FORSTER LANCASHIRE PLATE FINAL 1993
Merseyside Police v Sefton
at Waterloo RUFC – Sunday 11th April – Kick-off 3.00 pm

Merseyside Police	v	Sefton
Blue, Black and White		Red and White

Merseyside Police		Sefton
Peter Smith	15	Robert Earwaker
Ray Jones	14	Dominic Heron
Roy Galloway	13	Terry Clark
Richie Davies	12	Paul Walker
Tim McCabe	11	Paul Evangelides (Capt)
Paul Hornby	10	Ian Wood
Paul Kendrick	9	Charlie Breen
Gareth Howells	1	Frank Harper
Neil Shaw	2	Tom Kinloch
Paul Leeman	3	Kevin Byrne
Kevin Quinn	4	Keith Westcott
Geoff Huxley (Capt)	5	Paul Daley
Colin Roberts	6	Dave Neary
Mark Woods	7	Stuart Irvine
Andy Ward	8	Simon Jeans
Replacements		Replacements
Phil Wright		Nigel Willington
Jim Shields		Steve O'Reilly
Simon Thompson		
Phil Atherton		
Paul Rogers		

Match Officials
Referee
Mr. S. Lander (Liverpool Society)
Touch Judge No. 1
Mr. M. Buck (Liverpool Society)
Touch Judge No. 2
Mr. N. Shenton (Liverpool Society)

PATH TO THE FINAL		
Prel. Round – Didsbury Toc H (H)	38 – 0	
1st Round – Manchester YMCA (A)	17 – 3	
2nd Round – St. Mary's OB (H)	34 – 7	
3rd Round – Birchfield (A)	20 – 12	
Semi-Finals – Old Aldwinians (H)	17 – 0	

PATH TO THE FINAL		
Prel. Round – Bye		
1st Round – Littleborough (A)	14 – 11	
2nd Round – Eccles (A)	10 – 7	
3rd Round – Metrovick (H)	8 – 0	
Semi-Final – Eagle (H)	14 – 12	

Peter Moloney remembers former chairman Jim Alexander's funeral 1994

The Catholic Times   *Sunday, July 3rd, 1994*

PETER'S PENN'ORTH

I AM UNFIRMLY CONVINCED that the beauty of Christianity and glory of Catholicism can be expressed in the sublime absurdity of the ordinary, better than by scholarly polemic. This dates from my first reading of Leo Rosten's lovely book *Hooray for Yiddish*, in which he explains that Yiddish is 72% German, 18% Hebrew, 16% Slavic tongues, 5.6% Romance languages, and 3.55% English.

He adds: '…these figures add up to more than 100%…I KNOW they are to be trusted…I made them up myself.' Now, that's the spirit that inspires belief.

Searching for the Spirit behind the belief of Catholics, I asked a recent convert friend what had been the milestones on his Damascus Road. He said that, over the years,

D. P. BOHL B.Sc

he had attended baptisms, weddings, and even first communions of Catholic friends, but the blinding flash had come at Jim Alexander's requiem, when he heard the voice of God, though the bystanders had only heard a Rugby Song!

I knew exactly what he meant, for though it is some years ago now, and the celebrant, Father Tony Hodgetts, is now away in Rome, I suspect the scene is still as vivid in his memory as it is crystal clear in mine.

It was a fairly typical RC funeral, with a decidedly untypical congregation. Jim had spent many years at Sefton Rugby Club as player, coach, selector, chairman, president, *et al*, so a host of his rugby friends had turned up to pay their last respects.

A sensitive and balanced liturgy included a homily which was a nice mixture of sermon and panegyric. But the memorable climax was the final hymn. 'Jim's favourite hymn,' the celebrant announced, was *Cwm Rhondda*. 'It is not usually sung at funerals, but Pennie has approved it as our recessional hymn.'

Then, looking round at the throng of veteran loose forwards, and looser backs, he added with a smile: 'And let's try to stick to the words on the hymn sheets.' And we did. And it was superb.

Not the singing, you understand, but the spirit of the singing. Quite a few of the good pagans present told me that they would love, one day, to deserve a requiem like that. I was not at all surprised to learn later that it had brought some of the congregation into the arms of Holy Mother Church. Sent off for an early baptism.

I especially enjoyed the spirit of that particular muscular hymnody because when God created me, He breathed into me a great love of singing, but forgot to supply any of the necessary skills which would have made me any good at it.

Rather as though He had given me an expensive present which I could not use, since it was marked: 'Batteries not included'.

I also particularly enjoyed the spirit of that Requiem

Mass because it manifested something which Christians ought always to proclaim, but seldom do, namely that death is coming home.

The further away we've been and the longer the trip with however many changes and diversions, the greater the anticipatory joy must be. After all, Heaven is not a brief post-script to Now: Now is merely a short prologue to Everlasting Life.

The New Catechism, even under MASS, see *Eucharistic Sacrifice*, has no reference to REQUIEM, but under funerals is the advice: 'The litany of the Word during funerals demands very careful preparation because the assembly present for the funerals may include some faithful who rarely attend the liturgy, and friends of the deceased who are not Christians.'

Then, swing lo and behold, closing the section on sacraments, St. Symeon of Thessalonica sums up the lesson of Jim's Requiem: '... we sing for his departure from this life and separation from us, because there is a communion and a reunion. For, even dead we are not at all separated from one another, because we all run the same course, and will find one another again in the same place. We shall never be separated because we live in Christ...'

Oh, and it doesn't say so, but purgatory is only a scrum-down on the twenty-two with the try-line in sight.

D. P. BOHL B.Sc

*Peter Shallcross sketch of the Clubhouse
for Xmas Cards 1994*

SEFTON
R.U.F.C.

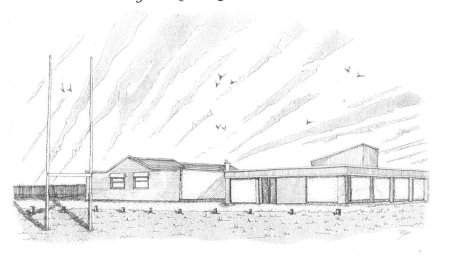

Photograph of the Clubhouse 1995

(ALIAS THE ALIENS)

Ex-Chairman Ron Langshaw surveys the new ceiling and carpet inside the clubhouse

Sefton Pitch

This picture was taken from the top of the now demolished Winterburn Heights by Graham Price who cast aside all thoughts of his well-being to capture the image. The flats, on the left, almost demolished in 1999.

D. P. BOHL B. Sc

The fire is the most welcome sight after watching mid-winter games

Bobby refurbishes 'The Tommy Donnelly Bar'

Sefton Ladies Team 1995

In 1995 Sefton offered coaching and playing facilities to the girls from Liverpool University. For some unknown reason there was huge increase in demand for places on courses to become fully qualified rugby coaches.

Club Dinner 1997 – The late Scotland and British Lion forward Gordon Brown

'Broon frae Troon' presents Neil McFarlane with his 3rd Team Player of the Year. Gordon Lamont Brown, born 1947 in Troon, was probably Scotland's greatest forward. Brown was capped 30 times for Scotland, touring Argentina in 1969 and Australia in 1970, and appeared nine times for the British Lions who were victorious in New Zealand in 1971 and South Africa in 1974. Brown holds the world record of eight tries scored by a forward on an international tour.

D. P. BOHL B.Sc

Club dinner 1999 – President Bill Jones with former England player Mike Slemen

Mike Slemen, pictured on the left, is a biology teacher at Merchant Taylors School in Crosby, Liverpool. He spent most of his career playing for Liverpool RUFC (which merged to become Liverpool St Helens) and in the late 70s and 80s was a regular England International playing on the wing. He was also guest speaker at the Club Dinner in 1987 and was a familiar face at Junior/Mini coaching sessions at Sefton on Sunday mornings.

(ALIAS THE ALIENS)

World Cup 1999 – Former player Ron Lowe with the Trophy

Ron Lowe, former Sefton player in the 1950s and 60s, photographed handling the Webb Ellis Trophy won by Australia in the World Cup 1999, milli-seconds before the security guards pounced. *Inset*: Ron in his playing days for Sefton in 1957/58

Sefton 8 v Didsbury TocH 16 – Lancs Plate Final 9th April 2000

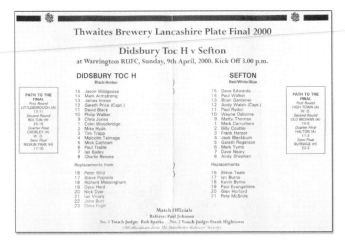

Sefton's brave bid to win the Lancashire Plate Final ended in heartbreak at Warrington on Sunday. Two late second half penalties for Didsbury proved the decisive scores after Sefton had battled back from seven points down after only five minutes. A Wayne Osborne penalty kept them in the game and a try by Gareth Rogerson closed the gap to two points.

D. P. BOHL B.Sc

Club Dinner 2001— Guest Speaker and Former England player John Bentley

SEFTON
R.U.F.C.

John Bentley, second on the left, presents club captain Andy Walsh with his player of the year award. Bentley, a Great Britain rugby league favourite, crossed codes to union and never really looked backwards. Playing for Leeds Tykes he was selected for the British Lions tour of South Africa and replaced Ieuan Evans on the wing in the 2nd Test. He later went on to be Director of Rugby at Nottingham.

Sefton 11 v Ruskin Park 19 –
50th Anniversary Game of the ground reopening

SEFTON
RUFC
Founded 1907

SEFTON
v
RUSKIN PARK
50 Years after the restoration of the ground
Saturday 14th December 2002 - 2:30 pm

A Message from the President of Sefton RUFC

On Behalf of the members and committee of Sefton I would like to extend a warm welcome to all who have attended this special occasion. We are grateful to our sponsor for the day and hope that our relationship can grow in the future. It is particularly pleasing to welcome back so many people who made a significant contribution to the club as administrators, players and club captains. The club would not be in the healthy position it is today without the efforts you put in during your active days.

Our fixtures with Ruskin Park are well established; games are always closely contested and full of good rugby. I am pleased that representatives of their committee are here to celebrate this special occasion. You and your team are most welcome, especially if our first team can reverse the result of the recent league game, which we lost 12-10.

The reason for our celebration is the 50th anniversary of the official handing over of the ground by the military after WWII. As you will be aware it was taken over by the army and although we had access before 1952, it was on this weekend five decades ago that we were given total control of our facilities.
I hope that everyone enjoys the lunch, the drinks, the game, the match and the atmosphere.

Many thanks for coming and supporting Sefton.

Brian McDonagh
President

Forthcoming events

December 15	**Children's Xmas social**
December 21st	**Club Xmas Social**

Sefton 11 Ruskin Park 19
The stars for Sefton were John Stitt and Gareth Rogerson. A try was scored by skipper Andy Walsh with Phil Evans adding a penalty and Wayne Osborne a drop goal. Ruskin Park's winners were Stuart Fisher with four penalties and a conversion and Mike O'Keefe with a try.

D. P. BOHL B.Sc

Memories of Sefton

Peter Moloney

MEMORIES OF PEOPLE AND EVENTS recalled from more than half a century ago are necessarily blurred and confused, but some remain vivid. Here are a few to add to the fond litanies of all the other nostalgic Seftonians.

I FIRST PLAYED for Sefton in the late '40s when my brothers and I were home on holiday from school. In those post-war years the club was re-building, literally, on the reconstituted ex-army anti-aircraft battery site, and by recruiting new players. Some of the new recruits were army personnel from the Deysbrook barracks, at the rear of the club grounds. Some were still schoolboys, while many were teachers, continuing the pre-war tradition in the club

Back row, left to right: W. Collins, Brendan Moloney, L. Scott, Michael Moloney, D. Taylor, D. Raynor, J. Snape. *Middle row, left to right*: T. Murphy, J. Griffiths, N. Kelly, K. J. Ashley (Captain), T. Donnelly, F. Barnwell. *Front row, left to right*: Peter Moloney, A. Edwards.

which had no direct school affiliation, it was never an 'Old Boys' club but had many teachers on the playing, administrative and coaching staff.

Over the following decades, recruitment was boosted from undergraduates at Liverpool University, including me, and trainee teachers such as those from Hopwood Hall teacher training college in Middleton, Manchester, including two of my brothers, Michael and Tony. Included among the Hopwood players were some of the DeLa Salle Brothers who were on the teaching staff. This occasionally had unexpected consequences, as on one of the occasions when Dixie Raynor was sent off. When the referee joined the players in the bar, half-an-hour after the game, he was confronted by a very irate Dixie proudly sporting a 'borrowed' dog-collar and clerical stock under his unruly beard. Dixie greeted the ref with a torrent of very unclerical Saxon expletives, followed by gales of laughter and drinks-all-round.

In the early fifties I was elected Captain, but my captaincy was sporadic because I was also playing for the University. I suspect that I was tolerated so that Sefton could claim to have had the only tee total captain in the whole of Rugby Union. Only with hindsight have I come to learn just how much time and organisation went into the club from stalwart members of the Committee, especially Chairmen and Secretaries. Legendary figures like Barney Wall and Jack Moore, and 'Crocky' Croxford seldom got the thanks they deserved. As Barney once said at a players' meeting: "We are the backbone of the club. You are a little lower down!"

These founder-rejuvenators of the club were gradually reinforced and eventually replaced by player-committeemen and ex-players like Jim Alexander and Tom Daley.

Outstanding memories of those years include Easter tours, one of which, in Ireland, was a joint tour with Liverpool University. My favourite story from that tour is of the 'Bridge Card School' which operated in hotels, on coaches and trains, and even in clubhouses as the bridge

D. P. BOHL B. Sc

fanatics honed their skills. The climax came, so the story goes, when some players went to confession in a Dublin Church on Good Friday. One of the bridge school was Bernard Wright, superb full-back of New Brighton fame, the end of whose confession dialogue was overheard as follows:

Priest: "Three Hail Marys."
Bernard: "Four no trumps."

Like most good rugby stories, it may be apocryphal, but Bernard has often heard me tell the tale since at his legal gatherings, so far without protest or denial. My fondest Easter-Tour memory is of one to the South of England, which included a stopover in London. In those days, Lyons Corner House advertised: 'As much as you can eat for a pound'. This, of course, amounted to a direct challenge to any self-respecting rugby club in strict training. I still have pangs as I recall laughing helplessly into the tear-stained face of the Manager as he begged me, after an hour or so: "Please, ask them all to go away."

There were Moloney brothers in the first fifteen throughout the fifties and into the sixties. There were also Moloney sisters and girl-friends on the 'refreshment staff' for home games. I don't think that the five brothers ever appeared in the first team together, but three of us certainly did. I played in the three-quarters alongside Tony and Michael until Tony went off to Canada. Terry played occasionally with Michael and Brendan while I was away at University, or being a Trappist novice at Nunraw in

Scotland, or doing an extended National Service with the Parachute Regiment in Cyprus, Egypt and Jordan. (A propos the newspaper piece 'The Monk in the Red Beret' a caricaturist of the time portrayed it as per the attached portrait. The reality was as per the 'On Active Service' photo) As a regular first-team scrum-half, I enjoyed the back-up of Michael at full-back and the protection of Brendan at prop-forward all during the late fifties and early sixties. (As per the attached team-photo from about 1960.)

After my rugby days ended, I mixed a media career with teaching. My newspaper articles often featured nostalgic stories of Sefton RUFC, as did my three semi-autobiographical books: *A Plea for Mersey* published by Gallery Press in 1966, *Football Mad*, also published by Gallery Press, in 1968,and *Tales You Win*, published by Countywise Press in 2001.

For a good example of journalistic Seftoniana see the piece on the requiem mass for Jim Alexander which celebrated all aspects of his life, including his family, career and long service to Sefton RUFC as player, coach, selector, chairman, etc.

Football Mad is actually a jaundiced rugby player's analysis of the quirks, liturgies and general incunabula associated with Association Football. To get a flavour of the text, complete the following sentence: "If God had intended man to play with a round ball..."

A frequently re-hashed story from *Plea for Mersey* is a true account of the most perilous moment in Dixie Raynor's long engagement to be married. With many weekend players, home games posed no great problems, but away matches put severe strain on the relationships of engaged or newly-wed couples. Dixie was renowned for stopping the return coach at any one of a series of hostelries and calling for 'hush' as he rang his fiancée to explain why he was unfortunately 'held-up' and therefore would not be able to keep their date for that evening. On the day in question, the chosen pub was half-way between Wigan and

D. P. BOHL B.Sc

SEFTON
R.U.F.C.

Dixie Raynor with beloved pint.
Dixie on 'the stand'. Dixie in Fancy Dress 1973.

Liverpool on the East-Lancs Road. The lounge-bar was eventually shushed into silence as Dixie made his phone-call. Surpassing himself in imagination and pathos he moaned gently: "I'm terribly sorry, dear, but I won't be able to make it tonight. In fact I've broken my leg and am ringing you from Wigan Infirmary." At that dramatic moment the bar door swung open and Dixie's fellow prop staggered in with a tray of pint glasses and a loud shout of "What are you having, Dixie?" With a mournful cry, Dixie groaned: "Gas, I think, doctor." And hung up.

In *Tales You Win* there are vestigial traces to be found of both the club and the code. Since my brothers and I sired only girls, the line, if not the line-out, has ceased to grace the West Derby turf. Our youngest daughter did actually play rugby at Oxford. She claims she "got a Black-and-Blue". The Sorto-Biography *Unconscious Nine-Irony* also records my last appearance in the red-and-white hoops of Sefton. In another chapter 'We Leave No Turn Unstoned' I tell the tale of my traumatic experience as Guest Speaker at a Sportsmen's Dinner at Wigan Rugby League Club.

(ALIAS THE ALIENS)

Bill Beaumont, Peter Moloney, President,
Secretary and Chairman of the RFU

My final public acknowledgement of my debt to the club came when I was invited to be Guest Speaker at a 'Sportsman of the Year' Presentation Dinner in London. Chief Guest of Honour was the retiring English, and British Lions, Captain Bill Beaumont. The Chairmen and Captains of most of the Southern clubs and some of the Northern ones were in the audience. The top table guests had large ornate place-cards in front of them, announcing their clubs and positions. Mine read simply: SEFTON RUFC. This caused some wry amusement and I was subjected to much ribald banter until Bill got up to make his acceptance speech, which began: "The first serious game of rugby I played was for Fylde seconds, on the wing, against the Vale of Lune. My final game was a Lancashire cup game, on a Sunday against Merseyside Police at SEFTON." The club thereafter got the praise which it deserves. And not just from me!

I never thought I would get another chance to record personal and family thanks to the club and all those who help to keep it going, but I am delighted to be given this

D. P. BOHL B.Sc

chance to 'say my piece' by Geoff Daley, who followed in his father's footsteps as a loyal Seftonian on and off the field, and is now relishing the task of being archivist and historian.

SEFTON R.U.F.C.

Ad multos annos, or as generations of learned-teacher-players would say:

"*Quemadmodo tunc, hunc, nunc,*"
or
"Howsabout that, then, now."

The University of Life
by
John Davies

IN THE AUTUMN OF 1958 I arrived as a history student at Liverpool University. I looked forward to pursuing my education in every sense of the word. I certainly did gain a great deal from five years as a university student but little did I think that a great deal of my 'further education' would come from a totally unexpected source, Sefton

Back row, left to right: T. Donnelly snr, J. Alexander, W. F. Jones, V. R. McDonald, W. Collins, J. Wilson, A. Bonner, G. Carroll, J. Dunne, W. Ryan, J. H. Daybell. *Front row, left to right:* T. Donnelly, A. Corlett, C. Lyons, J. Davies (Captain), W. Evans, T. Roberts, M. Gilmore, J. Bailey, G. Nelson, B. Mordyke (*inset*).

(ALIAS THE ALIENS)

Rugby Club. Although, coming from St Helens and a keen rugby player, I did not play in my first term at the university. But, one bleak Wednesday in January 1959 I played for an arts faculty team. By chance in the same team were two Sefton players, Peter Moloney and Bro. Wilfrid (David Burns). I had never heard of Sefton but Wilfrid persuaded me I should give the club a try. The following Saturday I played my first game for Sefton, for the fourth team against Orrell at Orrell. The captain, Joe Plumpton, asked me what position I played. I replied that I was a wing forward. I played fullback that afternoon. We took something of a hammering but I must have done something to impress Joe for he recommended me for promotion and the following week I played, at wing forward for the seconds under the captaincy of Jack Daybell, soon to be appointed as headmaster at St Philomena's. I played two further games under Jack's leadership and was then picked for the first team to play away at Fleetwood. I assumed my performances on the pitch had justified this call up but having set out on the coach trip to Fleetwood I realised that in those days when the M6 consisted of the Preston by-pass the trip to Fleetwood was an away game too far for some senior players. (We arrived late — the local edition of the *Sporting Pink* carried the banner headline that evening — 'Sefton Late'. Not a lot happened in Fleetwood in February.) We were clearly a few key players short but I took my chance and as we won I kept my place for the following week. That was the first of over 500 games for the first team (or so Ron Langshaw, Sefton's own spin doctor, claimed to the local press in the 1970s) and the beginning of my education in the university of life at Sefton.

Sefton started as a club for schoolteachers and during my time as a player there was always a strong core of teachers and lecturers. Peter and Mike Moloney, Les Scott, Joe Griffiths, Tom Donnelly, John Snape, Jim Bailey, Warwick Evans, Tony Edwards all taught at one time or another. Tom McMath was a college of education lecturer, Joe Dunn became a professor of engineering at Liverpool John

D. P. BOHL B.Sc

Jack Daybell   Les Scott   Jim Bailey

Ron Langshaw   Joe Griffiths   Warwick Evans

Peter Moloney   Tom Donnelly Jnr   Tony Edwards

Mike Moloney   John Snape   Joe Dunn

SEFTON
R.U.F.C.

(ALIAS THE ALIENS)

Barry Mordyke

John Stevens

Dave Baines

Tom McMath

Moores and Barry Mordyke a professor of metallurgy in Germany. Among the senior members of the club were teachers such as Jack Daybell and the post-war club captain, Bill Williamson, originally from Cumbria but a local headmaster when I joined. Bill was a real guru, a deep thinker about rugby and life. A lifelong socialist, he had visited the Soviet Union in the 1930s and a couple of years before he died in the 1980s he travelled across the country on the Trans-Siberian Railway. Fortunately, not everyone was a teacher and what struck me when I started at the club was that the players came from such a wide variety of social backgrounds. Coming from working class St Helens, where Rugby Union was a middle class game, I was pleasantly surprised that Sefton in no way conformed to the public stereotype of rugby clubs. The rich social mix of the club was one of its great attractions for me. There were very strong bonds between lads from different educational and social backgrounds and life long friendships were made. Also there was a very inclusive ethos at the club. All were welcomed from wherever they came. If you could play and paid your match fees you were in.

IT WAS ALSO GREAT FUN to play for Sefton. How could it not be when the club was stuffed with so many larger than life characters? Peter Moloney had been a Trappist monk and a captain in the paratroopers. Frank Barnwell was a public health inspector by day, pub bouncer (at the Palatine in Dale St) by night, part-time member of the *corps de ballet* at the Empire whenever the ballet companies visited Liverpool, and archetypal hard man on and of the field. Frank eventually married into the aristocracy and the notice of his marriage to the Hon. Florence Stevens appeared in the court news in *The Times*. John Snape was fruit porter on the docks, later teacher and eventually full-time organiser on Merseyside for one of the teaching unions. Tom Donnelly, perhaps the most naturally talented player I played with, was brought to the club by John Stevens after National Service on Christmas Island. Originally a fitter, he became a teacher, and a fine rugby analyst. Sadly he died of a massive brain tumour while still in his thirties. Les Scott, another teacher, later head of the largest primary school in the north of England, was always the level-headed one among us and peace-maker when things threatened to get out of hand after a few too many pints. There were many others but the largest of these larger than life characters was undoubt-edly Thomas Dixon, 'Dixie' Raynor.

IN 1959 DIXIE WAS STILL a career soldier, Corporal Raynor, stationed at Deysbrook Barracks across the field from the ground at Thornhead Lane. Later he would drive lorries and furniture vans before becom-ing a pub landlord, first in West Derby village and later in Stanley by the abat-toir. Dixie, sadly, like Frank Barnwell, died relatively young but the stories about

SEFTON
R.U.F.C.

'Dixie' Raynor

Frank Barnwell

George Nelson

Bill Williamson

him are legion. All of us will have our own favourites. In a team stuffed with university graduates Dixie was the sharpest of them all. Dixie was an orphan and he had come through life the hard way. I always felt his rapier-like wit was a weapon he had developed and used to protect himself. Dixie, and we sometimes forget this, was a massively talented rugby player. He never trained, and ceremoniously vomited on the centre spot at the beginning of every game, but he had a wonderful pair of hands and, in today's parlance, he was brilliant at off-loading the ball in the tackle as well as being a wonderful place-kicker, and a prop forward who knew every ruse in the book when it came to the scrum.

On the field also he was the great enforcer. I remember in an early game being persistently obstructed when trying to break from the scrum — wing forwards were allowed to break before the ball was out in those days — and being on the point of lashing out. Dixie told me to calm down. He would sort it. Five minutes later Dixie on the blind side of the scrum and of the referee delivered a short right arm jab which removed the offender for the rest of the match. The poor lad never saw what was coming and only woke up in the dressing room.

On another occasion, at Southport, he was sent off for a similar incident, which unfortunately was reported in the local press — 'Raynor Gets Marching

SOUTHPORT GAME MARRED

Raynor gets marching orders

SOUTHPORT 6, SEFTON 6

Periodical flare-ups of temper by both sides particularly among the forwards, culminating in Sefton's prop forward Raynor being sent off after a line-out scuffle near the end, marred a fast, open game under ideal conditions.

Southport had the edge over Sefton in speed and ability but were handicapped after ten minutes by an ankle injury to Watkinson which put him out of the game.

Sefton rarely seemed able to co-ordinate their resources so well but spotted Southport's failure in the first half to cover quickly in defence and twice nipped in to score surprise tries against the run of play.

SPLENDID MOVE

A splendid move by winger P. Roston paved the way within a few minutes for Girvan to go over for Southport who continued to press hard with their backs seeing plenty of the ball.

Sefton skipper Snape made an interception near half-way to outpace the thin defence to level the points. Shortly afterwards Sefton scored again with an almost identical move. Bailey snatching a wild Southport pass to send Corlett over.

A determined attack by Southport immediately after the turn round resulted in Ostick diving across the line to score from a scrum.

D. P. BOHL B.Sc

SEFTON
R.U.F.C.

Orders'. Unfortunately, his boss read the paper and was not too pleased. Dixie was off work, sick, at the time. When he returned he received another set of walking orders! Another famous Dixie incident occurred at Tyldesley. At one point in the match a woman ran from the touchline — there was always a volatile crowd in this Rugby League stronghold - and hit Dixie with her umbrella, alleging an assault on her son. Dixie responded by suggesting that she got back to her bingo. The final Dixie story concerns the sweep he organised whenever we played a local club who boasted a former international player in their side. The first one to hit the international got the kitty, deplorable no doubt but everyone took part. Dixie was certainly not the fleetest of foot but he always managed to win.

APART FROM THE PLAYERS there were a group of stalwarts, mainly former players, who ran the club and supported us. Along with Bill Williamson, there was Jack Wilson, holder of numerous patents for his inventions, Barney Wall, Fred Telfer and Les Wilkinson. As a result of Les Wilkinson's ingenuity Sefton was the first club to have collapsible corner flags. One of our players, Norman Kelly, suffered an horrendous injury to his leg when he collided with a rigid corner flag. Les decided to do something about it. Collapsible flags are now universally used. Did Les Wilkinson ever get any recognition for his invention? Perhaps the greatest service to the club in my time was given by Jim Alexander. Jim had moved up from Birmingham to Merseyside to become chief executive and works manager of BICC Prescot. He and his wife, Pennie, a local magistrate, were indefatigable community workers. As well as running the local tennis club in Childwall where they lived they were involved in a whole range

Les Wilkinson

Barney Wall

Fred Telfer

Norman Kelly

Jim Alexander

Robbie McDonald

of activities, but foremost among these was Sefton. Jim was chairman of the selection committee. He refereed the third or fourth team each Saturday. Before doing that he opened up the club, got the fire going which heated the bathwater, unblocked the toilets and made sure that the changing rooms had been cleaned since the previous match day. In addition to all of this he always had a welcoming word for those like myself who had stumbled upon the club. Later as Team Secretary I worked closely with him, particularly on Saturday mornings when I was often faced with a host of 'cry-offs'. We had to juggle the players and try to get out at least a semblance of four teams. Years later when Jim was retired I used to see him driving pensioners (probably younger than himself) to the afternoon club at Christ's College (Liverpool Hope) where I was then a lecturer. Without such stalwarts — and some of my own generation now fall into that class, Robbie Mac, Geoff Daley, Bill Jones, Bryan McDonagh - clubs such as Sefton would cease to function. All of us who enjoyed playing owe them a huge debt of gratitude.

ONE OF THE FEATURES of games played in the 1960s was the away trip by coach. We often travelled to local away games by train but for further afield the coach was used. In retrospect I feel a little sorry for the coach drivers who had to suffer us. After the game we would have a few beers in the clubhouse. The coach would then move on. The drivers often felt this was

D. P. BOHL B.Sc

the time to go home. Understandably they wanted to get back to Liverpool. Usually however, we wanted to stay out. We would stop at a pub or club en route for Liverpool. If we were lucky we would make it back into town for last orders. More often than not it was much later. I was still living in St Helens and on many Saturday nights after away games by coach I was on the last train, 12.45, home.

At one stage in the late 1960s Bill Collins, (another one of our team mates who sadly died young) who was a budding entrepreneur with a small engineering company that sub-contracted for the big car manufacturers, took to entertaining his Japanese business contacts by taking them on the coach to away matches. I often wondered what these guests from Osaka, Yokohama and Tokyo made of an afternoon in the middle of February watching us play at Tyldesley, followed by a night in the Leigh British Legion. What did they make of John Dooris (another who sadly died young) singing 'Ebb Tide' and 'Red Sails in the Sunset', not to mention Dixie singing his version of the Alphabet Song and the rest of us bawling out 'The Harlot of Jerusalem' as the coach arrived back in Liverpool?

WHAT ABOUT THE RUGBY? In the period I played there were no leagues. All matches were negotiated with individual clubs by the fixture secretary. We were a junior club but we had some talented players and we played some decent teams. Orrell

SEFTON R.U.F.C.

Geoff Daley

Bill Jones

Bryan McDonagh

John Dooris

Bill Collins

Ken Ashley

Brendan Moloney

were certainly the strongest of the sides we played regularly. We managed to beat them on a few occasions and although clearly they were a club on the way up we always gave them a decent game. Orrell continued to play Sefton up until they received national status. This was a favour returned. When Orrell had first been founded it found it difficult to get fixtures. Sefton had been one of the first clubs to give them a regular fixture. There was something of a special bond between the clubs and after our hard fought games there was always a friendly drink with Des Seabrook and the Lyons brothers. John Snape was regularly twitted by Dixie that he sent the Orrell back row Christmas cards. Among the other Lancashire teams we played were West Park, my old school old boys team, Tyldesley, Leigh, Wigan, Newton le Willows and Widnes. All of these teams would have a sprinkling of ex Rugby League players. This was strictly illegal as anyone who had played Rugby league over the age of eighteen was banned from playing Rugby Union. This rule was bitterly resented in the Rugby league heartlands of Lancashire. It was thought ridiculous that lads who had played perhaps half a dozen games for Widnes or Leigh A teams should be prevented from playing Rugby Union as amateurs. Sefton had a couple of ex-Leaguers. In my early days I remember Frank Nash, a very polished centre from Widnes, playing for us until someone reported him. I remember also Sefton being reported for playing an ex-Rugby League player, Ged Marshall, in a Lancashire cup match against Fylde, in which a young Billy Beaumont played. It turned out that

SEFTON
R.U.F.C.

our fly half had played for Blackpool Borough and was well known in the Fylde area. Of course we knew nothing of his previous playing career!

As for our style of play, in my first full season Frank 'this is a hand ball game' Barnwell, our captain, forbade kicking. We threw the ball about with wild abandon, sometimes with disastrous consequences. A season later with Ken Ashley as captain and Peter Moloney at fly half we reverted to a kicking game. That season I played several games at inside centre. My duties were entirely defensive. In six weeks I got six passes from Peter. From every scrum and lineout he planted the ball downfield and into touch. I always thought that it was a result of Peter's activities that season that the law was changed to prevent teams kicking directly into touch outside their own twenty-two (twenty-five in our day).

Coming to play for Sefton was an accident. I had never heard of the club. But it was a happy accident. At the beginning of the 1959-1960 season I was approached to play for the University but despite some pressure (A friend of mine who was the sports editor of the student newspaper, *Guild Gazette*, ran a campaign against those who like me refused to play for the University and opted for outside clubs.) I declined to leave Sefton. I was also asked on a number of occasions to return to my roots and play at West Park. But Sefton had something which neither the University Rugby Club nor West Park had. The University team was solely a students' team and West Park was then an old boys' club. Sefton's membership was socially diverse and offered such a rich experience of life, especially for a 'woolly back' such as me. The club also had a wonderful camaraderie, which could even survive the infamous occasion when the Barnwells fought the Moloneys during a match at Port Sunlight. Terry Moloney, who was deaf, failed to respond to a call for a quick throw-in from Frank Barnwell, captain at the time, and got involved in an argument with Frank, which led to an exchange of blows. Peter, Mick and Brendan Moloney came to Terry's aid and Terry

Barnwell joined in on Frank's side. The rest of us, the Port Sunlight team and the referee watched in amazement. Dave Earnshaw, the referee said that the laws of the game did not cover such eventualities and when calm returned he re-started the game, which we went on to win, with the throw-in which had caused the trouble. A team and club spirit, (encapsulated in John Stevens' expression 'The boys'), which could survive that, was worth treasuring. I certainly treasured it and have been grateful ever since for what I learned in the 'University of Life' at Sefton Rugby Club.

John Davies, Sefton, 1958–1959 to 1973–1974.

D. P. BOHL B.Sc

Team Photographs

Team Photograph – First Team Season 1963–64

Back row, left to right: M. Talbot, P. Vidamore, T. O'Shea, J. Smith,
R. Allen, J. Daybell, J. Alexander. *Front row, left to right*: T. Roberts,
D. Craggs, T. Jaynes, J. Snape (Captain), J. Stevens, I. Holden, K. Reid.

Team Photograph – First Team Season 1969–70

Back row, left to right: W. Collins, T. Donnelly, D. Ireland, J. Dunn,
P. Vidamore, M. Gilmour, W. Ryan. *Front row, left to right*: K. Langshaw,
W. F. Jones, A. G. Daley, V. R. McDonald (Captain), J. Stevens,
R. Fitzpatrick, W. Evans.

Team Photograph – First Team Season 1973–74

Back row, left to right: G. Carroll, W. F. Jones, N. Kelly, M. Shields,
I. Walker, F. Lee, B. Langshaw, A. Bonner. *Front Row, left to right*:
K. Langshaw, G. Owen, A. Corlett, P. Merriman (Captain), J. Davies,
D. Ireland, P. Scully.

D. P. BOHL B. Sc

Team Photograph – First Team Season 1974–75

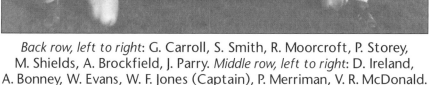

Back row, left to right: G. Carroll, S. Smith, R. Moorcroft, P. Storey, M. Shields, A. Brockfield, J. Parry. *Middle row, left to right*: D. Ireland, A. Bonney, W. Evans, W. F. Jones (Captain), P. Merriman, V. R. McDonald. *Front row, left to right*: K. J. Langshaw, A. Corlett.

Team Photograph – First Team Season 1976–77

Back row, left to right: P. Kavanagh, S. Smith, A. Stewart, J. Shields, K. Westcott, W. F. Jones, R. Schenk, P. Forshaw, F. Routledge. *Front row, left to right*: A. J. Murray, P. Flaherty, M. Shields, J. Scully, R. Langshaw, G. L. Nichols (Captain), G. Slee, D. Ireland, P. Osborne.

Team Photograph – First Team Season 1977–78

Back row, left to right: T. McMath, V. R. McDonald, A. Stewart, N. Kelly, K. Westcott, P. Rendalls, T. Kinloch, R. Branch. Guest D. York (Ref). *Front row, left to right*: W. F. Jones, P. Flaherty, D. Ireland, A. J. Murray (Captain), A. M. Pennington, F. Routledge, B. McNutt.

Team Photograph – First Team Season 1978–79

Back row, left to right: T. McMath, T. O'Hara, R. Warlow, J. Nye, W. F. Jones, P. Lund, K. Sweetin, A. Stewart, P. Greenalgh. *Middle row, left to right*: M. Grieves, C. Breen, A. M. Pennington (Captain), P. J. Roberts, J. Shields, T. Kinloch. *Front row, left to right*: A. Murray, J. Feenam.

D. P. BOHL B.S

Team Photograph – First Team Season 1981–82

Back row, left to right: D. Fields, W. F. Jones, L. Jackson, K. Westcott,
A. Stewart, T. Kitts, P. Flaherty, G. Spencer. *Front row, left to right*:
A. Murray, J. Orme, C. Breen, A. Pennington (Captain), J. Shields,
E. Pinder, J. White.

Team Photograph – First Team Season 1985–86

Back row, left to right: H. Price, D. Neary, R. Cunliffe, K. Westcott,
S. McMillan, D. Hawkyard, R. Earwaker, S. O'Reilly. *Front row, left to right*:
G. Jones, C. Breen, F. Harper, T. Kinloch, J. White, T. Hughes,
A. Pennington.

Team Photograph – First Team Season 1989–90

Back row, left to right: T. Kinloch, D. Edwards, I. Crawford, P. Daley, K. Westcott, P. Hood, P. Evangelides, J. Rogers, M. Evangelides, A. Pennington. *Front row, left to right*: F. Harper, D. Neary, G. Walsh, I. Wood (Captain), C. Breen, S. Woods, P. Newnes, D. Conlan.

Team Photograph – First Team Season 1991–92

Back row, left to right: C. Breen, A. Sheehan, J. Parr, G. Walsh, D. Heron, M. Whipp, K. Westcott, P. Hood, R. Earwaker, P. Newnes, G. Edwards. *Front row, left to right*: S. O'Reilly, G. Childs (Captain), J. Rogers, P. Evangelides Ref.

D. P. BOHL B. Sc

Team Photograph – First Team Season 1992–93
Lancs Plate Final at Waterloo

SEFTON
R.U.F.C.

Back row, left to right: F. Harper, D. Neary, S. Jeans, T. Clark, K. Westcott, C. Breen, K. Byrne, M. Carruthers, P. Daley, S. Irvine. N. Willerton, E. Nichols, J. Turner, T. Kinloch. *Front row, left to right*: S. O'Reilly, I. Wood, P. Walker, P. Evangelides (Captain), D. Heron, R. Earwaker.

Team Photograph – First Team Season 1993–94
at Preston Grasshoppers

Back row, left to right: T. Collins (Coach), I. Wood, C. Hudson, R. Earwaker, P. Evangelides, T. Clark, D. Edwards, M. Steene, G. Childs, C. Jordan, V. R. MacDonald. *Front row, left to right*: E. Nichols, S. Trotter, T. Kinloch, D. Neary (Captain), M. Carruthers, K. Westcott, P. Walker, M. Tyms.

Team Photograph – Ladies Season 1994–95

Back row, left to right: A. Leatherbarrow, A. Lowther, S. Christie,
L. Duncan, C. Sloane, S. Evans, S. Swift, A. Purefoy, S. Hancock. *Front
row, left to right*: S. Thomas, C. Mulhearn, E. Awat-Odoko (Captain),
H. Prior, S. J. Heaps, N. Huran.

Team Photograph – First Team Season 1995–96

Back row, left to right: A. Pennington, K. Byrne, N. Willerton, S. Pringle,
L. McGowan, W. Coulter, D. Neary, M. Tyms, M. Carruthers, R. Earwaker,
S. Trotter. *Front row, left to right*: D. Stretton, L. Warwick,
P. Evangelides, B. Gardner, B. Wilkes, R. Carter.

D. P. BOHL B.Sc

Team Photograph – First Team Season 1996–97

SEFTON
R.U.F.C.

Back row, left to right: W. Osborne, G. Jones, P. Hood, C. Breen, S. Teale,
K. Byrne, T. Kinloch, P. Evangelides, R. Earwaker, R. Spencer, B. Wilkes,
A. M. Pennington. *Front row, left to right*: F. Harper, N. Willerton,
M. Carruthers, M. Thomas, A. Sheehan (Captain), I. R. Wood,
D. Keegan, S. Smith.

Team Photograph – First Team Season 1997–98

Back row, left to right: D. Lee, K. Byrne, D. McCann, I. Burns, R. Spencer,
P. Hood, S. Teale, B. Wilkes, W. Osborne, M. Carruthers, B. Eden,
A. Pennington. *Front row, left to right*: E. Jones, A. Walsh, L. Warwick, F.
Harper, Dr T. Kinloch (Captain), J. Stitt, P. Evangelides, S. Smith,
M. Thomas, W. Coulter.

Team Photograph – First Team Season 2001–02

Back row, left to right: R. Webster, P. Evans, M. Jones, A. Harper, G. Cann, A. Sheehan, G. Rogerson, P. Walker, D. Griffiths, S. Bailey, M. Carruthers, W. F. Jones, G. Scully, S. Barrett, B. McDonagh.
Front row, left to right: W. Osborne, P. McBride, J. Stitt, M. Thomas (Captain), D. Neary, B. Gardner, P. Wynne.

D. P. BOHL B. Sc

Sefton Officials

Season	President	Chairman	Treasurer	Secretary	Fixture Sec.	County Rep.	1XV Capt.	2XV Capt.	3XV Capt.	4XV Capt.	5XV Capt.	6XV Capt.	7XV Capt.
1907–08				Applebee			Taylor						
1908–09				Applebee			Johnstone						
1909–10				Applebee			Johnstone						
1910–11				Applebee			Johnstone						
1911–12				Applebee			Croxford						
1912–13	Legge		Applebee	Applebee		Croxford	Jones	Flint					
1913–14	Legge		Bayliss	Applebee		Croxford	Croxford	Whittle					
1914–15	Legge			Applebee		Croxford	Jones						
1914–18	First World War – Club disbanded during hostilities												
1919–20	Legge		Milbourn	Applebee	Helme	Croxford	Helme						
1920–21	Knipe		Milbourn	Applebee	Helme	Croxford	O'Donnell	Williams					
1921–22	Knipe		Milbourn	Applebee		Croxford	Snape	Bayliss	Martinez	Daulman			
1922–23	Smith		Milbourn	Applebee		Croxford	Hutchings	Kay		Bateman			
1923–24	Smith		Milbourn	Applebee	Munroe	Croxford	Webley	Porter	Martinez	Bateman			
1924–25	Kay		Milbourn	Applebee	Munroe	Croxford	Hutchings	Bacon	Hemmingway	Bateman			
1925–26	Kay			Applebee	Lockier		Taylor						
1926–27	Taylor		Applebee	Applebee			Howard						
1927–28	Taylor		Applebee	Applebee			Howard	Thompson					
1928–29	Croxford		Applebee				Howard						
1929–30	Croxford		Applebee				Kilburn						
1930–31	Applebee		Applebee				Parkinson	Gosling	Nelson	Parle			
1931–32	Applebee		Applebee	Lewis	Paisley	Croxford	Winter	Dane	Jones	Boyle			
1932–33	Munroe		Applebee				Stephens						
1933–34	Munroe		Applebee				Parkinson						
1934–35	Parkinson		Nelson	Moore		Parkinson	Winter						
1935–36	Parkinson		Nelson	Moore			Winter						
1936–37	Marr-Orr		Nelson	Moore			Parkinson						
1937–38	Marr-Orr		Hulme	Moore		Parkinson	Mawson						
1938–39	Harlow		Hulme	Moore		Parkinson	Mawson	King	Scott	Ripley			
1939–45	Second World War – Club suspended												
1945–46	Bulmer			Moore			Williamson						
1946–47	Parkinson		Hulme	Moore		Parkinson	Williamson						
1947–48	Parkinson		Nelson	Moore		Parkinson	Williamson		McLoughlin				
1948–49	Birchall		Jones	Moore	Nelson	Parkinson	Williams	Barton	Williamson				
1949–50	Birchall		Williams	Moore	Nelson	Parkinson	Williams	Wright	Scott				
1950–51	Nelson		Williams	Moore	Nelson	Moore	Williams	Wright	Jones				
1951–52	Nelson		Williams	Moore	Nelson	Moore	Griffiths	Wright	Jones				
1952–53	Graley		Robbins	Moore	Nelson	Nelson	Griffiths	Wright	Jones				
1953–54	Graley		Robbins	Moore	Nelson	Nelson	McGrail	Wright	Jones	Smith			

Season	President	Chairman	Treasurer	Secretary	Fixture Sec.	County Rep.	1XV Capt.	2XV Capt.	3XV Capt.	4XV Capt.	5XV Capt.	6XV Capt.	7XV Capt.
1954–55	Barry	Wall	Robins	Moore	Nelson	Nelson	McGrail	Wright	Jones	Smith			
1955–56	Barry	Wall	Robins	Moore	Nelson	Nelson	Johnson	Robins	Whitefield				
1956–57	Moore	Wall	Robins	Moore	Nelson	Nelson	Griffiths	Robins	Whitefield				
1957–58	Moore	Wall	Robins	Moore	Nelson	Nelson	Barnwell	Daybell	Plumpton	Fraser			
1958–59	Wall	Williamson	Alexander	Robins	Wright	Nelson	Barnwell	Daybell	Robins	Smith			
1959–60	Wall	Williamson	Alexander	Robins	Wright	Nelson	Moloney	Daybell	Robins	Plumpton			
1960–61	Wilkinson	Williamson	Alexander	Robins	Wright	Nelson	Ashley	Daybell	Robins	Holden			
1961–62	Wilkinson	Williamson	Alexander	Robins	Wright	Nelson	Ashley	Daybell	Robins	Holden			
1962–63	Williamson	Wilkinson	Alexander	Proctor	Wright	Nelson	Moloney	Garnett	McCormack	Smith			
1963–64	Williamson	Wilkinson	Alexander	Telfer	Robins	Nelson	Snape	Garnett	Fitzpatrick				
1964–65	Wilson	Alexander	Crichley	Telfer	Robins	Nelson	Snape	Garnett	Daybell				
1965–66	Wilson	Alexander	Crichley	Telfer	Daybell	Nelson	Bailey	Cliff					
1966–67	Baines	Alexander	Bonner	Blackburn	Daybell	Nelson	Bailey	Evans					
1967–68	Baines	Alexander	Bonner	Blackburn	Daybell	Nelson	Scott	Evans	Fitzpatrick	Cooper			
1968–69	Daybell	Alexander	Nelson	Blackburn	Daybell	Nelson	Davies	Dooris	Snape				
1969–70	Daybell	Alexander	Bonner	Blackburn	Daybell	Nelson	McDonald	Blackburn	Street				
1970–71	Alexander	Daybell	Wilson	Evans	Mordike	Nelson	Collins	McMath	Rotherham	Reilly			
1971–72	Alexander	Rotherham	Wilson	Blackburn	Mordike	Nelson	Mordike	McMath	Street	Fitzpatrick	Young		
1972–73	Telfer	Daybell	Wilson	Blackburn	Mordike	Nelson	Langshaw	McMath	Webster	Morgan			
1973–74	Telfer	Wilson	Hardiman	Blackburn	Mordike	Nelson	Merriman	Reid	Fitzpatrick	Fletcher			
1974–75	Nelson	Mordike	Bonner	Blackburn	Daybell	Daybell	Jones	Collins	Street				
1975–76	Nelson	Langshaw	Bailey	Lee	Daybell	Daybell	Clitheroe	Purland	Warlow	Houghton			
1976–77	Donnelly	Langshaw	Bailey	Lee	Daybell	Daybell	Nichols	Morgan	Warlow	Makinson	Fitzpatrick		
1977–78	Donnelly	Langshaw	Nichols	Bailey	Merriman	Daybell	Murray	Corlett	Ledsham	Davenport	Evans		
1978–79	Blackburn	Langshaw	Nichols	Shenton	Merriman	Daybell	Pennington	Jaynes	Ledsham	Lee	Devaney		
1979–80	Blackburn	Langshaw	Nichols	Davenport	Merriman	Daybell	Roberts	Warlow	Ledsham	Lee	Devaney		
1980–81	McDonald	Langshaw	Nichols	Davenport	Merriman	Daybell	Pennington	McDonald	Young	Lee	Byrne		
1981–82	McDonald	Langshaw	Alexander	Davenport	Merriman	Daybell	Pennington	Nye	Young	Lee	Crate		
1982–83	McDonald	Langshaw	Alexander	Davenport	Houghton	Daybell	Flaherty	McEvoy	Jenkins	Spencer	Lewis		
1983–84	McDonald	Langshaw	Alexander	Davenport	Houghton	Daybell	Flaherty	Murray	Poulson	Young	Lewis	Yes	Yes
1984–85	Daley	Langshaw	Alexander	Griffiths	Houghton	Daybell	Westcott	Walsh	Poulson	Young	Povey	Yes	
1985–86	Daley	Daley	Alexander	Bryne	Houghton	Bryne	Sweetin	Pennington	Poulson	Law	Povey	Yes	
1986–87	Langshaw	Daley	Alexander	Bryne	Houghton	Heaney	Westcott	Pennington	Beggs	Bradley	Devaney		
1987–88	Langshaw	Pennington	Alexander	Beggs	Houghton	Heaney	Westcott	Harper	Young	Doherty	Grace		
1988–89	Houghton	Pennington	Conlan	Beggs	Houghton	Heaney	Walsh	Wood	Parr	Doherty			
1989–90	Houghton	Pennington	Lee	Jones	Houghton	Heaney	Wood	Coleman	Poll	Simpson			
1990–91	Pennington	Coombes	Lee	Jones	Houghton	Heaney	Wood	Law	Turner	Simpson			
1991–92	Bryne	Coombes	Lee	Jones	Houghton	Heaney	Childs	Parr	Thomas	Spencer			
1992–93	Merriman	Jones	Lee	Price	Houghton	Heaney	Evangelides	Turner	Jones	Eden			

(ALIAS THE ALIENS)

	President	Chairman	Treasurer	Secretary	Fixture Sec.	County Rep.	1XV Capt.	2XV Capt.		
1993–94	Merriman	Jones	Lee	Price	Houghton	Byrne	Neary	Turner	Cully	Eden
	Eden	Byrne	Lee	Price	Houghton	Heaney	Stewart	Wood		
1995–96	Eden	Byrne	Lee	Price	Houghton	Heaney	Walker	Willerton	Parr	Gladden
	Lee	Eden	Lee	Spencer	Houghton	Merriman	Jones	Harper		
1997–98	Lee	Eden	Lee	Spencer	Houghton	Merriman	Kinloch	Wood	Parr	Gladden
	Jones	Eden	Lee	Spencer	Houghton	Merriman	Walsh	Wood		
1999–2000	Jones	Eden	Lee	Spencer	Houghton	Merriman	Walsh	Smith	Parr	
	Stewart	Eden	Lee	Spencer	Houghton	Merriman	Walsh	Smith		
2001–02	Stewart	Eden	Lee	Spencer	Houghton	Merriman	Walsh	Stitt	Shaw	
	McDonagh	Eden	Lee	Spencer	Houghton	Merriman	Walsh	Gladden		

D. P. BOHL B.Sc

Past Presidents

J.G. Legge,
1912–15, 1919–20

R.L. Knipe,
1920–22

W.J. Smith,
1922–24

S.J. Kay, 1924–26

J.W.A. Taylor,
1926–28

W.B. Croxford,
1928–30

F.J. Applebbe,
1930–32

H.A. Munroe,
1932–34

J. Parkinson,
1934–36, 1946–48

W. Marr Orrr,
1936–38

H. Harlow, 1938–39

G.J. Bulmer,
1945–46

J. Parkinson, 1934–36, 1946–48

J. Birchall, 1948–50

G.E. Nelson, 1950–52, 1974–76

G. Graley, 1952–54

F.R. Barry, 1954–56

J.F. Moore 1956–58

B. Wall, 1958–60

L. Wilkinson, 1960–62

W. Williamson, 1962–64

J.T. Wilson, 1964–66

D. Baines, 1966–68

J. Daybell, 1968–70

J.W. Alexander, 1970–72

F.G. Telfer, 1972–74

T. Donnelly, 1976–78

G.N. Blackburn, 1978–80

D. P. BOHL B. Sc

SEFTON
R.U.F.C.

V.R. McDonald,
1980–83

A.G. Daley,
1983–85

R. Langshaw,
1985–87

B. Houghton,
1987–89

A.M. Pennington,
1989–90

R. Bryne, 1990–92

P. Merriman,
1992–94

B. Eden, 1994–96

D. Lee, 1996–98

Bill Jones,
1998–2000

A. Stewart,
2000–02

(ALIAS THE ALIENS)

Past Captains

J.W.A. Taylor,
1907–08

J.D. Johnstone,
1908–11

W.B. Croxford,
1911–12

R.W. Jones, 1912–13

W.B. Croxford,
1913–14

S.S. Jones, 1914–15

World War One,
1914–18

J.H. Helme, 1919–20

R.A. O'Donnell,
1920–21

H.E. Snape,
1921–22

N.W. Hutchings,
1922–23

H.G.C. Webley,
1923–24
1924–25

J.R. Taylor, 1925–26

W.E. Howard, 1926–29

A.C. Kilburn, 1929–30

J.C. Parkinson, 1930–31

E. Winter, 1931–32

A.L. Stephens, 1932–33

J.C. Parkinson, 1933–34

E. Winter, 1934–36

J.C. Parkinson, 1936–37

W. Mawson, 1937–39

W. Williamson, 1939–40

World War Two, 1939–45

W. Williamson, 1946–48

J. P. Williams, 1948–51

J.N. Griffiths, 1951–53

J. McGrail, 1953–55

(ALIAS THE ALIENS)

E.T. Johnson,
1955–56

J. Griffiths,
1956–57

F. Barnwell,
1957–59

P. Moloney,
1959–60

K.J. Ashley,
1960–62

P. Moloney,
1962–63

J.J. Snape, 1963–65

J. Bailey, 1965–67

L.M. Scott,
1967–68

J. Davies, 1968–69

V.R. McDonald,
1969–70

W.J. Collins,
1970–71

B.L. Mordike
1971–72

K.J. Langshaw,
1972–73

P.A. Merriman,
1973–74

W.F. Jones 1974–75

D. P. BOHL B.Sc

C. Clitheroe,
1975–76

G.L. Nichols
1976–77

A.J. Murray,
1977–78

A.M. Pennington
1978–79

P.J. Roberts,
1979–80

A.M. Pennington,
1980–82

P. Flaherty, 1982–83

K.T. Westcott,
1983–84

K. Sweetin,
1984–85

K.T. Westcott,
1985–87

G. Walsh, 1987–88

I.R. Wood, 1988–91

G.H. Childs,
1991–92

P. Evangelides,
1992–93

D. Neary, 1993–94

C. Rowlands-
Stewart, 1994–95

(ALIAS THE ALIENS)

P. Walker, 1995–96   G. Jones, 1996–97

T. Kinloch,   A. Walsh,
1997–98   1998–2003

D. P. BOHL B. Sc

The Sefton Website

WWW.SEFTONRUFC.CO.UK

SEFTON NOW ADVERTISES its activities on the world wide web and tries to capture would-be players when they arrive on Merseyside, 'Give us a try!'

A great thank-you is due to its web author Paul Hood, pictured below demolishing Guinness in Ireland.

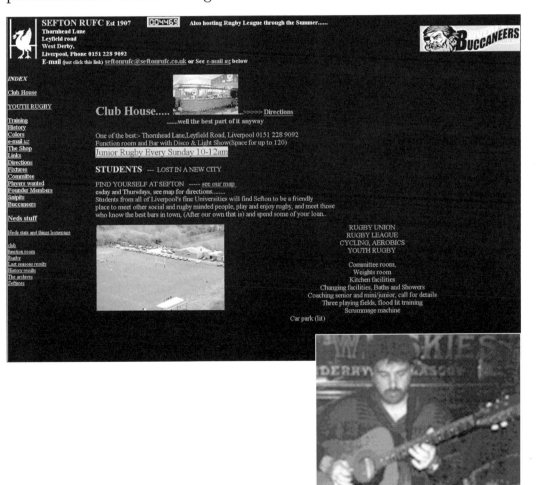

SEFTON RUFC Est 1907   004469   Also hosting Rugby League through the Summer......
Thornhead Lane
Leyfield road
West Derby,
Liverpool, Phone 0151 228 9092
E-mail (just click this link) seftonrufc@seftonrufc.co.uk or See e-mail us below

INDEX

Club House

YOUTH RUGBY

Training
History
Colors
e-mail us
The Shop
Links
Directions
Fixtures
Committee
Players wanted
Founder Members
Snipits
Buccaneers

Neds stuff

Neds stats and things homepage

club
function room
Rugby
Last seasons results
History results
The archives
Seftimes

Club House..... ......>>>>> Directions
......well the best part of it anyway

One of the best:- Thornhead Lane,Leyfield Road, Liverpool 0151 228 9092
Function room and Bar with Disco & Light Show(Space for up to 120)
Junior Rugby Every Sunday 10-12am

STUDENTS --- LOST IN A NEW CITY

FIND YOURSELF AT SEFTON ----- see our map
esday and Thursdays, see map for directions.......
Students from all of Liverpool's fine Universities will find Sefton to be a friendly
place to meet other social and rugby minded people, play and enjoy rugby, and meet those
who know the best bars in town, (After our own that is) and spend some of your loan..

RUGBY UNION
RUGBY LEAGUE
CYCLING, AEROBICS
YOUTH RUGBY

Committee room,
Weights room
Kitchen facilities
Changing facilities, Baths and Showers
Coaching senior and mini/junior, call for details
Three playing fields, flood lit training
Scrummage machine
Car park (lit)

On A Sad Note

ON TUESDAY 19th November 2002 our beloved Chairman and a great pal, Brian Eden, passed away after a long illness.

We will miss you!

Widnes Vets, Liverpool University Veterinary, Sefton 3XV and Sefton 2XV observe one minute's silence